362.2 BA1

19.99

Interdisciplinary Working in Mental Health

DATE DUE			

Interdisciplinary Working in Mental Health

DI BAILEY

palgrave
macmillan

First published 2012 by
PALGRAVE MACMILLAN

Palgrave Macmillan in the UK is an imprint of Macmillan Publishers Limited, registered in England, company number 785998, of Houndmills, Basingstoke, Hampshire RG21 6XS.

Palgrave Macmillan in the US is a division of St Martin's Press LLC, 175 Fifth Avenue, New York, NY 10010.

Palgrave Macmillan is the global academic imprint of the above companies and has companies and representatives throughout the world.

Palgrave® and Macmillan® are registered trademarks in the United States, the United Kingdom, Europe and other countries.

ISBN: 978–0–333–94802–6

This book is printed on paper suitable for recycling and made from fully managed and sustained forest sources. Logging, pulping and manufacturing processes are expected to conform to the environmental regulations of the country of origin.

A catalogue record for this book is available from the British Library.

A catalog record for this book is available from the Library of Congress.

10 9 8 7 6 5 4 3 2 1
21 20 19 18 17 16 15 14 13 12

Printed and bound in Great Britain by
CPI Antony Rowe, Chippenham and Eastbourne

Contents

Tables

Figures

Key Concepts

List of Practice Focus Boxes

Acronyms

AC	Approved Clinician
ACCT	Assessment, Care and Custody in Teamwork
AO	Assertive Outreach
AMHP	Approved Mental Health Professional
ASW	Approved Social Worker
CAMHS	Child and Adolescent Mental Health Services
CAIPE	Centre for Advancement of Interprofessional Education
CBT	Cognitive Behavioural Therapy
CCA	Community Care Act
CCfW	Care Council for Wales
CHC	Community Health Council
CIPW	Creating an Interprofessional Workforce programme
CMHC	Community Mental Health Centre
CMHT	Community Mental Health Team
CMHT-OP	Community Mental Health Team for Older People
CPA	Care Programme Approach
CPN	Community Psychiatric Nurse
CRT	Crisis Resolution Team
CTO	Community Treatment Order
DALI	Dartmouth Assessment of Life Inventory
DAT	Drug Action Team
DH	Department of Health
DHSS	Department of Health and Social Services
ECT	Electro Convulsive Therapy
EIP	Early Intervention in Psychosis
FG	Focus Group
FGM	Focus Group Managers
FGSU	Focus Group Service Users
FST	Family Support Team
GP	General Practitioner
GSCC	General Social Care Council
HoNOS	Health of the Nation Outcome Scale
ICP	Integrated Care Pathway

IMCA	Independent Mental Capacity Advocate
IMHA	Independent Mental Health Advocate
IPE	Interprofessional Education
LIT	Local Implementation Team
MCA	Mental Capacity Act
MDO	Mentally Disordered Offender
MHA	Mental Health Act
MHRT	Mental Health Review Tribunal
MMHP	Manchester Mental Health Partnership
NHS	National Health Service
NHS&CCA	National Health Service and Community Care Act
NICE	National Institute of Clinical Excellence
NSF	National Service Framework
NSF-OP	National Service Framework for Older People
NWW	New Ways of Working
OT	Occupational Therapist
PCG	Primary Care Group
PCMHW	Primary Care Mental Health Worker
PCT	Primary Care Trust
PHCT	Primary Health Care Team
PQ	Post-qualifying
PRAMS	Person centred, Risk Assessment and Management System
RC	Responsible Clinician
RL	Received Learning
RMO	Responsible Medical Officer
SAP	Single Assessment Process
SEU	Social Exclusion Unit
SOAD	Second Opinion Appointed Doctor
SSD	Social Services Department
SSI	Social Services Inspectorate
STR	Support Time and Recovery
SURGE	Service Users Research Group England

Preface

This book is the first of its kind dedicated to interdisciplinary working in mental health. The proceeding chapters take as their reference point a definition of interdisciplinarity that includes contributions from service users and carers alongside professional and non-professionally affiliated staff who comprise an increasingly diverse mental health workforce.

Whilst the term 'service user' is adopted throughout the book to signify the status and contribution increasingly afforded to individuals with direct experience of using services the term 'patient' is used in Chapter 1 to intentionally reflect the comparatively powerless status of individuals who received mental health treatment between 1900 and the 1980s.

The book draws on the extensive experience of the author as a mental health practitioner and the lessons learned from the many years of working as a member of multidisciplinary teams. The messages in each of the chapters reflect an overriding policy agenda in mental health, that as effective treatment approaches diversify and contemporary services are reconfigured to respond to the heterogenic mental health needs of service users, a combination of discipline-specific and shared ways of working are required.

As well as the challenges for interdisciplinary working some solutions and suggestions for how to achieve this to better effect are offered. These insights are offered based upon the invaluable expertise gleaned from working collaboratively with service users and colleagues in a range of practice and education settings.

Acknowledgements

I would like to thank the following people:

Linda Kemp for her expertise in the craft of referencing. Her patience and diligence in chasing up queries on my behalf has been invaluable.

To colleagues including Chris Ring and Sara Moore for supplying case material that is included in Chapters 9 and 10 respectively.

To all those colleagues and service users who I have worked with over the last 28 years and who have enabled me to develop my ideas regarding the fundamental need for collaborative working to promote better mental health services.

This book is dedicated to Guy Wishart a trusted friend and valued colleague who travelled a 10 year journey in mental health education alongside me and died on 11th August 2011.

The author and publishers would like to thank the following publishers for granting permission to reproduce copyright material in the main body of this book: SAGE Publications Ltd., London, Los Angeles, New Delhi, Singapore and Washington DV, for Figure 2.1, originally from Golightley, R.: *Social Work and Mental Health*, (Exeter: Learning Matters, 2006); Jessica Kingsley Publishers for Figure 5.1, originally from Carson, D. and Bain, A.: *Professional Risk and Working with People: Decision Making in Health, Social Care and Criminal Justice*, (London; Philadelphia: Jessica Kingsley Publishers, 2008); and Cengage Learning EMEA Ltd for Figure 12.6, originally from McNichol, E. and Hamer, S.: *Leadership and Management: A 3-Dimensional Approach* (Cheltenham: Nelson Thornes, 2006; *Page 18: A 3-dimensional approach to leadership and management*).

Introduction

The landscape of mental health services in Britain has been subject to unprecedented change since the introduction of the National Service Framework for mental health in 1999. Not only have community-based services been reconfigured to include increasingly specialist teams working with those with the most severe and enduring mental health needs, but also new roles and new ways of working for existing professionals have been introduced into the mental health workforce. The mental health care system remains in a state of flux with the expectation that embedding the changes of the Mental Health Act (2007) will bring about further challenges for mental health workers, people who use mental health services and their families.

Despite this level of complexity, the message from these combined developments is simple. Contemporary mental health care is predicated upon a greater degree of service integration that draws from a range of disciplines, combining skills, theories and expertise in response to the diverse needs of service users. The flurry of government policies such as the Care Programme Approach (1991 and 2008), the NHS Plan (2000) and the New Ways of Working initiative (NWW) (2005) are amongst the strongest determinants that can foster or undermine such collaborative practice.

The move towards increased partnership working and collaboration in mental health care is also inevitable because of the cost and complexity of services together with the more informed demands and expectations of the people who use them and their families. The alternative according to Horder (2003) is confusion, duplication and inefficiency. By bringing together professionals from the range of disciplinary backgrounds in mental health it is expected that they will engage in an open exchange of ideas and skills to solve service users' problems in cost-effective ways (Colombo, 2002).

Whilst, in principal, there are few counter arguments to this approach, which is now broadly accepted as the blueprint for mental health teams and services, problems with interdisciplinary working arise because of a number of interrelated factors that are particular to mental health care delivery.

Firstly there is an absence of a shared philosophy of practice between mental health workers. This has arisen largely because of the tensions between social, psychological and medical explanations for mental distress.

In addition, the growth of the survivor movement in psychiatry has encouraged the recovery model as an alternative to more traditional explanations of signs and symptoms. These tensions are reflected in mental health professionals' preoccupation with their own identity either as a nurse, social worker, or psychiatrist and their propensity to practise in a uniprofessional manner. The result is that workers resist a greater blurring of professional boundaries and shared areas of expertise.

In addition, the lack of a common language to define and describe interdisciplinary working does little to assist mental health professionals articulate how their respective unique contributions can be augmented by collaborative practice for the benefit of service users.

Finally, comparatively speaking, community mental health services have a brief history of development compared with hospital provision that dominated since the asylum era of the 1800s. It is therefore not surprising that despite political moves to support a more seamless approach to services, care provided in the hospital setting continues to be construed as separate from the increasingly diverse range of community provision.

Book Structure and Chapter Outline

This book is written with the explicit intention of unpacking the above issues in a way that makes interdisciplinary working more understandable and accessible. The content is tailored to a readership of mental health students and practitioners of all disciplines who are currently working or destined to work in mental health services in the future. The book is divided into two parts.

Part one outlines the development of interdisciplinary working including the policy and legislative contexts. It identifies the recovery model of mental health as synonymous with an interdisciplinary approach.

Chapter 1 chronicles the evolution of interdisciplinary working, drawing upon the changing policy context and the language used to describe how mental health professionals work together. In Chapter 2 the exploration of models and values that underpin interdisciplinary working are explored with the intention of helping readers develop a shared philosophy on which to build collaborative practice.

The legislative context for mental health is discussed in Chapter 3 including the recent changes to the Mental Health Act 1983 and the impact of these on practice. Chapter 4 provides a more focused discussion of the Care Programme Approach (CPA) as the mechanism underpinning interdisciplinary care planning and related to this Chapter 5 addresses the specific issue of risk assessment, planning and management as part of the remit of the CPA.

Part two provides a more in-depth look at interdisciplinary working with different groups of people who use mental health services. This begins in Chapter 6 with a consideration of the issues for involving service users in general in mental health service design and delivery. Chapter 7 focuses on people using primary mental health care as the largest group with more common mental health problems. The needs of young people with mental health issues are explored in more detail in Chapter 8 before moving on in Chapter 9 to consider how older adults experience interdisciplinary mental health care delivery. Chapter 10 discusses some of the issues of working with people with complex mental health needs drawing upon issues explored in earlier chapters around issues of risk and inter-agency working.

The final chapters focus upon the current agenda for workforce change in mental health and suggest some ideas and practical strategies for leading and developing an increasingly interdisciplinary mental health workforce. Thus Chapter 11 draws together the growing body of literature in interprofessional education and training while Chapter 12 focuses upon how to lead and manage increasingly diverse teams and services.

Learning Features

In order to assist readers to make links between the conceptual issues being explored in each of the chapters and how these impact on mental health practice, key issues for interdisciplinary working are set out at the start of each chapter. In addition, case studies are used as illustrative examples of interdisciplinary practice throughout. These case examples are provided as suggestions of good practice but it is acknowledged that readers may have their own strategies and ideas for contributing effectively to collaborative working with mental health professionals, service users and their families.

The Contexts of Interdisciplinary Working

The Evolution of Interdisciplinary Working: Definitions and Policy Context

---

Key Issues:

- A definition of interdisciplinary working needs to reflect contributions from professionals, service users, carers and the increasing number of non-professionally affiliated staff in the mental health workforce.
- Over the past century, interdisciplinary working has evolved – beginning with uniprofessional working synonymous with the asylum era of care and the dominance of the disease model for understanding mental ill health.
- The 1983 Mental Health Act marked a significant legislative milestone in promoting multidisciplinary practice.
- Many services are now at different stages of developing interdisciplinary ways of working depending upon the extent to which they include professionals and service users interacting in order to work collaboratively.

This chapter seeks to explain how the practice of interdisciplinary working has evolved in mental health services. In order to explore this journey it is first of all necessary to define what is meant by interdisciplinary working and the related concepts of professions and professionalism. As McClean (2005) neatly puts it:

> It is not possible to understand interdisciplinary practice without first understanding the phenomenon of professionalism. (McClean, 2005, p. 324)

Defining Interdisciplinary Working

Farrell et al. (2001: p. 281) refers to an interdisciplinary health care team as 'a group of colleagues from two or more disciplines who co-ordinate their expertise in providing care to patients'. In Britain, Marshall et al. (1979) use both interdisciplinary and multidisciplinary to refer to teams of individuals with different training backgrounds. According to Lethard (2003, p. 5) multi-professional and multidisciplinary are preferred terms to denote a wider team of professionals and she suggests that interprofessional is a key term to refer to interactions between these groups.

A mental health professional is a person who provides care and treatment for the purpose of improving an individual's mental health. In Britain, mental health professionals have traditionally included:

- Psychiatrists who are medical doctors specializing in the treatment of mental illness using a biomedical or disease model approach to understand signs and symptoms.
- Clinical psychologists with an undergraduate degree in psychology and postdoctoral training to understand and intervene with people with psychologically-based distress and dysfunction.
- Mental health social workers who have received additional post-qualifying training with a focus on social causation and labelling as explanations for mental distress, some of whom will have completed additional training to become 'approved' to undertake statutory duties as defined by the 1983 Mental Health Act.
- Psychiatric nurses who specialize in a branch of nursing that provides skills in psychological therapies and the administration of psychiatric medication.
- Occupational therapists who assess and treat psychological conditions using specific, purposeful activity to prevent disability and promote independence and wellbeing.

These professionals often deal with the same symptoms and issues and deliver the same types of interventions but their approach and scope of practice will differ as a result of their education, training and professional codes of conduct. Their roles are also associated with different statutory responsibilities.

The difficulty therefore with the use of terms like multi or interprofessional working is the assumption that this is solely the business of professionals, qualified as such because of their membership of a particular group as a result of their training and in some cases their license to practice by a particular professional body.

This negates the contribution to contemporary mental health care of the growing numbers of non-professionally affiliated staff such as Support Time and Recovery (STR) Workers and graduate Primary Care Mental Health Workers. It also excludes people who use services, who as such are experts by their own experience, together with their families and carers who by virtue of their crucial support role also have a contribution to make.

According to the Oxford English Dictionary a discipline is defined as 'a branch of instruction or learning, shaped by the mental, moral and physical training undertaken'. Such learning can be acquired and influenced by a person's lived experience of using mental health services and is as valid as that taught on professional courses or through reading textbooks. Given the growth of the service user movement in mental health since the 1950s, contemporary mental health care can no longer be anything other than inclusive of service users and carers' disciplinary contributions.

Lethard helpfully points out that Latinists translate 'inter' as between and 'multi' as many (2003, p. 5) and Barr et al. (Barr, 2003, pp. 265–79) defines interprofessional work as reliant upon *interactive* learning. Similarly McClean (2005, p. 323) differentiates as follows:

- *Multidisciplinary practice* – a team of professionals working together but retaining their professional autonomy.
- *Interdisciplinary practice* – a team of professionals working as a collective.

It is this 'betweenness' and interaction that delineates collaboration in contemporary mental health care as distinct from the fragmented joint working seen in the past. No longer are service users and their carers passively involved with services and so the boundaries between professional groups and between community teams and hospital care are becoming increasingly porous.

Thus because of the expanding range and complexity of mental health services across the care spectrum the system becomes increasingly dependent on effective interactions between the different elements and groups that contribute. This is why a step beyond *many working together* to *many interacting to work collaboratively* is required.

In the light of these issues the remainder of this chapter will discuss the historical developments towards this more interdisciplinary way of working as the cornerstone of contemporary mental health practice.

Uniprofessional Working in the Asylum Era

The nineteenth century marked the beginning of the uniprofessional era of mental health care: *professional* because it lay in the hands of professionals and *uni* because of the dominance of the medical discipline. Although initially the large number of asylums built in England provided confinement and physical restraint of those considered to be criminally insane or morally defective, between about 1830 and 1860 a period of therapeutic optimism paved the way for a greater reliance on the contribution of medical doctors to the treatment of the mentally disordered. The introduction of the 1828 Madhouses Act saw mentally ill people moved from depraved, poverty stricken communities into the closed but more humane and disciplined asylum environment that aimed to cure their disorder particularly if caught early on, thus reducing the numbers dependent on poor relief.

Reflecting the greater emphasis on the moral conditions in which the mentally insane were kept, together with a greater emphasis on more human treatment approaches, asylums built under the 1808 and 1828 Country Asylums Acts tended to be managed by doctors. By the late 1800s doctors openly recognized mental disorder as a form of illness and the symptoms of schizophrenia were first described by Kraepelin in the 1890s.

In the second half of the nineteenth century although the emphasis on curing insanity was revisited in the light of Darwinist beliefs that being insane was the result of a person's genetically inherited biology, interest still continued in medical procedures such as post-mortems to unearth the physiological lesions in the brain that were to blame.

The reliance on psychiatry as a profession, intertwined with medicine as a discipline, was reinforced by the 1930 Mental Treatment Act that provided voluntary treatment and psychiatric outpatient clinics. Many men who displayed symptoms of shell shock and were discharged from the army in the First World War on psychiatric grounds were believed to be suffering as a result of physiological damage to their brains caused by explosions rather than the psychological impact of war which was completely ignored in favour of a medical response.

Post-War Developments in Uniprofessional Working

Between the 1940s and the late 1970s there were a number of developments that signified a yo-yoing between support for hospital care and moves to undermine it.

Following the Second World War, the National Health Service Act of 1948 defined hospitals as places of treatment for people suffering from illness or defectiveness and the NHS inherited a system of over 100 'mental hospitals' with an average population of 1,000 people in each. However, in order to deal with the psychological dysfunction experienced by those returning from war in the armed forces, psychological treatments rooted in psychodynamic psychology found favour. These included the beginnings of psychometric tests, small group psychotherapy and the establishment of therapeutic communities.

By 1955 bed numbers had risen to a peak of 150,000 after which they began to decline so that by 1992 this figure had dropped to just a third at 50,000. This was largely because the plans to reduce bed numbers and increase discharges had been put in place prior to 1955 and needed time to take effect. The introduction of drugs like chlorpromazine and imipramine in the mid 1950s supported these moves to reduce the hospital population of people with mental health problems.

The medicalization of mental disorder was legally recognized by the Royal Commission on the Law Relating to Mental Illness and Mental Deficiency which resulted in the Percy Report in 1957. The key themes were that mental disorder should be regarded 'in much the same way as physical illness and disability' (para 5) and that mental hospitals should be run as nearly as possible like hospitals for physical disorders. This message was reinforced by Enoch Powell's famous Water Tower Speech in 1961 and the ensuing Hospital Plan in 1962 that increased the role of psychiatry in District General Hospitals and emphasized re-institutionalization albeit in different settings, not community care.

The 1959 Mental Health Act provided the legal framework for compulsory admission to any hospital facility thereby retaining medical decision making. This Act also introduced informal admission for psychiatric disorders and separated out social care for people who did not need inpatient treatment by handing over this responsibility to local councils.

By the 1970s, the asylums were in crisis as largely isolated institutions with significant political concerns being expressed about the standards of care delivery. Visiting multiprofessional teams set out to improve care standards by highlighting poor practices which were fed into a Department of Health and Social Services working group. The outcome of this process was the Nodder Report (DHSS, 1980) which recommended more clearly defined management structures for services with management teams working to embed clear objectives, standards and targets. The Nodder Report underlined joint planning at a strategic level between health and the Local Authorities, together with the involvement of community groups such as Community Health Councils and voluntary organizations. This, together with the emergence of psychological treatments, was perhaps the first suggestion that uniprofessional working in mental health was on the wane.

Against such a backdrop of ambivalence regarding hospital versus community care it is therefore understandable that the uniprofessional approach to treating mental ill health continued from the early 1900s to the 1980s. Although 35 hospitals closed between 1980 and 1990, 89 were still open in 1993. Medical treatments continued to be controlled by the psychiatrists with day to day administration of drugs on the wards provided by nurses as 85 per cent of government funding for mental health continued to be spent on hospital services (Sayce, 1989).

The psychiatric social work departments that had developed following increasing Local Authority involvement in social care services as a result of the 1959 Mental Health Act continued to remain separate and occupational therapy input was confined to workshops notoriously associated with basket weaving or work-based schemes concerned with menial tasks. Despite the emergence of a more psychologically oriented discourse within psychiatry

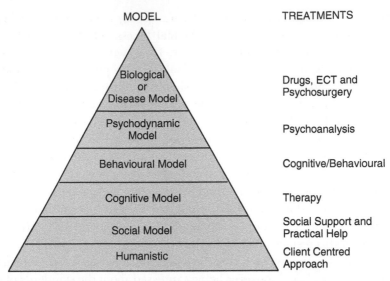

Figure 1.1 Hierarchy models of mental distress in mid 1900s

with the work of Freud, Jung and Skinner giving rise to a mix of psychodynamic and behavioural theories of mental distress, psychologists were still rarely involved in treatment plans. Patients were passive recipients of a regime of containment and medical interventions imposed in 'their best interests' in the absence of consultation and discussion.

The disease model of mental illness dominated the continuation of the institutional era supported by advances in psychotropic medication and medical treatments such as Electro Convulsive Therapy (ECT) and psychosurgery. According to Bond and Lader (1996, p. 4) 'The notion of an illness implies that there is a fundamental difference from normal, and a categorical rather than a dimensional approach is therefore preferred'. This approach rests on the premise that once the illness is medically treated this will negate the need for other forms of intervention as the signs and symptoms will improve. Thus even where other professional groups made a contribution to this uniprofessional approach, each one was bounded by their own codes of conduct, philosophies and models for understanding mental illness that were subsumed within the disease model reflecting the differential status of the other professions relative to psychiatry.

The Introduction of a Multiprofessional Approach

From the 1980s onwards, the configuration of mental health services reflected the developments that had occurred in the previous 30 years and a separation of care between services for people with acute presentations of mental illness and more chronic conditions. Financial infrastructures were revisited to redress the balance of care between the National Health Service (NHS) and Local Authorities (DHSS, 1981).

There was therefore a mix of old, unclosed, large psychiatric hospitals, purpose-built units for acute care in new general hospitals and designated psychiatric wards in older general hospitals. In addition provision included community residential services, such as hostels, group homes and therapeutic communities, Community Mental Health Centres and day centres run by the NHS and Local Authorities. For individuals at high risk with offending histories in addition to their mental health needs treatment was provided in regional secure units and the special hospitals.

Against this backdrop, the introduction of the 1983 Mental Health Act (MHA) reflected a concern with how mental disorder was defined and sought to clarify under what conditions people should be compulsorily detained. This piece of legislation influenced a move from *uniprofessional* to *multiprofessional* working characterized by 'many' sharing the care of the mentally ill because as (Pilgrim and Rogers, 1996, p. 88) point out its main accomplishment seemed to be 'the formal codification of existing professional roles and practice in relation to compulsory detention of patients'. This was achieved in a number of ways.

Firstly, the 1983 MHA introduced the right for patients to apply for representation by a lay or legal advocate at a Mental Health Review Tribunal that would review the legality of their detention. Tribunal panels established by the 1983 MHA included representatives from lay professionals as well as legal advocates and doctors. This gave a clear mandate to a multiprofessional panel of individuals to combine their expertise from different backgrounds to ensure the safeguard of patients' rights.

Secondly the delineation of professional roles, both within and between disciplines was made more apparent by the 1983 MHA. Under section 5 registered mental nurses in addition to doctors were given new 'holding powers' in order to prevent patients detained informally from leaving hospital. These orders allowed for compulsory detention for short periods of time (up to 72 hours) so that further assessments to explore whether compulsory admission was deemed necessary, could be undertaken.

Finally the Act specified in detail how professional roles and responsibilities should be exercised. For example Approved Social Workers (ASWs) were required to make the application for admission under section whilst two medical doctors had to provide a recommendation that this course of action was in the best interests of the patient. ASWs were required to interview people being assessed under the Act in a suitable manner to ensure that detention was the most appropriate way of providing the care and treatment which they needed. By specifying professional responsibilities in this way the 1983 MHA provided a much clearer demarcation of skills and roles of the professional groups than previously and contributions from viewpoints other than from the medical perspective were acknowledged.

Not only did the 1983 MHA influence multiprofessional contributions on a one-to-one and team level it also set out to change multi-agency working primarily between health and social services. According to Hudson (1987) agencies do not naturally collaborate, striving instead to maximize their level of autonomy. However the Act introduced in section 117 the provision of 'aftercare' for patients being discharged from compulsory treatment in hospital. Providing this type of aftercare was identified as a joint responsibility between health and social services who were required to contribute to coordinated packages of care on discharge. Similar messages regarding multi-agency working were reinforced by the subsequent National Health Service and Community Care Act (Great Britain, National Health Service and Community Care Act, 1990) that changed the traditional territory of psychiatric services, setting out more clearly the responsibilities of Local Authorities for providing community mental health care.

These changes should be viewed as developments in multiprofessional and multi-agency working as they perpetuated the status quo of professional groups working together albeit in ways they had not done previously. The professionalization of mental health care was still clearly demarked from a more inclusive approach that sought contributions from people who were using mental health services, to their care and treatment. As Perkins and Repper (1998, p. 3) point out, service users were excluded from service planning meetings and were 'only invited to ward rounds to demonstrate their symptoms and hear the doctor's prescription'. Thus whilst joint working between professionals could be deemed to have moved on a stage, the involvement of service users remained at an impasse. It is this crucial dimension of service user involvement that marks the difference between multiprofessional and multidisciplinary working.

Multidisciplinary Working in the 1990s

According to Rogers and Pilgrim (1996) the 1983 MHA was 'flimsy' in its impact on service development because of the focus on improving the rights of forcibly detained patients at the expense of promoting a more community oriented response to care delivery generally. It was not until the introduction of community care policies in the late 1980s that this balance was redressed.

Community Care, Agenda for Action (DHSS, 1988) and Caring for People (DH, 1989a) embodied the principles of care in the community that were enacted through the 1990 National Health Service and Community Care Act

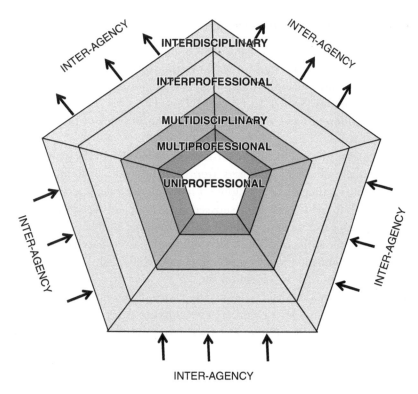

Figure 1.2 Stages of multidisciplinary working

(NHSCCA) and the subsequent Care Programme Approach (CPA) guidance in mental health (DH, 1990).

These policy developments encouraged a first phase in *multidisciplinary working* (see Figure 1.2) that continued as the NHSCCA was implemented. Both this legislation and the CPA emphasized the need to involve people who used services in the ways in which they were designed and delivered. The NHSCCA explicitly introduced the requirement for 'needs-led' as opposed to 'service-led' assessments and embodied the principle that people who receive help should have a greater choice in what is done to assist them.

This stage in the evolution of joint working is thus flagged as *multidisciplinary* in contrast to *multiprofessional* because of this more overt involvement of service users and their carers in the planning and development of community-based mental health care. Even though in the 1990s this involvement may have been tokenistic there was an emerging acceptance that service users could no longer be regarded as passive recipients as they had a valid perspective to offer about mental health services, based on their direct experience of using them.

Multidisciplinary Teamworking

According to Woodcock (1989) a team is a group of people who share common objectives and who need to work together to achieve these. From the 1990s onwards, multidisciplinary practice was increasingly delivered through Community Mental Health Teams (CMHTs). However these were configured in very different ways across Britain because of a lack of prescription in government policy.

At one end of the spectrum was the Community Mental Health Centre (CMHC) where all team members from the different disciplinary groups were brought together in one building often with a single 'operational manager'. Referrals to the team were discussed at a team meeting where decisions were made about the most appropriate team member to take on the referral and undertake the individual work with the service user. Service user groups were usually established locally and linked to CMHCs while inpatient beds were generally retained on a hospital site.

At the other extreme CMHTs existed in name only. Community psychiatric nurses (or CPNs) and social workers continued to work from separate uni-professional team bases and conduct their own referral and assessment procedures. Often CPNs were still based on the hospital site with psychiatrists. Psychology input usually remained scarce and available only via a referral from the CMHT. Occupational therapy also tended to remain within the domain of the hospital provided as therapeutic activities to inpatients. In these kind of teams service user involvement was much less developed and at a tokenistic level.

Table 1.1 The relationship between team communication and collaboration, adapted from Gregson et al. (1992)

Level of communication	Extent of collaboration
1. No direct communication	Team members who never meet, talk or write to each other
2. Formal brief communication	Team members who encounter or correspond but do not interact meaningfully
3. Regular communication and consultation	Team members whose encounters or correspondence include the transfer of information
4. High level of joint working	Team members who act on that information sympathetically, participate in general patterns of joint working, subscribe to the same general objectives as others on a one-to-one basis in the same organization
5. Multidisciplinary working	Involvement of all workers and service users as team members in a mental health setting

Parallels can be drawn between the spectrum of multidisciplinary working that existed in the CMHTs in the mid to late 1990s and Gregson et al's taxonomy (1992) which aimed to explain a link between the level of collaboration between team members and their related patterns of communication (see Table 1.1 above). Where CMHTs existed in name only, communication was non-existent or very brief and formal with little meaningful interaction between team members ensuing (levels 1–2). Where CMHTs adopted the CMHC model communication and collaboration was more akin to levels 3–4 with level 5 being reserved for those exceptional CMHTs where service users were actively involved in teamwork and service planning.

Between the CMHTs at opposite ends of the spectrum were any number of variations with many teams engaging in communication and collaboration characteristic of level 3. As a result the majority of teams had some common elements of joint working that typified *multidisciplinary* as opposed to *interdisciplinary* working. These are outlined in Key concept 1.1 below.

Key concept 1.1:   Elements of the first phase of multidisciplinary working in mental health from the early to mid 1990s

- Separate duty systems operated by CPNs and social workers.
- An emerging demarcation between community and hospital provision such that nurses working in inpatient settings were increasingly seen as distinct from their counterparts in the community.
- Alternative philosophies shaped care in the community as different from institutional care to the extent that the mental hospital was not regarded as included in 'community care'.
- The biomedical model of mental illness continued to dominate.
- The mental hospital continued to be regarded as the place for treatment and medical interventions.
- Service users' involvement was tokenistic, often limited to consultation regarding service development and service users were excluded from involvement in key decision making about service planning and delivery.

Throughout the 1990s a number of mental health inquiries began to highlight the flaws in the CMHT approach including the problems with professionals recording and passing information, poor risk management, a lack of bed availability, poor ward environments and management. In an attempt to strengthen discharge arrangements for service users considered most at risk of losing contact with services the *Mental Health (Patients in the Community) Act* (1995) was passed by parliament. This legislation introduced new paragraphs into section 25 of the 1983 MHA in order to provide aftercare under supervision (or supervised discharge), reserved for individuals who had been compulsorily detained on a section 3 for treatment in hospital and who would receive section 117 aftercare on discharge. Both psychiatrists and ASWs were identified as the professionals who would assess and apply for individuals to become subject to this increased level of multidisciplinary discharge planning.

Alongside this legislation was a renewed emphasis on the Care Programme Approach (CPA) as the mechanism for promoting a more integrated approach to multidisciplinary working (DH, 1995) and several training aids were developed to improve practice in line with policy. In addition, service user involvement in the care planning process began to be more explicitly promoted as an indicator of good practice (Carpenter and Sbaraini, 1996).

As a result many CMHTs did embark on a training programme and implemented strategies to improve integration. Where teams were fragmented across different sites they were brought together into the same building and arrangements for CPA, supervised discharge and existing section 117 aftercare procedures were revised and agreed locally between mental health Trusts and Local Authorities.

Single operational managers for the teams were appointed although as Onyett and Ford (1996) point out these managers were often nurses, social workers or psychologists who had little or no management experience. This resulted in particular tensions between the management of day to day caseloads and staff resources and the delivery of professional supervision where managers were from a different disciplinary background to the worker being supervised. Such issues led to the management of many CMHTs being perceived as weak and a criticism that the focus on individuals with the most severe mental health needs was lacking in some teams.

Whilst there was therefore some evidence that multidisciplinary working in the CMHTs was evolving from the early stages in the mid 1990s in response to the critics, there was a political view that mental health and social care needed more radical modernization (DH, 1998a, 1998b). To this end the National Service Framework (DH, 1999a) and related Mental Health Policy Implementation Guide (DH, 2001) set out the standards for contemporary mental health care and the service models that must be in place. The specialist teams identified in the Policy Implementation Guide are detailed in Table 1.2 overleaf.

Interventions offered by the specialist teams include psychological therapies such as Cognitive Behavioural Therapy in addition to relapse prevention, family work, problem solving and education about signs and symptoms of mental distress. These 'talking' treatments were to be offered alongside the prescribing of medication which focused on the use of newer neuroleptic drugs and antidepressants in line with guidelines from the National Institute of Clinical Excellence (NICE).

Table 1.2 Specialist teams identified in the Mental Health Policy Implementation Guide 2001

Team	Population Covered and Caseload Size	Focus	Disciplinary Composition
Crisis Resolution Teams (CRTs)	150,000 caseload 20–30 service users per worker	Crisis intervention to prevent relapse and hospital admission	Multidisciplinary, named worker plus a team approach
Assertive Outreach (AO)	Caseload 10–12 per worker	A strengths-based approach with individuals with severe and enduring mental health problems who are likely to disengage with services	As above
Early Intervention in Psychosis Teams (EIP)	A population of a million in total served by between 3 and 4 teams with links to respite services	Individuals between 14 and 35 years with their first episode of psychosis or within 3 yrs of symptom onset	Multidisciplinary team integrated with Child and Adolescent Mental Health Services (CAMHs), primary care, education and youth services.

Multidisciplinary Working from 1999 Onwards

The impact of these developments on CMHTs has resulted in several changes that have required a more sophisticated level of multidisciplinary working. Some CMHTs have disbanded completely to form the specialist teams identified above and a team approach is favoured over a single worker being accountable. In other areas CMHTs have retained a gatekeeping role between primary care mental health services for people with more common mental health problems and those who require more specialist interventions.

With the introduction of new non-professionally affiliated staff such as Support Time and Recovery (STR) workers into these teams, the effect of these developments has been to encourage each disciplinary group to 'add' their particular contribution to achieve the objectives of the team. Rawson (1994) would describe this as an example of the 'additive effects model' where multidisciplinary working can be regarded as the sum of the disciplinary perspectives. Represented mathematically this would look like $2 + 2 + 2 + 2 + 2 = 10$.

However, whilst many of the above developments have been positive, and heralded a further step towards increased integration of mental health care and treatment, they have raised a number of challenges that need to be addressed if interdisciplinary working is to be achieved.

Firstly, the raft of new roles and new ways of working has been introduced simultaneously and at such a pace that services have struggled to keep up with the policy changes. According to Øvretveit (1993, p. 105) formal work-role responsibilities are 'the work expected of a person by his or her employers; the ongoing duties, and the tasks which are delegated by higher management from time to time'. The roles taken on by staff within mental health services have become increasingly blurred as the range of knowledge and skill is spread across traditional professional boundaries and extended to include workers in a more hands on support role.

Secondly, organizational structures have become more complex to accommodate the diversification of teams, a factor which, according to Miller and Freeman (2003), has the potential interfere with effective teamworking. Thirdly, as multidisciplinary team membership diversifies, interpersonal relationships can be hindered by power structures and differences in commitment to teamworking. Finally a whole set of issues, marked by ambivalence, surround attempts to allow service users and carers more influence in the way that services are organized and the choices of treatment available.

Taken together these factors can all detract from the sum of the different disciplinary perspectives as postulated by Rawson. Mathematically this would look like $2 + 2 + (-2) + 2 + (-2) = 6$ and would result in mental health care struggling to move beyond multidisciplinary delivery.

Interdisciplinary Working: The Utopia?

For all the above reasons it is important to remain cautious about the extent to which mental health services and teams are working together collaboratively, demonstrating purposive interaction *between* disciplines and teams within the service system. This is reinforced by Miller and Freeman's study in 2003 which found that out of six so-called interdisciplinary teams in a range of settings including community mental health only one was demonstrating effective collaborative working.

This team was characterized by a highly developed vision of teamworking and shared philosophy of care that encouraged a shared responsibility for team actions. Communication was multilayered and all team members were expected to contribute to problem solving and decision making in respect of their service users. Role understanding was also multilayered with team members knowing what each other's role comprised, how it was performed and the underpinning rationale for action. However, role boundaries were also flexible and team members learned new skills and knowledge to contribute to better continuity of care. Joint practices were therefore evident in the team in respect of joint assessments, monitoring service users and evaluating therapeutic interventions.

While Miller and Freeman didn't consider the actual or potential contribution from service users and carers in the teams they studied, they did find that collaboration was increased by a wide range of knowledge being used on which to base team decisions and a problem solving approach. The greater this level of collaboration, the more frequently practices such as continuity and consistency of care, together with appropriateness and timeliness of referrals were upheld.

Applying this to an Assertive Outreach team provides a case example of what contemporary interdisciplinary working could look like.

Key concept 1.2:   Case example of Interdisciplinary working in an Assertive Outreach (AO) team

- Clear guidance would be evident about referrals to and from the team and about how the team connects and communicates with other community teams and inpatient services.
- There would be formal and informal arrangements for communicating within the team about day to day care of service users.
- There would be integrated pathways of care across the service with the AO team being clear about their distinctive contribution to the care system in terms of their philosophy of approach.
- The team approach would be rooted in the original model of Stein and Test (1978) that emphasizes working with each individual's strengths to promote engagement and continued participation in psychosocial interventions alongside medication compliance.
- A shared flexible responsibility for working with individuals rather than a single worker, reinforced by a good understanding of each other's role in the team and the specific roles of Care Coordinator and Responsible Medical Officer.
- Service user's awareness of their own signs and symptoms would be encouraged and such knowledge together with carers' perspectives would contribute to the team decision making process re: care planning allowing for a more shared responsibility of care.

According to Gregson et al. (1992) such combined integrated effects of disciplines working together generates new potential and enhances rather than undermines the input of individual team members. The result is a level of 'magic' or synergy within the team such that the whole becomes greater than the sum of the parts. Gregson refers to this as the multiplicative effects model which he represents mathematically as $2 \times 2 \times 2 \times 2 = 32$.

It is this level of interdisciplinary working for which contemporary service should be striving and which is possible if the policy developments are implemented creatively in practice. This shift ultimately requires a more inclusive approach across individual care, teamworking and organizational service delivery levels.

Summary

This chapter has attempted to define how interdisciplinary working differs from the ways in which mental health professionals have worked together since the early part of the last century.

Over the last 100 years systems and structures in mental health services have evolved to a point where they can support interdisciplinary practice. The Policy Implementation Guides have identified the service elements that are required of a modern mental health system and changes to the mental health workforce mean that services are poised on the brink of greater collaboration in the future.

The difference between interprofessional and interdisciplinary working is the extent to which non-professionally affiliated staff and service users and carers are involved in care planning and delivery alongside the traditional mental health professionals. A truly interdisciplinary approach hinges upon such involvement to respond to the diversity of service users' needs in the twenty-first century and reflect the wider social inclusion agenda in contemporary mental health and social care.

Models and Values for Interdisciplinary Working in Mental Health

---

Key Issues:

- Interdisciplinary working in mental health requires teams and services to establish a shared value base for collaborative care delivery.
- Power dynamics and professionalism need to be explored in relation to an increasingly diverse workforce.
- The 'recovery model' combines team members' perspectives, skills and expertise and supports interdisciplinary working.
- Dimensions of interdisciplinary working span the organizational/strategic, team and individual practice levels. Change must be supported at all levels for interdisciplinary practice to be effective.

As outlined in Chapter 1, the location of mental health care and treatment has resided within the professional domain for over a century. In addition, terms such as multiprofessional or interprofessional perpetuate and collude with the professional tensions and power struggles that emerge as hospital-based mental health care is reconfigured into community provision and Community Mental Health Teams (CMHTs) are further specialized. In order to adopt a more inclusive approach, synonymous with interdisciplinary care delivery, it is important to consider what creates and perpetuates these divisions and how they might be transcended effectively in future. As McClean (2005) states:

> Integrated care is only possible if the divisions created by professional specialisms are transcended. (McClean, 2005, p. 324)

Power, Culture and Professionalism in Mental Health Care

Loxley (1997) explains that power and culture are central themes in a process whereby professional specialisms seek permanence and autonomy in their job role. Professional groups achieve the power to maintain these autonomous positions by acquiring social and political influence and by being perceived

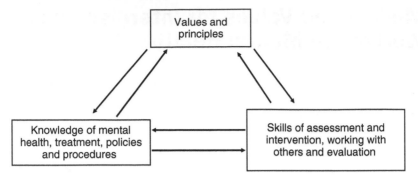

Figure 2.1 Values, knowledge and skills (Golightly, 2006, p. 6). Reproduced with kind permission

by government as pivotal in meeting their welfare agenda. Professional power is also maintained by the language and models that the different professional groups use to understand and describe mental distress. In turn these are underpinned by different value systems that influence the knowledge and skills of mental health workers and the relative importance attached to professional versus service user contributions to care and treatment approaches.

Golightly (2006) provides a diagrammatic representation to explain the interrelationship in mental health between values, knowledge and skills and practice. This is reproduced in Figure 2.1.

Since the introduction of the mental health National Service Framework in 1999 the government has been dedicated to a parallel process of changing the workforce and occupational culture in mental health services through the New Ways of Working initiative (DH, 2007). This agenda has also been reinforced by the White Paper, *Our Health, Our Care, Our Say* (DH, 2006) that embodies the concept of 'personalization' to put people who use services more than ever at the centre of the care they receive.

The key developments as a consequence of these policy changes are as follows:

- Service users have political support in their quest for services that promote recovery. They are therefore much less accepting of services that fail to listen and take account of their individual needs.
- Psychiatrists are being encouraged to prioritize their 'consultant' role and delegate hands on care and treatment decisions to other team members.
- New roles for non-professionally affiliated staff such as Support time and Recovery Workers and Carers' Support Workers are being introduced in the existing mental health workforce.
- The Approved Social Work Role is being extended to other professionals who will become the Approved Mental Health Professionals of the future.

The Ten Essential Shared Capabilities Framework (DH, 2004) was produced in an attempt to define the shared areas of knowledge, skills and values that would be required of *all* staff in the mental health workforce, including both professional and non-professionally affiliated workers (see Key concept 2.1 below). The capabilities are intended to complement other discipline specific occupational standards such as those for nursing and social work and guide mental health education and training at the pre-registration and qualification stages.

Key concept 2.1:   The Ten Essential Shared Capabilities (DH, 2004)

- Working in partnership
- Respecting diversity
- Practising ethically
- Challenging inequality
- Promoting recovery
- Identifying people's needs and strengths
- Providing service user-centred care
- Making a difference
- Promoting safety and positive risk taking
- Personal development and learning

Taken together, all the above factors have the potential to increase role blurring and the erosion of professional identities which have remained unchallenged in mental health for so long. The anxiety that professionals may experience as a result of this process can perpetuate existing power dynamics in mental health teams as members are reluctant to collaborate. This leads to less flexible ways of working and rigidity regarding each profession's contribution (see Figure 2.2).

Paradoxically then, for effective interdisciplinary working to occur it becomes even more important for workers to develop a clear sense of their unique professional identity and disciplinary contribution in order to be confident about their role when working collaboratively with others. The New Ways of Working initiative is not about all professional groups being able to do the same thing. It is about each group having a basic foundation of shared skills, knowledge and values that coexists with an openly acknowledged disciplinary contribution. It is these discipline specific contributions that allow for an interdisciplinary response to the increasing diversity of need within the service user population who seek help and assistance for a whole range of mental health problems. Bronstein (2003, p. 299) offers a helpful summary of such interdisciplinary collaboration which she describes as 'an effective interpersonal process that facilitates the achievement of goals that cannot be reached when independent professions act on their own'. She outlines the five components of interdisciplinary collaboration as follows (p. 301)

Key concept 2.2: Bronstein's five components of interdisciplinary collaboration

Interdependence: the existence and dependence on interactions between different professionals where each is dependent on the other for the successful completion of roles and tasks.

Newly created professional tasks: collaborative acts, initiatives or projects that can achieve more than could be achieved by professionals acting independently.

Flexibility: that goes beyond interdependence and refers to the deliberate occurrence of role blurring. Examples of flexibility would include seeking productive compromises and the modification of roles as professionals, thereby responding creatively to a changing context.

Collective ownership of goals: shared responsibility for the whole process of design, delivery and achievement of goals.

Reflection of process: practitioners' attention to the process of working together, including explicit discussion of working relationships and processes and providing productive feedback in order to strengthen collaborative relationships and effectiveness.

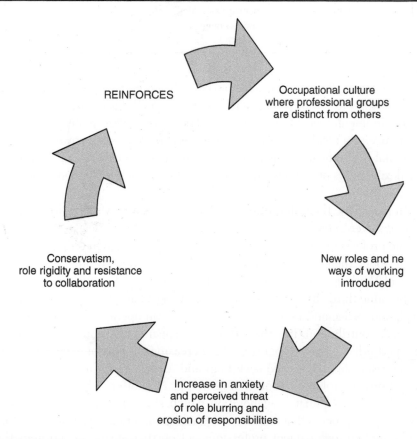

REINFORCES

Occupational culture where professional groups are distinct from others

New roles and ne ways of working introduced

Increase in anxiety and perceived threat of role blurring and erosion of responsibilities

Conservatism, role rigidity and resistance to collaboration

Figure 2.2   Cycle of power dynamics and professional roles

Models of Mental Distress

For teams attempting such increased integration and collaboration they will need to revisit the tension between managing and containing mental illness on the one hand and collaborative approaches to fostering the promotion of mental health on the other. Bracken and Thomas (2004, p. 6) explain that 'the world of mental health is replete with models ... and we invest much energy in developing models, elaborating them and more importantly, arguing that one is better than the other'.

This energy (or the ϵ factor) that professionals invest is just one of the factors that can influence interdisciplinary working and can detract from the multiplicative effect of working collaboratively that was identified in Chapter 2 e.g. $2 \times 2 \times 2 \times 2 = 32 - \epsilon$.

This phenomenon has been demonstrated in practice by Colombo and colleagues in 2002. They undertook studies with multidisciplinary mental health teams to explore why, when contributions were added to a process of shared clinical decision making, problems of communication arose that hindered rather than supported collaboration as an outcome.

In their work Colombo et al. asked participants from different professional groups in mental health (including social workers, service users, carers, nurses and psychiatrists) to respond to 12 open-ended questions after reading a case resumé for a person called Tom whose behaviour suggested that he had schizophrenia. The 12 questions sought to establish which models of mental distress the different groups used to make sense of what was happening to Tom. Not surprisingly Colombo et al. found that psychiatrists and nurses clearly favoured the medical approach which received overall most support. In contrast social workers showed support for the social model to explain Tom's signs and symptoms. Amongst the service users, there was some degree of consensus across a range of perspectives and carers endorsed the medical and family models.

These findings led Colombo et al. to conclude that as a consequence of such implicit models competing for recognition the interdisciplinary decision making process can become highly contested with the likelihood that cooperation between colleagues and with service users and carers is undermined.

Alongside the development of more specialist mental health services in Britain since 1999, there has been a shift away from the dominance of the disease model described in Chapter 1 to more holistic frameworks for understanding why people's mental health deteriorates. These include the stress vulnerability model (Zubin and Spring, 1977), the biopsychosocial model (Engel, 1977; 1980) and the recovery model (Deegan, 1988; Anthony, 1993). The latter, in particular, reflects a recognition that practitioners increasingly need to adopt a 'being with' rather than 'doing to' approach when working with service users (Hinshelwood, 1998).

The emphasis on psychosocial interventions in contemporary mental health services is a key component of the recovery model that seeks to acknowledge that individuals may continue to experience symptoms of mental distress whilst retaining a high degree of control over their lives. The strength of this approach is that it places equal value on social, psychological and medical interventions thus embracing contributions from the different disciplinary groups including the person using the service and their family. This inclusive approach allows for a more holistic perspective about how best to intervene and solve the difficulties being experienced by the service user.

This is perhaps most clearly articulated by Perkins and Repper (1998, p. 25) who assert that 'different people adopt different models for understanding what has happened to them... organic constructions... psychological, social, religious or spiritual formulations. People have a right to define their own experiences for themselves and it is rarely helpful and more likely to be alienating for the clinician to insist that their understanding is correct'.

By allowing for a combination of social, psychological and medical interventions to be provided from the interdisciplinary team at any one time this approach fits with Bronstein's components of interdependence, newly created professional tasks and flexibility. For example if a person wants to be able to cook they may need practical help to identify ingredients and prepare

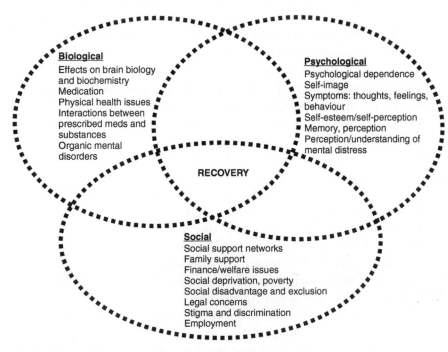

Figure 2.3   Recovery model of mental distress

a meal rather than an understanding of their neurotransmitters or intrapsychic processes (Perkins and Repper, 1998). Such assistance is likely to be provided most effectively by a support worker who has the time to spend with a service user in their own home and on a trip to the supermarket. Similarly, whilst an individual may need practical help to ensure they collect appropriate benefits and manage their income, they may also need medication to control psychotic symptoms so that they are not unduly distracted from such important day to day tasks. This way of working is embodied in an interdisciplinary approach that combines perspectives, skills and expertise from team members and in contemporary services this should be the rule rather than the exception.

The recovery model (shown in Figure 2.3) allows mental health teams and individual practitioners to work towards a more inclusive agenda that places the needs of service users, families and communities at the centre of their approach. As a result the professional power bases and boundaries are rendered intrinsically less valuable thereby reducing the negative ∈ effect that detracts from collaborative care delivery. Bracken and Thomas (2004) identify this 'thinking outside' traditional models in a quest for greater inclusivity as characteristic of what they refer to as 'post psychiatry' of the twenty-first century. They see this as inextricably linked with the concept of citizenship which they define as 'being free from discrimination, exclusion and oppression' and 'being able to define one's own identity and celebrate this in different ways' (Bracken and Thomas, 2004, p. 6). This is important as individuals often report that their experiences of discrimination and exclusion as a mental health service user are often more serious than the signs and symptoms of their mental distress that they cope with on a day to day basis.

According to Bracken and Thomas (2004), as full citizens, service users are entitled to the best medical interventions, well-resourced and effective support services and clear information about the risks and benefits of different treatments. This agenda enhances rather than negates the professional contribution to care delivery as it requires mental health team members to constantly reflect upon their working practice with service users. This approach is synonymous with Bronstein's (2003) fourth and fifth elements of interdisciplinary collaboration as for it to occur there needs to be a collective ownership of goals and reflection on the process of care delivery.

Value Systems and Value-based Practice

As Colombo et al. (2002) have shown, different models for understanding mental distress are inextricably linked with different value systems. Fulford et al. (2002, p. 25) share this view and explain that 'a social worker may be concerned with risk, a nurse or psychiatrist with compliance and a manager with client throughput'. Looking at the contributions to teamworking in this way it seems logical why the additive effects model identified in Chapter 1 is too simplistic for interdisciplinary working when workers are concerned with different elements of the care process that are at times likely to contradict each other. In an attempt to meet targets for service user throughput, team members may have inadequate time and resources to engage individuals effectively to develop a shared responsibility to risk taking which includes psychoeducational interventions and informed negotiation about medication issues.

Thus where these respective value systems of disciplinary groups remain unexplored and unacknowledged they have the potential to hinder effective communication, disempower team members, increase resistance to change and foster conflict rather then collaboration. One reason why it is important to uncover value issues as teams strive to work in a more interdisciplinary way is because they impact on practice at a number of levels.

Fulford et al. (2002) point out that at a policy level the National Service Framework (NSF) sets the value base for mental health care by defining the key standards such as combating stigma and discrimination and promoting choice, that services must meet. At an organizational level agencies will differ in the extent to which corporate values reflect a concern with statutory mental health care that aims to ensure public safety versus independent provision where services are targeted at promoting service users' autonomy and citizenship. Differences at this level will undoubtedly influence inter-agency working. At an individual level, Fulford points out that service users are a heterogeneous group and thus what is experienced as an acceptable intervention and good outcome for one person may be unacceptable for another. This makes it difficult for team members to translate service user-centred values generally into one-to-one practice.

In interdisciplinary teams research has also shown that different professional groups hold different views about the value of working together as a team. In some teams this is coloured by a disciplinary mix that remains biased towards nurses and psychiatrists. Assertive Outreach teams are often prime examples. Occupational Therapists (OTs) continue to occupy a cursory attachment role or take on a gap filling role to assert an identity as a competent all rounder (Fortune, 2000). Psychologists, as a profession, are most strongly convinced that their contribution to mental health care is best provided as a uniprofessional service which can be accessed through referrals (Mistral and Velleman, 1997). In the midst of the New Ways of Working initiative, the development of a role for support workers recruited from a background of direct experience of using services has been compromised with the introduction of Support, Time and Recovery (STR) Workers, the majority of whom do not have such experience. This has occurred more by default than design but nevertheless detracts from the contributions service users can make when employed in a paid or volunteer capacity to the delivery of services at a strategic level (Haswell and Bailey, 2007).

According to Fulford's (2002) work, one factor that seems to make the difference between teams that are able to collaborate effectively and those beleaguered by conflict is collegiate respect for the distinct values disciplinary groups hold. Thus in order for interdisciplinary teams to move forwards it is not about striving for the right values, rather it is about developing a healthy respect for the different values that team members bring. These operate at both a personal and professional level as a result of individuals' life experience and professional training and are an important and valuable aspect of the diversity of human beings.

In some areas teams have progressed to what was outlined in Chapter 1 as phase 2 multidisciplinary working by attempting to be more explicit about the shared values to which the team subscribes. For example, 'Rehabilitation and Recovery' teams in parts of the West Midlands in the early part of this decade adopted an explicit value base which embodied principles of hope and personal recovery. Fulford and his colleagues have used 'values awareness' workshops with teams to embrace diversity and build on this so that they are able to adopt a more service user-centred approach to interdisciplinary working. Where this awareness raising has taken place it should be possible for teams to agree a shared value base or philosophy developed collaboratively with service users that supports principles such as inclusivity, citizenship and anti-discriminatory practice.

In such teams it is possible for individuals who have personal experience of using services to take a more integral role in directly supporting other service users or representing the views of service user groups collectively (see Haswell and Bailey, 2007) thereby adding to the disciplinary contributions made by professionals. This important contribution is highlighted by several research studies that have identified how much service users value practical support that is not provided from a professional power base (Mental Health Foundation, 1997; Care Services Improvement Partnership, 2005) and the opportunity to exert a greater influence over the care they receive (Sainsbury Centre for Mental Health, 2006).

Integrated Service Elements

The perceived failure of multidisciplinary working in CMHTs contributed to the need for the contemporary service models such as Assertive Outreach and Crisis Resolution Services, and Early Intervention Teams. However, because of the prescriptive nature of the Policy Implementation Guides, more attention has been paid to their specific remits rather than the skill mix required to deliver these services successfully. If these teams are to avoid problems of professional rivalry, role confusion and overlap some consensus needs to be reached about which disciplines, including service users and carers, should be represented and what specific and interchangeable skills are required of the different disciplinary groups.

One of the drawbacks of these specialist teams is the issue of care continuity particularly when service users are in contact with more than one team at any given time. This requires a whole mental health care system to support interdisciplinary working that operates both within and between teams. For example, assessment procedures prior to hospital admission and follow-up after discharge need to be revisited to redress the artificial boundary between hospital and community services and to facilitate rather than constrain interdisciplinary working. Where a member of an Assertive Outreach Team holds care coordination responsibilities it seems cumbersome to suspend their involvement and transfer care coordination to the Crisis Resolution Team to facilitate admission to hospital, then subsequently to pass this on again to ward staff. This sequential approach is highlighted in a recent systematic review by Bailey et al. (2012) and seems counter to the aim of the Care Programme Approach. The review highlights that a clearer analysis is needed regarding the range of relationships being referred to within and between teams and disciplines and the level at which these operate.

Within the review some studies have attempted to describe inter-team relationships using the concepts of horizontal integration (Leichsenring, 2006; Nies, 2006; and Peck, 2002) to refer to connections at the team or single area of service level, and vertical integration to denote links between different areas of services e.g. primary and specialist mental health care. This distinction is supported by Lester (2005) who found that in mental health there is a difference of emphasis depending upon whether there is linkage between teams and services, coordination or full integration. Leutz (1999, p. 83) explains that: *'You can integrate all of the services for some of the people, some of the services for all of the people, but you can't integrate all of the services for all of the people'*. According to Leutz the first part of this statement is characteristic of the ideal interdisciplinary team that has a mandate to cut across the traditional boundaries of the mental health system.

Within an overall interdisciplinary approach outlined in Chapter 1 there will inevitably be instances when individual workers, service users and carers will need to adopt a unidisciplinary perspective or approach. This may be because of specific responsibilities associated with a professional's role or because a particular discipline is charged with delivering an essential contribution within the wider team approach. One way of thinking about the distinction between unidisciplinary and uniprofessional working is that the former is always delivered with reference to the wider team culture, which fundamentally sees users and carers as involved in decision making about care delivery. The latter is discharged with reference to a particular professional culture or model only (for example the disease model of mental distress). An interdisciplinary approach, therefore, should be viewed as fluid with the flexibility for teams and workers to move between the different domains of collaborative working depending upon a number of factors. These could include the degree of support for team culture, individual personalities, personal and professional values, leadership within the team and management structures.

Where care coordination takes place across agency boundaries as multi or inter-agency working the extent of integration will depend upon the extent to which agencies are able to collaborate to explore their diverse value systems and the interchangeability of workers' roles and skills. Integration is likely to be fostered when the agencies working together have joint policies including shared aims and objectives and a recognition of each other's frameworks for understanding and responding to mental distress.

The case example in Key concept 2.3 below highlights the importance of planning for increased service integration and the need to resolve issues of clinical and professional leadership for inter-agency working to be successful. It is also apparent from this case example that putting structures in place to support interdisciplinary and inter-agency working is a time consuming process that requires organizational support at a strategic level.

Key concept 2.3:   Case example of inter-agency working: The Manchester Mental Health Partnership (MMHP)

Recognizing that inter-agency working can be hampered from the outset if it is perceived as being imposed, the Health Act Partnership in Manchester *evolved* over a period of three years allowing for relationships to develop in advance of integrating financial arrangements. From 1996 the Health Authority and Local Authority began working in a more integrated way which culminated in the development of a joint strategy for adult services. A staged approach to strategic development is advocated as the best way forward for promoting collaboration (Valios, 2000).

Whilst a number of studies have identified difficulties in promoting inter-agency working at an organizational level due to the continued boundaries between health and social care (Hannigan, 1999; Beecham et al., 1996) the MMHP modelled strategic joint working across the health and social care interface from the outset through a *Joint Commissioning Board*. This was subsequently subsumed into a multidisciplinary partnership board comprising both executive and non-executive roles and led to the Manchester Health and Social Care Partnership Trust being established.

In an attempt to address some of the disagreements that have been documented as hindering inter-agency working, particularly in response to the detail of service models and ways of working, the MMHP engaged in various stages of consultation

Key concept 2.3 – *continued*

through the evolutionary period. This optimized the active participation of a whole range of stakeholders including people who used services and increased the likelihood that the emerging service reconfiguration would be 'owned' by a range of disciplinary groups. The *consultation exercise* included:

- An external review to ascertain the views on the appropriateness of the new model of service.
- A public consultation exercise undertaken jointly in 1999 by the Health Authority and Local Authority regarding the effective management of adult mental health services.
- A consultation document distributed at stakeholder conferences and meetings to explore how services could be provided in a more 'integrated' way building upon the development of the joint strategy for adult services.
- A multidisciplinary approach to consultation involving service user groups, staff, non-statutory providers, NHS Trusts and Community Health Councils (CHCs).

Another challenge facing the MMHP was how to resolve issues of professional versus clinical leadership as services became integrated, particularly as this required the blurring of traditional disciplinary boundaries with the increased sharing of common tasks and responsibilities. The partnership addressed this by placing an emphasis on professional leadership as integral to inter-agency working achieving it through:

- The appointment of professional leads for the disciplines of nursing; psychiatry, OT, psychology and social work that advise the Partnership Board through a shared governance structure. Despite shared roles and tasks the professional leads continued to be professionally accountable to their own discipline and each professional group had its own mechanism for ensuring high performance standards.
- Consulting the professional leads on practice and training developments related to their profession and on matters relating to the appraisal system to ensure that through this route specific performance issues could be addressed together with more generic ones relating to shared roles and responsibilities.
- A shared statement of purpose to improve the mental and emotional well-being of the partnership's population, thereby regarding service users and carers as integral players in the planning and delivery of services and the partnership approach.

The case example demonstrates that delivering joined-up mental health services has become an increasingly complex interdisciplinary activity operating across different dimensions within and between organizations. Systems and structures are required that facilitate organizational development so that strategic aims and objectives for collaboration can be realized, underpinned by organizational values that support interdisciplinary practice. This in turn will

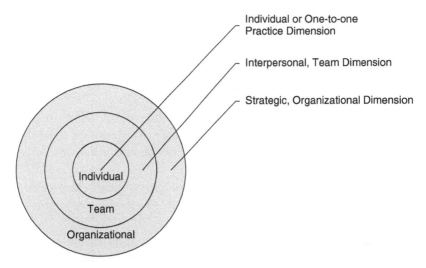

Individual or One-to-one
Practice Dimension

Interpersonal, Team Dimension

Strategic, Organizational Dimension

Individual

Team

Organizational

Figure 2.4   Dimensions of interdisciplinary and inter-agency working

allow for a repositioning of the workforce in line with strategic and operational requirements and improve the effectiveness of teams and services as experienced by those who work in them and people who use services. As modern mental health services become further specialized, as evidenced by the MMHP case for example, the importance of such linkage, coordination and full integration as espoused by Leutz (ibid) becomes even more central to effective, contemporary, coordinated care.

Consequently the dimensions of interdisciplinary and inter-agency practice that need to be addressed are the strategic or organizational dimension, the interpersonal or team dimension and the individual practice dimension with service users. These are shown diagrammatically in Figure 2.4 and discussed in more detail in the remainder of this chapter in an attempt to offer some suggestions about how each dimension can be realized to support enhanced collaboration.

Dimensions of Interdisciplinary and Inter-agency Working

The Organizational Dimension

The organizational dimension is important as it sets the strategic agenda for inter-agency working with other mental health establishments and the implementation agenda for care delivery within the agency itself. If there is a lack of support for interdisciplinary working at this strategic level then it will limit the change that individual practitioners and teams can effect on a daily basis. The mental health policy framework that has developed since the NSF in 1999 supports increased collaboration at this level and thus offers the opportunity for translation into organizational policy locally. What might this look like in reality?

- Interdisciplinary and inter-agency structures for the planning of local services reinforced through each organization's in-house policies and procedures.
- Integrated financial systems that underpin contributions to mental health services from health and social care. As shown by the MMHP case example above, the Health Act 1999 should make this easier to achieve than previously.
- An integrated framework of organizational accountability that embraces hospital and community provision and all disciplinary groups and teams.
- Each organization's mission and vision that supports the ideology of discipline inclusivity and a shared value base that enshrines respect for the diverse disciplinary contributions necessary to deliver contemporary mental health practice.
- Organizational human resource procedures that provide for staff cover but also support the interchangeability of skills and roles within teams.
- Opportunities (possibly through honorary contracts) to support the contribution of service users and carers as key partners in a strategic interdisciplinary approach including their involvement in the planning and commissioning of services.
- Leave of absence procedures that support rather than penalize employees if they are absent from work as a result of their own mental health needs.

Interdisciplinary Working in Teams

For interdisciplinary teams to work effectively they need to be able to implement practice that accords with the strategic vision and mission of the organization, and its goals and objectives. This will require effective communication and agreed referral routes and care pathways. The involvement of team members in the development of a series of indicators that will help them to identify that improved interdisciplinary working is taking place should be a starting point. A shared value base for interdisciplinary working within the organization will promote team ownership of their areas of responsibility and support flexible collaborative approaches.

Through team away days, team meetings and training and development, events teams should be encouraged to set aside time to:

- Agree ways of working both with core team members and colleagues who are part of the team's wider network. For example workers in independent sector agencies, service users who may be acting as

independent advocates and 'attached' staff such as occupational therapists and pharmacists. Particular agreement needs to be reached about
team versus practitioner accountability and confidentiality procedures
especially where team members are subject to different legal and policy
arrangements.

- Reach a consensus about how interdisciplinary working within the team
  will be managed and lead alongside the delivery of professional supervision. This is important to support team members in managing individual
  and shared caseloads and retain ownership of their unique disciplinary
  contribution.
- Create opportunities for interdisciplinary decision making, to explore
  issues around risk and referral for hospital treatment and access and exit
  routes between teams spanning the hospital/community interface.
- Clarify procedures for interdisciplinary working between CMHTs
  where they continue to exist and the specialist teams such as Assertive
  Outreach, Crisis Resolution and Early Intervention teams. These procedures will need to include guidance on information sharing about service users and transfer of care coordination responsibilities.
- Recognize and challenge inherent racist and discriminatory approaches
  that exclude service users from team decision making and team
  approaches to care delivery.
- Create a team culture that is open to a range of mental health discourses
  and seeks to promote citizenship and recovery.

Interdisciplinary Working at a Practice Level

Interdisciplinary working at a practice level is often easier to implement as it
is more within the control of individual workers than team tensions or strategic organizational constraints. However, without support from the wider team
or the organization as a whole, acting as an individual change-agent can be
potentially isolating. Practitioners will need to feel supported to work collaboratively and have the skills, values and knowledge required to effect change.
This means that they will need to have a degree of autonomy that allows them
to take some responsibility for their own practice. Emancipatory relationships
with service users that seek to acknowledge service users as citizens who have
a right to a recovery-orientated approach will be fostered when all these conditions are favoured. They can be fostered by the following:

- Practitioner's feeling comfortable with increasingly fluid professional
  boundaries whilst being clear about their specific disciplinary contribution to the team as a whole.
- Team members who are confident in their own unique skills, knowledge
  and values and have the ability to articulate and demonstrate these to
  other team members and in their work with service users.

- Clear administrative procedures for integrating interdisciplinary care packages for service users through the Care Programme Approach.
- Identification of a shared model for understanding mental distress that hinges upon a recovery approach with service users whilst recognizing the inevitability of risk issues.
- Team members who understand that the uniqueness of service users and the diversity of groups that access mental health services requires a collaborative culture in which one-to-one practice can be responsive and promote defensible rather than defensive practice.

Summary

Interdisciplinary working is synonymous with the modernization of mental health services. It hinges upon a shared model for understanding mental distress that places the service user and their family at the centre of care delivery, and a value system that promotes flexibility in relation to issues of professionalism, power and occupational culture. Interdisciplinary working spans organizational, team and individual dimensions of practice and allows service users to choose how they understand and take responsibility for managing their mental distress on a day to day basis. Interdisciplinarity is underpinned by approaches that seek to enhance recovery and promote citizenship and inclusivity.

Inter-agency working is reserved for integrated approaches that straddle agency boundaries and promote partnership working at structural and strategic levels. Where services are moving towards increased integration a staged approach is favoured that includes all stakeholders as partners in the consultation and implementation phases. Collaboration within and between mental health agencies will be encouraged if issues relating to interdisciplinary management and professional leadership accountability are debated and clarified and founded upon a shared value system that seeks to improve care delivery for service users, their families and communities.

3

Interdisciplinary Working and the Mental Health Legislation

Key Issues:

- The Mental Health Act (MHA) (1983) is revised as a result of the MHA 2007 which came into being on 1st October 2008.
- The 2007 MHA has implications for interdisciplinary working because of the way it redefines mental disorder and widens the definition of treatment.
- Professional roles are subject to change as a result of the new legislation that fits with the overall New Ways of Working initiative, having the biggest impact on Consultant Psychiatrists and Approved Social Workers (ASWs).
- The new role of the Independent Mental Health Advocate (IMHA) is introduced which has the potential to increase service users' contributions to interdisciplinary decision making about their care and treatment.

Mental health law forms the foundations of the mental health care which according to Unsworth (1987, p. 5) influences the *'intricate mechanisms of control, surveillance and discipline'*. As outlined in Chapter 1, the 1983 Mental Health Act marked a systemic shift towards multiprofessional working by outlining the legally defined duties of doctors, nurses and Approved Social Workers (ASWs).

On 19th July 2007, the Mental Health Act 2007 received Royal Assent and came into being on 1st October 2008. This Act does not replace the 1983 MHA, which continues to be the mainstay of legislation governing the compulsory treatment of individuals with a mental disorder. Rather the main purpose of the legislative change is to amend sections of the earlier Act. The 2007 MHA is also being used to extend the rights of victims under the Domestic Violence, Crime and Victims Act of 2004 and to revise the Mental Capacity Act (MCA) (2005) by introducing 'deprivation of liberty' safeguards.

This chapter seeks to outline the main changes to the law that occur as a result of the Mental Health Act (2007) and consider these in relation to their potential impact upon interdisciplinary working.

Defining Mental Disorder and Treatment

The first change made by the 2007 Act is that it introduces a singular definition of mental disorder as 'any disorder or disability of the mind'. This should result in the abolition of the 1983 categories of mental illness, psychopathic disorder and mental impairment. The latter now being dealt with as mental capacity under the 2005 MCA.

Whilst this change may not seem particularly significant it signals a more inclusive approach to defining mental distress that was identified in Chapter 2 of this book as integral to a more interdisciplinary way of working. By incorporating this wider definition, the mental health legislative framework will be able to move away from an emphasis on mental illness per se and its association with psychiatry as the dominant discourse.

This shift is strengthened by an extension of the definition of medical treatment which has also been extended by the 2007 MHA to include: 'nursing, psychological intervention and specialist mental health habilitation, rehabilitation and care'.

The notes which accompany the 2007 Act (Great Britain. Mental Health Act 2007) explain that practical examples of psychological interventions include cognitive therapy, behaviour therapy and counselling. Habilitation and rehabilitation refer to specialized services provided by a range of professional staff including nurses, psychologists and social workers with the overall aim of improving service users' physical and mental abilities and social functioning.

Such an approach accords with the biopsychosocial model of mental health that was explored previously in Chapter 2 which necessitates a combination of these interventions tailored to the needs of the individual. A revised s. 3(2)(d) of the 1983 MHA introduces the concept of an 'appropriate medical treatment test' that applies equally to all mental disorders. This means that an individual cannot be deemed to meet the criteria for being detained under the Act unless the appropriate treatment is available. A widening of the concept of treatment to include nursing, psychological and social interventions accords with the idea that for some service users treatment will be more effectively delivered in the community rather than in the hospital, coordinated through an interdisciplinary care package.

Whilst the widening of the definition of mental disorder can be interpreted as a step forward towards interdisciplinarity other amendments to Part 1 of the 1983 Act are perhaps less helpful. Rather surprisingly, a new section 1(3) makes it explicitly clear that dependence on alcohol or drugs is not considered to be a disorder or disability of mind. This reinforces the position of the original Act that, as suggested in Chapter 8, has contributed to a division of service between statutory mental health care and drugs work.

Although the guidance notes seek to flesh out the position regarding people with substance use issues they do so in a rather confusing way. Firstly the guidance states that: dependence on alcohol and drugs *is* regarded as a mental disorder (this appears to contradict the legal definition). Then the guidance states that the mental disorder may arise out of the dependency on or the actual use of alcohol or drugs. The notes also state that a person who is dependent on alcohol or drugs may also suffer from another disorder that does warrant action under the Mental Health Act 1983.

This unhelpful position reinforces an approach that is often referred to in the dual diagnosis literature as the 'primacy of condition'. This means that individuals who have complex interrelated needs must be identified as *either* having a primary mental disorder *or* a substance misuse problem. In the past this divisive position has contributed to a group of very vulnerable individuals falling through the network of care services. The 2007 MHA will therefore do little to challenge practitioners' pre-occupation with the aetiology of dual diagnosis and seems to contradict the requirements for effective mainstreaming of services to people with this presentation (DH, 2002) which is explored in more detail in Chapter 9.

According to the explanatory notes, organic disorders that affect the physiological make-up of the brain are not considered to be mental disorders unless they give rise to a disability or disorder of the mind as well. This relates mainly to service users with dementia who therefore should continue to be protected by the 1983 legislation and should receive integrated mental health care as set out in the NSF for older adults (DH, 2001a).

Treatment in Hospital and in the Community

One of the reasons that the 1983 Mental Health Act was increasingly considered outdated and in need of replacement was because it was conceived and passed as a statute when the psychiatric hospital was the main place of treatment. Following the trend towards care in the community that began in the 1950s, culminating in the National Health Service and Community Care Act (1990) and the Care Programme Approach (DH, 1990) community mental health services have become the cornerstone of care provision. As a result, today only people with severe and enduring mental health problems, who are considered a significant risk to themselves or to others, are likely to end up compulsorily detained in hospital. In relation to risk management this raises a key concern: how to ensure that people who do have severe mental health needs continue with their treatment on discharge, and do not lose contact with services and become 'revolving door patients'. Perhaps more importantly, as the numbers of beds have reduced, how can more risky individuals be maintained in the community to prevent hospital admission becoming necessary in the first place?

In the early 1990s the response to these concerns was to introduce compulsory treatment in the community. Understandably when Community Treatment Orders (CTOs) were initially proposed they were met with considerable resistance not least because their whole ethos seemed to conflict with the Human Rights' legislation. Under Article 5 of the European Convention on Human Rights (1950), individuals have a right to liberty and security, and under Article 8 a right to respect for private and family life. In the light of the Human Rights Act (1998) nursing staff in particular were concerned about potentially having to use force to treat resistant individuals. In support service user groups and the survivor movement in mental health lobbied against the proposed legislative reform arguing that if they were so ill as to require treatment against their wishes then this should be provided in a hospital setting where their rights to a Mental Health Review Tribunal and potential redress remained intact.

As a result of these issues, the Mental Health (Patients in the Community) Act (1995) was implemented as a 'compromise' legislative change, amending the 1983 MHA by introducing aftercare under supervision (supervised discharge) through revisions to section 25. The main thrust of the change was to ensure that a service user discharged from a treatment section of the 1983 MHA continued to receive aftercare by requiring them to:

- Reside at a specified location;
- Attend at specified places and times for the purpose of medical treatment, occupation or training and;
- Allow access to the mental health professionals involved in their care and treatment.

The requirements of aftercare under supervision did not therefore go as far as compulsory treatment in the community and were instead based upon the requirements for a guardianship order set out in section 7 of the 1983 MHA, with one important difference. Under the revised section 25, aftercare under supervision allows for a service user to be taken and conveyed in order to receive the care and treatment that they are deemed to need.

Section 17 leave arrangements, as originally outlined in the 1983 MHA, were also amended in 1996 at the same time as aftercare under supervision came into effect. This meant that the length of time that a patient could be on leave was increased. The 2007 MHA deletes sections 25A to J of the 1983 MHA that dealt with aftercare under supervision. In its place are further revisions to section 17 that introduce the new legal framework for Community Treatment Orders (CTOs).

Supervised community treatment differs from aftercare under supervision in that it will allow individuals who do not need to continue receiving treatment in hospital to be discharged into the community but with powers of recall to hospital if necessary. Section 17(2A) requires the clinician responsible for the service user's care to consider using a CTO in any situation when granting leave of more than seven consecutive days.

However, CTOs primarily relate to service users being discharged following treatment rather than offering a realistic mechanism for preventing admission to hospital in the first place. In addition individuals who are subject to a CTO are referred to in the legislation as 'community patients', which unhelpfully reinforces a distinction between hospital *and* community care rather than supports an integrated system where hospital care is part of an inclusive community approach. This is identified as a barrier to the effective interdisciplinary implementation of the Care Programme Approach which is discussed further in Chapter 4. Consequently the onus will continue to rest with Assertive Outreach and Crisis Intervention teams to bridge the gap between care provided in hospital and community settings but, as has been recently shown, this is difficult in the absence of a systemic approach (Bailey et al., 2012).

Professional Roles

Undoubtedly the biggest impact of the legislative changes will be upon the professionals who will be responsible for implementing these in practice. These roles are set out in Chapter 2 of the Mental Health Act 2007.

Two of the most significant changes are in respect of the Responsible Medical Officer (RMO) that is replaced by the Responsible Clinician (RC) and the role of the Approved Social Worker (ASW) which is replaced by the Approved Mental Health Professional (AMHP).

Changes to the RMO Role
Under the 1983 MHA, the RMO is the registered medical practitioner (usually a Consultant Psychiatrist) who is in charge of the treatment for the service user. Associated with this role are various responsibilities that include authorizing treatment, discharge and leave arrangements. In accordance with the legislative revisions the Responsible Clinician (RC) may be *any practitioner* who has been approved for that purpose as an Approved Clinician (AC). The guidance notes state clearly that approval need not be restricted to medical practitioners and maybe extended to professionals from other disciplines such as nursing, psychology, social work and occupational therapy.

The drivers for this change are the acknowledgement that treatment approaches in contemporary mental health care increasingly combine psychological and social interventions alongside, or in some cases instead of, medical treatment. Together with the changes to the role of Consultant Psychiatrists, as set out in the New Ways of Working initiative (DH, 2005), this means that their caseload numbers will reduce, paralleled by a delegation of responsibility to other team members (usually nurses). In some teams Advanced Practitioners with prescribing responsibilities have already been appointed ensuring that psychiatrists' input is preserved as 'consultancy' when complex treatment issues arise rather than diluted as standard case work with the majority of service users.

Section 9 of the 2007 MHA makes a number of amendments to part 2 of the 1983 Act that is concerned with compulsory admission to hospital and guardianship orders. It defines the RC as the Approved Clinician with overall responsibility for the service user's case where they are liable to be detained in hospital or as a community patient. In the case of guardianship the RC is defined as the AC authorized by the Local Social Service Authority to act in this capacity.

Given that in the past guardianship orders have predominantly been concerned with 'welfare' rather than medical treatment the position of the AC may be more appropriately held by social workers. It also affords authority to Local Authorities to sanction professionals other than social workers to undertake particular roles and functions in respect of individuals with mental health needs. This change also applies to Approved Mental Health Professionals (see below) and will require an increasingly integrated approach between health and social services to agree the detail and orchestration of the approval process.

Under the new section 17A, the RC may make a Community Treatment Order for a service user who is detained under section 3 of the 1983 Act or for a person who is not subject to restrictions under part 3 of the Act (concerned with individuals subject to criminal proceedings or under sentence). The RC can also recall the service user to hospital if they consider that their mental health has deteriorated and poses risks following discharge. The RC is responsible for renewing a service user's detention. Section 9 of the 2007 Act will insert a provision into section 20 of the 1983 Mental Health Act that requires the RC to gain the agreement of a professional from a *different* discipline that the conditions for renewal are met. This second professional must also have been concerned with the service user's treatment thereby retaining the potential for interdisciplinarity into the decision making process.

Section 5(2) of the original MHA dealt with doctors' powers to hold individuals in hospital, who were not detained compulsorily, for a period of up to 72 hours in order for a mental health assessment to be undertaken where it was felt that an application for a compulsory admission was necessary. Under a revised section 5(2) and (3) this power has been extended to Approved Clinicians suggesting that such action could be instigated by a member of staff from a discipline other than psychiatry. Where teams are adopting an interdisciplinary model of practice with shared decision making and shared responsibility for care delivery that transcends the input from individual team members, it is easy to see how the role of the Approved Clinician could be developed to ensure that decisions regarding compulsory care and treatment forms part of an overall care plan that responds quickly and effectively to the changing needs of the service user.

In reality it is likely that extending some elements of the Responsible Clinician's role to other disciplines will be met with resistance for a number of reasons.

Firstly, this change, taken together with the New Ways of Working initiative and the changes to how mental disorder and treatment are defined by the revised legislation, clearly signifies a culture shift away from the dominance of the psychiatric profession in mental health. This will take time to embed and will need to be supported at the individual, team and organizational levels of practice that were identified in Chapter 2.

Secondly, there may be some resistance from service users, who identify psychiatrists as the fixers when they are unwell (see Chapter 9). Where service users have been used to very traditional models of care delivery the idea that psychiatrists can delegate increasing aspects of care and treatment may be perceived as a reduction in the quality of service being offered. This is supported by research into the impact of New Ways of Working in which service users criticized the changes, particularly in respect of continuity of care. Some, whose care spanned hospital and community services, reported seeing a number of different psychiatrists which was unhelpful. Others emphasized the importance of the relationship between themselves and their psychiatrist as an aid to recovery and feared that the changes in the psychiatrist's role would result in longer stays in hospital. Also that their recovery would be slower than with a trusted relationship with one individual (Harrison et al., in preparation).

Finally, it is not easy to see why professions allied to medicine (psychology, social work and occupational therapy) would opt to take on increased responsibility for a service user's treatment in the role of an AC unless they were given additional training, support and renumeration. In particular, where service users present with very risky behaviours there may be concerns about litigation should the care and treatment plan fail to manage these. There may also be questions raised by medical colleagues over a different profession's level of competence to take on a remit that has been traditionally associated with medical training and the discipline of psychiatry.

Changes to the ASW Role

Section 18 of the 2007 MHA replaces section 114 of the 1983 MHA and the role of the ASW with that of the Approved Mental Health Professional. As with the Approved Clinician, this will mean that in practice a wider group of professionals, such as nurses, psychologists and occupational therapists (but not medical practitioners), will be able to carry out the role and functions traditionally held by one discipline, in this case social work.

The main drivers for this change have been purely logistical workforce issues rather than a move away from the need to combine professional perspectives regarding compulsory mental health care and treatment. Firstly, with the introduction of the Capable Practitioner framework (Sainsbury Centre for Mental Health, 2001) and the New Ways of Working initiative, the roles of mental health professionals have become increasingly blurred.

Secondly, many Local Authorities have struggled to recruit and retain a sufficient number of ASWs which has led to a perceived shortage in the workforce of staff willing to take on this role. In reality this has more to do with allowing time for the changes to social work education and training (in particular the requirements for the new degree and PQ1) to embed, than a lack of interest in mental health social work. In addition, there are concerns that ASWs are becoming an aging profession that is likely to impact upon succession planning.

The main change is that is that in future AMHPs may be employed by the NHS rather than by local councils; although safeguards will remain in place to try and ensure that they continue to provide the same independent social perspective that has been unique to the ASW role previously. An amended section 145 of the 1983 MHA refers to AMHPs who are *carrying out their functions on behalf of a Local Social Service Authority*. This reflects the political commitment to retain the mechanism, whereby an 'independent' practitioner can provide an objective assessment for admission unencumbered by the politics of working for the same organization as the doctor providing the medical recommendations. In the past social workers were also likely to have access to a different set of resources and services than those provided by the Trust, if the ASW decided to opt for a less restrictive alternative than hospital care. What is not clear is whether AMHPs will have access to this same range of services if they are not employed by the Local Authority. The real dilemma is whether these 'hybrid' measures will be sufficient to support continued robust multiprofessional decision making at the point of admission for compulsory detention.

Changes to section 13 of the 1983 MHA will mean that, at a strategic level, Local Authorities will continue to have a role in ensuring there is an adequate AMHP service and will have the latitude to decide whether they operationalize this themselves or enter into agreements with other LAs and/or NHS Trusts. If they opt for the latter this is likely to require some sort of inter-agency/partnership agreement about how this will work in practice. There are likely to be related, cross disciplinary tensions around pay and conditions that will need to be tackled as currently ASWs are paid on a very different scale compared with, for example, clinical psychologists. Interprofessional supervision for AMHPs who are not from a social work background is also likely to require attention as it is unlikely that other professions will have the skills or expertise to provide advice and guidance about the intricacies of AMHP practice in relation to the statutory requirements of the role.

Under the new arrangements AMHPs will have to demonstrate the skills and attitudes necessary to ensure they are able to provide the independent social perspective. To ensure this is the case Local Authorities will approve AMHPs but before doing so must be satisfied that the individual has the appropriate competencies for dealing with people with mental health problems and complies with the regulations for approval. The approval for the training for all AMHPs will continue to rest with the General Social Care Council (GSCC) in England and the Care Council for Wales (CCfW). However, the GSCC will disband in 2012 and will be replaced by the Health Professions Council.

In practice this means that where AMHPs are employees of a health service organization they will be required to demonstrate practice and standards approved by a Local Authority under the auspices of a social care professional body. This raises a rather confusing interdisciplinary issue in relation to the continued regulation of these individuals. Under section 114A(4) of the revised MHA 1983, the functions of the AMHP are not considered to be 'relevant social work' for the purposes of Part 4 of the Care Standards Act (2000). This means that unless AMHPs are social workers by professional background they will not be regulated by the codes of practice required by the GSCC and CCfW. Nurses, psychologists and occupational therapists all have their own professional organizations with their respective codes of conduct that could allow for disciplinary differences in the way that AMHPs carry out the role depending upon these uniprofessional requirements.

In practice such diversity could be counterbalanced by the overarching Code of Practice that will accompany the revised mental health legislation provided that it does not conflict or undermine guidance issued by the professional bodies and issues of interprofessional working are dealt with clearly and constructively.

The role of the AMHP in relation to admission to hospital will continue to be what it was for the ASW: that of making the application (unless it is made by the service user's nearest relative), and coordinating the overall assessment process, taking all factors into account to ensure that detention in hospital is the most appropriate course of action or whether there is a less restrictive alternative. In addition, AMHPs will be required to consider making an application for a guardianship order on the LA's behalf. In several other respects AMHPs will also have the same role and function as those previously discharged by ASWs. These include:

- Informing the service user's nearest relative that an application for admission for assessment is to be made.

- Consulting the nearest relative (as long as it is reasonably practicable and will not cause unreasonable delay) re: an admission for treatment or a guardianship application to check that they do not object to the application being made.
- Being able to apply to the County Court to displace or replace a nearest relative.
- Where a nearest relative is the applicant for detention, providing a social report.
- Ensuring that the service user is interviewed in a suitable manner.
- Applying for a warrant to search for or remove to a place of safety a person who is living alone or in need of care.
- Entering and inspecting premises where it is believed there is a person with mental health needs who is not receiving proper care.
- Assessing a service user with a view to making an application if requested to do so by the service user's nearest relative and informing them in writing if their decision is not to make the application.
- Where a service user is admitted to hospital, providing a report to the hospital managers on the service user's social circumstances.

In respect of Community Treatment Orders, the AMHP's role is to make a recommendation that the order should go ahead by stating in writing that they agree with the opinion of the Responsible Clinician and they are assured it is appropriate to make the order. Where CTOs are to be extended beyond their initial six month period, an AMHP must be in agreement with the RC that the criteria for extending the order are satisfied and it is the appropriate course of action before a report for extension can be made.

AMHPs are also likely to get involved in certain treatment decisions covered by Part 4 of the 1983 MHA where interprofessional decision making is required. One example of this is section 58A that relates to Electro Convulsive Therapy (ECT). Where a service user is detained in hospital and in need of this treatment but is incapable of giving consent to receive it, the Second Opinion Appointed Doctor (SOAD) cannot authorize ECT before consulting two other professionals, one of whom must be a nurse concerned with the service user's treatment and a second who must be neither a nurse nor a doctor. AMHPs could therefore find themselves in this latter position responsible for providing an additional professional perspective in relation to a service user's treatment plan.

The legal intricacies of the original ASW role are therefore retained and in some instances enhanced by the 2007 MHA as they transfer to the remit of AMHPs. In order for this change to be implemented effectively there are a number of key interlinked interdisciplinary issues that will need to be addressed through training and development programmes.

Firstly, there is the issue of uniprofessional training and post-qualifying experience. Before the introduction of AMHPs, the role of the ASW was exclusively held by professionally qualified social workers who, by virtue of the training and post-qualification work experience, were familiar with working within a statutory framework whether this was in relation to mental health, vulnerable adults or child protection work. Undertaking such statutory interventions is unique to the social work profession as a whole and provides a distinct foundation on which to build skills and knowledge for providing an independent social perspective re: care and protection that incorporates anti-oppressive and anti-discriminatory practice. Disciplines such as nursing, psychology and OT may have mental health experience relevant to the AMHP role but will not have this same level of exposure to statutory work. This needs to be addressed if they are to tackle the legal dilemmas associated with being an AMHP on a day to day basis.

This presents a challenge for the providers of ASW training programmes who will need to ensure that the programmes are tailored to meet the training needs of a wider range of participants. This is not simply a matter of exposing a mixed group of learners to the same input (Hewstone and Brown, 1986), rather for training to be effective it will need to respond to the different training needs of the different groups and address the disciplinary differences and similarities between the professions in how they execute the role. Some of the challenges of designing such shared learning programmes have been outlined previously (see Bailey, 2002; and 2002a).

The training programmes will also need to tackle head on the need for AMHPs to bring an independent perspective and model for understanding mental distress to a multiprofessional decision making process. In relation to Community Treatment Orders there are concerns about collusion and a lack of such independence if the AMHP is, for example, a nurse and a member of the clinical team, where it could be difficult to argue against a medical recommendation for community treatment.

Independent Mental Health Advocates

One of the ways in which service users may be supported in ensuring that the decisions made about their care and treatment are interdisciplinary is through the use of an Independent Mental Health Advocate (IMHA). This role was introduced by section 30 of the 2007 MHA and is available to service users who are liable to be detained under the Mental Health Act 1983 for assessment and/or treatment, or who are subject to a guardianship or Community Treatment Order. An IMHA may be requested by a service user's nearest relative, Responsible Clinician or AMHP to visit and interview the service user in order to assist that individual to obtain information and understand:

- The provisions of the Act and any conditions or restrictions that apply in their particular situation.

- The nature of the medical treatment being proposed, why and under what authority it is to be given.
- Their rights as an individual detained under the 1983 MHA and how they may obtain help to exercise these.

In order to fulfil their role and responsibilities IMHAs are able to conduct an interview privately with the service user. They are also entitled to interview anyone who is professionally concerned with the service user's medical treatment and with the service user's consent they may inspect any records relating to the service user's detention, treatment or aftercare plan that are held either by the NHS Trust or the Local Authority.

This new role provides for an additional disciplinary contribution to a decision making process that has been traditionally located in the hands of mental health professionals. It will be important to evaluate whether service users experience greater involvement in their care provided under the 1983 MHA as a result of this safeguard or whether the role of the IMHA is limited to tokenistic representation in order to preserve the multiprofessional status quo.

In respect of promoting interdisciplinary decision making it is noteworthy that the role of the IMHA does not explicitly extend to supporting a service user in a Hospital Manager's Hearing or Mental Health Review Tribunal (MHRT). However, it is highly likely that their input will be required by service users who are party to this process and need support to understand the decisions made by the professionals on their behalf. The make-up of the MHRT remains as it was in the original 1983 MHA with representation from a lay member alongside a legal advocate and doctor thereby retaining some opportunity for multiprofessional decision making. The question remains as to whether this could have been developed a stage further by the revised legislation.

PRACTICE FOCUS 3.1

Interdisciplinary Working According to the 2007 Mental Health Act

Robin was initially referred to a CMHT that has since specialized in working with service users with psychosis. Robin is 48 and has a diagnosis of schizophrenia. He is the eldest of three children all of whom live at home with their mother and all of whom have a diagnosed mental health problem. Robin has a CPN as his Care Coordinator as he receives his medication monthly by injection.

Robin first experienced the changes to the Mental Health Act when he was readmitted to hospital in crisis and his consultant psychiatrist changed. This was because the team was adopting the New Ways of Working approach and his Responsible Clinician came from the Crisis Resolution and Home Treatment Team that facilitated his admission.

Practice Focus 3.1 – *continued*

Following treatment in hospital Robin is now subject to a Community Treatment Order which means that he will continue to receive his medication at home but can be recalled to hospital if he refuses the injection or the risks to himself and his family increase. His care has reverted back to the psychosis team.

The role of the AMHP in the psychosis team is exclusively held by social workers even though it was opened up to other disciplines as a result of the 2007 MHA. Consequently Robin has experienced little change in the way that he was assessed for his last compulsory admission. Because of their specialist role in respect of mental health act assessments AMHPs in the team get a lower caseload than other Care Coordinators which is currently around 20.

Robin and his mother are involved in decisions about care and treatment mainly through their collaborative relationship with Robin's Care Coordinator, the CPN. At present the psychosis team do not have access to Independent Mental Health Advocates but Robin has been told this should happen in the not too distant future. In the meantime if Robin's CTO is renewed it is likely that the RC will consult with the AMHP to ensure that the conditions for renewal are met. As a key member of the interdisciplinary team providing care to Robin and his family it is essential that his Care Coordinator contributes information to this decision making process.

Summary

The Mental Health Act of 1983 has been revised as a result of the MHA 2007. It introduced the new roles of the Responsible Clinician, Approved Clinician, Approved Mental Health Professional and Independent Mental Health Advocate. These roles embrace professionals from a wider range of mental health disciplines than previously and therefore provide an opportunity for increased interdisciplinary working. However these new roles have been met with some resistance and have the potential to detract from collaborative working unless issues such as pay, conditions of service, interprofessional training and professional regulation are addressed. The changes in the way the Act defined mental disorder and medical treatment opened up the potential for a more inclusive model of mental health care delivery. The challenge is now to ensure this is provided in such a way that professional rivalries become a thing of the past, rather than a barrier to contemporary mental health care in the future.

4

Interdisciplinary Care Planning in Mental Health

Key Issues:

- The Care Programme Approach (CPA) provides the administrative framework for delivering effective interdisciplinary mental health care and consists of assessment, care plan design and delivery and monitoring/review.
- Since 2008, the government has refocused the CPA on people who have complex mental health needs and are likely to require an interdisciplinary response from a range of workers and agencies.
- The CPA may be strengthened by the implementation of integrated care pathways that seek to improve either elements of the care delivery process or specific intervention strategies for a specified mental health problem.
- The Care Coordinator should be a professional member of the relevant mental health team who has the skills, knowledge and influence to facilitate effective interdisciplinary working.
- Interdisciplinary care planning will need to transcend the boundaries of Community Mental Health Teams and the hospital-community interface to provide continuous care for individuals.

Historical Developments of the Care Programme Approach

The CPA was introduced in April 1991 (DH, 1990). Led by health and originally intended as a screening system imported from the USA it aimed to prevent people with severe and enduring mental health problems falling through the net of psychiatric care. In the beginning, decisions about which individuals were suitable for CPA were made almost exclusively by the Consultant psychiatrist reflecting a uniprofessional approach. Service user involvement in the process was on the whole disregarded as CPA was 'done to' rather than 'done with' the person accessing mental health services. Many service users were unaware that they had a care plan and received little in the way of information about the process.

At a strategic level an inter-agency approach to CPA was hampered from the outset when the 1990 NHS and Community Care Act gave Local

Authorities the lead role in implementing care management procedures for adults. Whilst this legislation did not relate specifically to people with mental health problems the intention was that it would provide a case management framework particularly for people requiring funding for long-term residential placements and community-based care packages. With the reprovision of mental health services from hospital to community settings gathering momentum in Britain in the early 1990s the almost simultaneous introduction of the CPA and care management impacted significantly on people with severe and enduring mental health needs. Whilst there was a growing recognition in health and social care that a more coordinated approach to assessment and care delivery was needed there was confusion over which framework should be used for people with mental health problems and which agency should take the lead. This perpetuated dilemmas and decision making at all levels of CPA implementation spanning organizational procedures, individual practice and teamworking specifically in respect of how the two approaches might be reconciled.

Not surprisingly, five years after its launch in 1991, the implementation of the CPA remained patchy (Audit Commission, 1994) and was struggling to keep pace with the developments in community-based care. As a result service users often experienced care continuity and coordination as fragmented. Consequently several policy documents and related guidance aimed to encourage a more coherent approach to care planning (DH, 1994a; DH, 1994; DH, 1995; DH, 1999b). The policy emphasis was clearly focused upon collaboration as reinforced by the DH in 2008.

> 'Services should organized and delivered in ways that promote and coordinate helpful and purposeful mental health practice based on fulfilling therapeutic relationships and partnerships between the people involved. (DH, 2008, p.7)'

A tiered approach to care planning was introduced to reflect that some service users needed a more 'multidisciplinary' care package than others and terms such as 'simple' and 'complex' or 'full' and 'minimal' CPA began to be used to differentiate between the different levels. The role of the *Key Worker* was clarified as being responsible for pulling together all the elements of an individual's care plan into a coherent whole. There was also a token approach to involving a service user in the care planning process as their signature on the care plan documentation was required. In these respects the CPA began to develop from a uniprofessional to a multidisciplinary activity, as defined in Chapter 1. This development reflected the moves towards multidisciplinary working more generally in mental health services during the same time period.

The desirable outcomes of the CPA have been identified in a number of publications and are summarized below. If the care planning process is implemented effectively all these elements should be in place, clearly documented and communicated to *all* parties involved see Key concept 4.1 below.

Key concept 4.1:   Desirable outcomes from a Care Programme Approach

- All needs for health and social care will be identified by competent assessors.
- Needs will be addressed through a well-designed care plan agreeable to service users and carers which coordinates the service involves.
- A Care Coordinator will take responsibility for coordinating care planning and care delivery.
- The service user and carer will know who to contact.
- The Care Coordinator will be responsible for convening reviews.
- The success of the care plan and changing needs of the client will be reviewed and plans amended as necessary.

The CPA as a tool for improving multiprofessional communication arose because a number of mental health inquiries had identified this as a weak link contributing to tragic homicides involving people with severe and enduring mental health problems in the late 1980s (Reith, 1998). The CPA was thus essentially a 'common sense' approach to care planning that was never intended to generate the significant issues with implementation that ensued.

Not surprisingly the tensions created between the NHS and Local Authorities at a strategic level and the dissent amongst mental health professionals about the CPA in practice started to be illustrated by a number of studies. One such example was Miller and Freeman (2003) in their study of a CMHT implementing care plans based on the three levels of CPA. They found that whilst at a senior management level the local mental health trust and social services department had developed joint documentation that included both psychological and social assessments for service users, only health professionals used it. The social workers, supported by their managers in the Local Authority, continued to use their own assessment forms which all team members agreed provided a much more comprehensive assessment of social needs. Having two types of documentation compounded confusion over the severity of a service user's mental health needs and contributed to buck passing within the team regarding the role of the key worker. This is a classic example of where the different professional perspectives in mental health detract from the sum of multiprofessional contributions resulting in poorer outcomes for service users.

In the light of these implementation issues the National Service Framework (DH, 1999) re-emphasized the CPA as the mechanism for care planning in mental health. Care providers were instructed to ensure the system was integrated with Local Authority care management procedures to avoid duplication of effort and improve care continuity and communication in line with the original outcomes identified. The NSF clearly delineated two levels of CPA: standard and enhanced and set out the areas of care that should be covered by the care plan which were reinforced by the Department of Health in 1999. This latter document described what the features of a truly interdisciplinary system of care planning would look like in an attempt to facilitate integration between health and social services (see Key concept 4.2 below).

Key concept 4.2: Features of an integrated Care Programme Approach between the NHS and social services departments

- A single operational policy.
- A single point of access to assessment, support and resources from both health and social services.
- Joint training for staff.
- One lead-officer to work across all agencies.
- Common and agreed risk assessment and management procedures.
- Shared information systems.
- Single complaints and serious incidents procedures.
- Shared budgets.

This level of detail was helpful in guiding mental health Trusts and Local Authorities towards increased integration. However, there were no clues about how this should be achieved between hospital and community services. With the emergence of the specialist teams such as Assertive Outreach and Crisis Resolution this gap became even more evident. Inpatient nursing staff complained of being a 'Cinderella' service compared with their community-based counterparts and low morale and workforce shortages followed. Consequently CPA did not operate seamlessly for those service users whose needs spanned periods of inpatient and community-based care.

The CPA as a tool for promoting a continuous service bridging the hospital and community interface has been hindered since its inception because of the tendency to reserve its application for discharge planning. Unfortunately the National Service Framework did little to help clear up the mismatch between the CPA approach 'in principle' and how it would be translated into practice. Whilst the NSF stated that 'all mental health service users on CPA should ... have a written care plan' it did not reinforce the message that access to the CPA was synonymous with access to specialist mental health services.

By stating that those service users 'who are assessed as requiring a period of care away from their home should have a copy of a written aftercare plan agreed on discharge' the NSF inadvertently colluded with the link between the CPA and hospital discharge.

In a further attempt to refocus the CPA on service users with the most complex needs once the specialist mental health teams were in situ, the Department of Health conducted a consultation exercise in 2006 that culminated in new guidelines in 2008. This guidance makes it clear that where a service user has straightforward needs and is in contact with only one agency their care will be facilitated through a uniprofessional approach. Formal paperwork for care planning, and reviewing the care delivery will not be required; although a statement of care agreed with the service user should be recorded in some way such as a letter or in individual medical notes. For this group of service users this form of documentation will constitute their 'care plan'. The 'new' CPA is reserved for service users who have more complex needs, requiring multi-agency support and under the previous arrangements would have qualified for an 'enhanced' interdisciplinary care package. Essentially however the elements of the care planning process are as set out in earlier guidance notably:

- A systematic assessment of health and social care needs for everyone in contact with the psychiatric services.
- A care plan, drawn up in consultation with the individual and their family/carers and also with members of the multiprofessional team.
- A nominated Care Coordinator who should keep in close contact with the service user and their family and coordinate the contributions to the care plan.
- Regular review and monitoring of the care plan to assess and respond in an ongoing way to any changes in need or circumstances.

The difference with the 'new CPA' is that everyone referred to secondary mental health services will receive an initial assessment of their mental health needs that will act as a screening process to decide what level of care delivery they require and what risks they present. The outcome of this initial screen will be communicated to the service user and a decision will be reached as to whether a more in-depth assessment is triggered as part of the new CPA. The guidance makes it clear on page 18 that the CPA does not cover the part of the care pathway prior to this decision being reached about whether secondary care or further assessment is necessary. This is shown diagrammatically in Figure 4.1.

Taking each stage of the CPA in turn it is possible to consider how interdisciplinary working can be promoted so that the approach is experienced as collaborative at each stage.

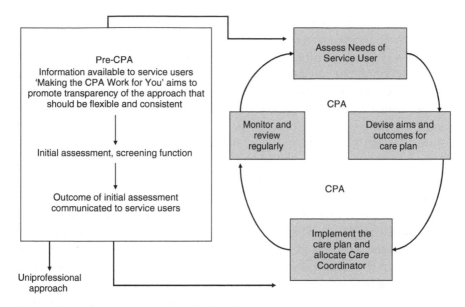

Figure 4.1   The process of care planning

The Care Programme Approach Process in Practice

Interdisciplinary Assessment

The first stage of the CPA is a comprehensive multidisciplinary and multi-agency assessment that includes the full range of needs and risks. It draws upon information from mental health professionals alongside the perspectives of the person using mental health services, their family and close social contacts. Establishing a shared approach to assessment should encourage people with mental health needs to continue to engage with specialist services particularly at times of increased vulnerability. It will also ensure that the desired outcomes from the care plan are owned by the range of disciplines involved. An assessment of social care needs should be conducted as part of the comprehensive assessment process in order to determine whether the service users meet the eligibility criteria for Fair Access to Care Services and Direct Payments.

In respects of risk issues relating to the service user it is also important to consider the safety factors that may reduce these risks and the strategies that service users and their families draw upon to cope with life on a daily basis. It is important that the assessment process does not undermine these skills. Interdisciplinary assessments therefore need to be sensitive to the service user's needs at the times when they are well which may be different to what they need during periods of increased mental distress. This is referred to in the most recent CPA guidance as crisis and contingency planning. Comprehensive assessments will also need to be conducted in such a way so that the range of professionals involved can collect information relevant to their contribution but which does not require the service user to repeat their story to several members of the same mental health team. This has been a common criticism from service users regarding the lack of joined-up assessments in the past.

The mental health National Service Framework sets out the areas that should be covered as part of a comprehensive assessment that reflect the recovery model for understanding mental distress that was outlined in Chapter 2. Good interdisciplinary assessments as part of the CPA should therefore dovetail with a recovery approach and cover the areas shown in Figure 4.2.

According to the DH guidance, the comprehensive assessment of a service user's mental health needs should be outcome oriented and not just focus on what professionals and services can offer. It is expected that for people on the new CPA the Health of the Nation Outcome Scale (HoNOS) ratings will be completed at least once a year and when any key changes are highlighted in a service user's needs as part of the ongoing assessment and monitoring process.

In addition to HoNOS (which has not been used consistently in mental health teams to date) there are also other outcome measures that can be used

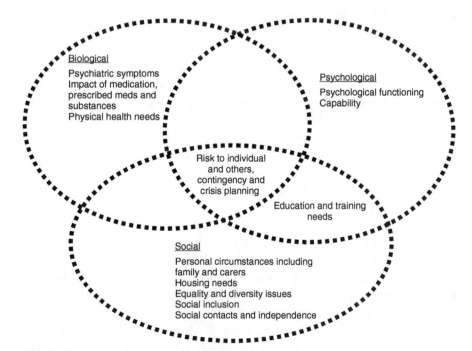

Figure 4.2 Areas included in a Comprehensive Care Programme Approach Assessment as set out in the National Service Framework

to detect improvement in an individual's mental health and social function. For example, the Lancashire Quality of Life tool (Oliver et al., 1996) includes a range of social outcomes as part of the assessment while the Beliefs About Illness Questionnaire (Birchwood et al., 1993) may be more appropriate for use with service users who experience a predominance of psychotic symptoms. Such tools can be used with other related assessments such as, for example, the Dartmouth Assessment of Life Inventory (DALI) (Rosenberg et al., 1998). This would be applicable where interdisciplinary assessment issues arise around a service user's interrelated mental health and substance use needs. If such outcome measures are to be used as part of the comprehensive CPA assessment, an interdisciplinary approach will be optimized where all team members are familiar with the measures being used and have reached agreement about how they contribute to the overall assessment process.

Devising and Implementing the Care Plan

A good comprehensive assessment should give rise to a series of objectives that form the basis of the care plan. Lloyd (2010) asserts that these should follow the SMART rule being Specific, Measurable, Achievable, Realistic and Timely.

In the case of a standard CPA involving only one agency or professional these can be relatively straightforward to negotiate with the service user. However, where enhanced care plans are necessary to meet the complex needs of people with severe and enduring mental health problems this poses more of a challenge. Integrated care pathways can provide an opportunity to ensure an enhanced CPA is delivered in a more interdisciplinary way. According to Lloyd (ibid, p. 8) 'a care pathway is a previously designed care process' that focuses upon either the mental disorder (for example, schizophrenia) or the service provision. In mental health there have been less care pathways that in other clinical areas (for example, diabetes) because of the diverse way that mental health problems present and the individualistic way people respond to their signs and symptoms.

Where care pathways are appropriate each discipline will need to collect information on what tasks they undertake and what interventions they provide along the care continuum. This allows some consensus to be gained within and/or between teams on what is agreed as best practice in interventions in respect of interventions and outcomes. Developing a care pathway provides teams with a useful opportunity to examine team member's roles and functions which can be especially important if moving from a generic CMHT approach to specialized teams such as Assertive Outreach.

Variations from the pathway can be coded according to the different staff groups involved which again highlights the unique and shared contributions between disciplines and allows an opportunity for reflecting on this. It also allows the team to see how the service users respond to different professional interventions. For example, if a nursing approach to medication compliance appears not to be working very well this can suggest to them team that an alternative approach should be tried.

Developing and delivering an enhanced CPA can often result in the service user being sidelined with the professionals' objectives dominating by virtue of the complexity of the plan and the different agendas of those involved. Lloyd (ibid) suggests that the five principles of the Mental Capacity Act 2005 should underpin the care planning process. Where users experience a lack of ownership of their care plan it can be difficult to agree who is taking responsibility for managing mental distress and any arising issues of risk. A perceived lack of involvement can also extend to professional colleagues and family members if they feel excluded from the decision making process that is part of the care plan implementation. Such a situation leaves the Care Coordinator open to criticism when the care plan is not complied with and, in a worse case scenario, he or she is held individually accountable if something goes wrong. This, in turn, can perpetuate further defensive practice which reinforces care planning as a professional obligation rather than as an aid to recovery for the service user.

One way to break this cycle and move towards a more interdisciplinary approach is to consider the following:

- With people with complex mental health needs it is virtually impossible for one member of the mental health team to be able to deliver all the interventions necessary all of the time.
- Arriving at shared objectives is only possible when the diverse interests and different agendas of the professionals, service users, their family and supporters are considered and respected.
- The skills, energies and expertise of a single professional seeking to implement a complex care plan entirely in isolation will invariably run out.
- To implement a care plan successfully in the long-term to meet individuals' complex needs the organizations' procedures and systems for CPA will need to be augmented through practices of leadership that draw upon the energies of an interdisciplinary 'team'.

Some mental health teams have looked to Integrated Care Pathways (ICPs) to provide 'structured multidisciplinary care plans' (Campbell et al., 1998, p. 133) that outline the optimal sequencing and timing of interventions (Ignatavicius and Hausman, 1995, cited in McQueen and Milloy, 2001, p. 45). The aim of an ICP is to have the right people, doing the right things, in the right order, at the right time. By tracking deviations from the original care pathway it allows for a comparison to be made between planned care and the care that is actually given. The approach hinges upon professional groups being 'willing to have their interventions and outcomes displayed in a deterministic sequence' (Jones, 2001, p. 65). This allows the contribution of different disciplinary groups to be scrutinized at various junctures along the pathway and provides a feedback loop about what professionals are doing that is unique to their profession and where they are implementing shared skills and approaches. One of the difficulties in moving teams to an ICP that promotes interdisciplinary working is that different professional groups may be unwilling to sacrifice their role autonomy.

In their investigation of assessment practice in the State Hospital in Scotland, McQueen and Milloy (2001) developed a version of the assessment care pathway for service users and their carers as a guide to what they should expect to happen by certain stages of the assessment process. Implementing an integrated care pathway either as a means of realizing a national guideline, for example, the NSF standards, or as a way of improving an area of practice that a team agrees must improve, can provide the impetus for examining the team's role and function and within it professional responsibilities. It can also assist in developing an interdisciplinary approach to record keeping; for example, through the use of a shared record which is either electronic or paper based where all professionals document their involvement. These records should then accompany the service users through the course of their care which facilitates information sharing and guards against individuals being asked to repeat their story to several different professionals.

Whilst a care pathway focusing on the CPA assessment process may help standardize the care service users receive there is a danger that this can have the adverse effect of undermining their autonomy which is so central to the recovery oriented approach. If care pathways become a deterministic mechanism to exercise control and compliance with service users deemed not to be conforming to the pathway of care this can undermine their rights to withdraw from mental health interventions. A fully integrated interdisciplinary care pathway is therefore only possible when there is active service user participation. However as Jones (2001, p. 65) points out this would require 'a political shift to empower the user'.

To date integrated care pathways have been more prevalent in the USA where user-centred values are perhaps less evident than in the UK and have been implemented in hospital settings. With the increasing focus on community-based care planning and the values of the recovery model these factors suggest opportunities for a variation on a theme to meet the needs of UK service users and service systems.

These requirements have been identified in a general sense by Moxley (2001) as leadership as partnership. Those involved in care plan implementation could learn something very useful from this particular approach; if for no other reason than because leadership and care plan implementation share one thing in common: they both involve a serious meddling in other peoples' lives.

Applying Moxley's (2001) five requirements for leadership as partnership to the care planning process offers a positive framework for greater interdisciplinary care plan implementation.

1. *There must be a balance of power.* Successful execution of a care plan will not happen when the professionals have power (some may have more than others) and the service users and their families do not. If coercive power is used to implement a care plan then partnership working will stop. The alternative is for each person involved in the care plan to claim their own personal power – for service users this is likely to draw upon their lived experience of mental distress and for their families the emotional involvement they have contributed over the years and the support they may be willing to offer in the future. Professionals will need to reflect on how they bring both their professional and personal power to bear in the approach (this may involve sharing their own personal experiences where relevant) to achieve the right balance of power at critical points in the service user's recovery.

2. *There must be a shared goal and objectives even though everyone may have different views about how to achieve these.* This focus can be especially helpful, as inevitably conflict about the care plan will surface from time to time. By acting to remind all parties that they are working towards a common aim the care planning process can allow for some areas of conflict to be accepted and accommodated i.e. agreeing to disagree in the interests of achieving the desired outcome.

3. *There must be a shared sense of responsibility and accountability.* This means that everyone including the service user and their families are responsible and accountable for realizing the care plan objectives. This helps to guard against an *us* and *them* approach, creates a climate for recovery and if something goes wrong the buck stops with everyone. This approach is more likely to lead to defensible rather than defensive practice from mental health workers by virtue of their increased confidence and energy.

4. *Partnership requires respect for the person.* A partnership approach to care planning values the diversity of inputs by celebrating the inherent worth and value of everyone involved.

5. *Partnership must be applied to important as well as unimportant issues.* It is easy to see how the above approach could work well with an individual who is compliant with medication and where risk issues are minimal. Such an approach is just as important with individuals who are

often seen as 'difficult' to engage and where their coping strategies may be considered risky.

The following case study is an attempt to illustrate the application of this approach in practice.

PRACTICE FOCUS 4.1

Philip

A comprehensive assessment with Philip (aged 43) reveals that he has complex mental health needs arising from auditory hallucinations symptomatic of a psychotic disorder. He also has moderate learning disabilities and epilepsy that is reasonably controlled with medication. Philip responds to his voices by talking 'to himself' and is often found giggling and preoccupied. Sometimes his voices do trouble him to the extent that he will shout a lot and become verbally aggressive to those around him. His physical health is poor, arising from a serious smoking habit and poor nutrition.

Philip has not worked since he was made redundant from a chicken-processing factory 10 years ago (he had worked there since leaving school). He relies on benefits and lives with his father and younger brother (aged 40). Philip's mother died eight years ago and his father has never remarried. An assessment of Philip's quality of life bears testimony to his lack of social activities, low self-esteem and poor social skills. His only interest appears to be in gardening which he pursues through a gardening group at a day centre where he attends twice a week.

A risk assessment has identified the following:

When Philip gets bored and unhappy he makes hoax calls to the emergency services. This has landed him in trouble with the police on at least two occasions.

Philip complains that his brother beats him and he has presented with physical injuries that support this. When this happens Philip will sleep rough for a couple of nights in the local town until the problems at home die down. On at least one occasion he was found in the early hours of the morning very drunk sleeping on a bench. The police were concerned that he would be an easy target for muggers and on this occasion took him home.

Philip has previously been barred from the day centre because of the safety risk posed by his smoking. On one occasion he deliberately set a litter bin on fire by dropping a lighted cigarette into it.

Whilst Philip's epilepsy and psychotic symptoms are fairly well controlled with medication he does have a tendency to stop taking his tablets at times when he is very stressed or unhappy. This has led to him experiencing a couple of seizures at the day centre and an exacerbation of feelings of persecution. In the case of the latter it is difficult to know whether these beliefs have a foundation in reality as a result of his brother's violent behaviour. The doctors have suspected on several occasions that Philip's injuries have been self-inflicted.

In attempting to implement a care plan with Philip there are two fairly important issues to grapple with. First is the glaringly obvious imbalance of power which lies exclusively in the hands of the professionals who have little hesitation in preventing Philip from attending the day centre when he 'misbehaves'. This perpetuates Philip's disengagement with services as it means he cannot attend his gardening group which is the only activity he enjoys. When his attendance is stopped he has no option other than to remain at home in a potentially violent environment. Secondly, Philip's coping

Practice Focus 4.1 – *continued*

strategies such as sleeping rough, fire setting and contacting the emergency services pose a significant risk to others but also to Philip himself. These risks are exacerbated when Philip disengages with services and compounds the difficulties in implementing a care plan in partnership.

In attempting to move on from this 'stalemate' situation it would be helpful to arrive at some shared objectives for a care plan that realize Philip's goal of pursuing his interest in gardening whilst meeting the professionals aim which is to prevent the cycle of disengagement and associated risk. Some skilled negotiation will be central to this process. For example, it will be important to establish with Philip the links between events which cause him distress (being unhappy and bored at home), his behaviour (fire setting at the day centre) and the consequences (being barred from the centre, missing the gardening group and so becoming even more frustrated and unhappy at home). This will pre-empt a more in-depth exploration of how Philip copes with his unhappiness currently and how he might try coping differently in future. It is also likely to require agreement from colleagues at the day centre that strategies other than barring need to be invoked if Philip is behaving in a risky way. Perhaps he would agree to leave his cigarettes with a member of staff until agreed break times when staff would be able to supervise. Exploring such options allows for a recognition that responsibility and accountability for managing risk and mental distress is a shared process which in turn may encourage Philip to feel more empowered by the involvement of professionals rather than powerless.

Obviously Philip's home situation needs further exploration and intervention and opportunities to engage with Philip's father will be key to this. In the longer-term it may be possible to meet with all three members of the household to explore how they communicate and deal with conflict and stress with a view to reducing the levels of hostility and aggression. If there is evidence to support Philip's reports of being physically abused by his brother it may be necessary to invoke adult protection procedures although again a balance will need to be reached between promoting Philip's safety and continuing to pursue the wider goals of the mental health care plan.

Ultimately it may be possible to support Philip to seek voluntary or paid employment using his gardening skills in the wider community rather than within a specialist mental health service. His previous work history shows that he has been able to make a long-term commitment to employment which should not be dismissed as impossible for the future. Such a long-term outcome would have the added benefits of reducing his time being bored at home, may ease the stress within the family and allow Philip to feel he is making a positive contribution either vocationally or financially to his family and wider community. This in turn may help to reawaken a sense of worth and purpose that currently seems missing from Philip's life and enable him to feel more valued as an individual rather than as, at present, everybody's problem.

Interdisciplinary Care Planning: Spanning the Hospital/Community Interface

According to the guidance issued in 1999 'the CPA as a framework is as applicable to service users in residential settings (including prisons) as to those in the community. Assertive in-reach is as relevant as assertive outreach as an underpinning principle of the CPA' (DH, 1999b, p. 5).

Following on from the initial assessment it may be decided that further assessment in a treatment or custodial setting is required. Alternatively it may be decided that the needs identified can only be met in hospital either by admitting the service user informally whereby they accept the recommendation to receive care and treatment in this way or on a formal basis where a compulsory order is used. Irrespective of the legal status of the individual, part of the care planning process is to identify the best place to provide the care. At this juncture hospital staff require relevant information about the individual's needs stemming from the assessment in order that they can begin to intervene appropriately. This requires an interdisciplinary approach spanning the service interface that views the hospital as part of the user's wider community.

This becomes even more important given the introduction of Community Treatment Orders in the 2007 MHA (see Chapter 3).

When the person has been admitted to hospital, Ryan et al. (1991) claim it is not clear whether the hospital-based multidisciplinary team will supply the Care Coordinator or whether they will more frequently be drawn from the community team. Where hospital admission is orchestrated through a Crisis Resolution and Home Treatment Team this adds an additional stage in the admissions process which can result in even greater confusion of roles and responsibilities. With the emergence of Community Treatment Orders and the specialist mental health teams the separation of hospital and community services is rendered increasingly 'artificial'. Therefore the CPA must be sufficiently portable to deliver a care plan embracing a range of settings, workers and services. Greater attention should to be given to how practitioners might work more flexibly to promote greater continuity. This is likely to mean that the role of Care Coordinator is retained during admission through the process of in-reach until discharge. This way of working will have a knock on effect on caseload management and workloads of inpatient and community staff which is likely to demand some creative human resourcing policies to promote the flexibility of the service.

The Care Coordinator Role

The care coordinating role thus becomes increasingly integral to the successful implementation of care plans for people with complex needs like Philip. Given his interest in gardening and a long-term goal of employment the involvement of an Occupational Therapist may be useful. An OT would be able to assess the skills gap that needs bridging if Philip is to return to work. This may involve a staged approach to rehabilitation and recovery in the medium-term. However, this is unlikely to be the only input necessary given the ongoing issues around medication. Also a more in-depth assessment of the family situation may lead to adult protection procedures being invoked which may give rise to other social issues such as alternative accommodation, benefits and social relationships.

The decision about who should be the Care Coordinator was initially discussed in para. 3.1.18 on page 50 of the Building Bridges guidance that aimed to support care plan implementation. A number of factors were outlined that should be taken into account including the service user's needs and wishes, workloads, authority to undertake the role and adequate training. Initially identified as the key worker, the role was spelt out quite clearly in Developing the Care Programme Approach (Clark et al.,1995, p. 32). The remit was to:

- Monitor and review the package of care agreed in the care plan.
- Liaise, coordinate and keep in regular contact with the service user and so be able to respond effectively and quickly to changing circumstances and needs.
- Be the focal point of contact for the other professionals involved with the GP and with any carers who may also be involved.
- Identify unmet need and communicate unresolved issues to appropriate managers.

Whilst the guidance is helpful in outlining the respective elements of the role, it omits to highlight the importance of reaching an interdisciplinary agreement about who is best placed within the team to take it on. Care coordination by coercion is unlikely to yield satisfactory results either for the service user or the worker. Similarly allocating the role to a colleague who is absent from the team discussion is likely to breed resistance unless the worker has been consulted previously and is willing and able to accept responsibility. Careful thought should also be given to the level of responsibility the professional carries as a consequence of their job role and the training they may need to be an effective Care Coordinator. In some areas a contentious issue has surfaced over whether it is appropriate for health care or social work assistants to act in this capacity. This hinges on the extent to which these workers are integrated into the interdisciplinary team and the level of influence they are able to have over colleagues who may be considered professionally superior.

When thinking about training for Care Coordinators there are two inter-related but specific parts to this role that requires a combination of skills and knowledge in respect of interdisciplinary and inter-agency working in addition to user involvement.

To coordinate the care plan the Care Coordinator needs to have the necessary span of responsibility to be able to influence networks with other professionals and services and to be able to negotiate effectively (Gupta, 1995). They need to be a key point of information about services and how to access them and about the service user, such that information flows in a two-way process. Care Coordinators also need a basic knowledge of the legal framework in which they are operating which includes both the legislation and policy guidance such as the 2007 Mental Health Act and associated Code of Practice.

To engage service users and their families in effective care coordination workers need to be able to obtain their trust, have frequent and meaningful contact and some freedom to act as an advocate on their behalf at CPA meetings and in negotiation about how their needs will be met (Gupta, ibid). Returning to Philip it may be decided that whilst a time-limited intervention from an OT may add significantly to his care plan another member of the mental health team may be more appropriate to develop a longer-term relationship with Philip and his family that acts as the bedrock for the greater acceptance of interventions. The National Service Framework states explicitly how carers should be involved in the CPA (DH, 1999a) which is further reinforced through the Carers (Recognition and Services) Act 1995.

Thus, whilst working with Philip, the Care Coordinator will also need to ensure that his father's needs are taken into account as part of the care planning process. This may reveal that Mr C has sufficient needs to require a local authority assessment under the NHS and CCA (Great Britain. National Health Service and Community Care Act 1990) which the Care Coordinator should be able to instigate.

Given the potential involvement of so many stakeholders in the care plan, Care Coordinators should be encouraged to reflect upon who benefits from their undertaking of the role. In the past there has been a tendency for care coordination to take place primarily to satisfy the requirements bestowed upon CMHTs, rather than to improve the delivery of care to the service user. However, the National Service Framework, despite its lack of emphasis on service user involvement generally, does make explicit the standards of care users can expect to receive in relation to care planning. This provides an impetus for Care Coordinators to fulfil their role in a creative way with improving service delivery as an agreed priority. However, evidence shows that differing professional perspectives on the nature of the role have at times acted to hinder such an approach.

When canvassed about their perceptions of the role CPNs in Shepherd et al's (1995) study said they should be aware of all the psychological, medical and social interventions being offered, in order to coordinate the respective inputs to a service user's care plan. However, they were clear that they would not be responsible for actioning these interventions. In addition, whilst they would do their own assessments they would leave the more complex assessment of social needs to social work colleagues. In contrast, social workers said they regarded the Care Coordinator role as akin to that of care manager which involved *both* coordinating and executing the care plan. They felt that CPNs should include more social awareness in their thinking and take on a social aspect to their professional contribution.

With the introduction of the Ten Essential Shared Capabilities in 2004 and the New Ways of Working initiative since 2005 the roles of mental health professionals have become increasingly blurred since Shepherd et al's study. There is emerging evidence that within newly reconfigured mental health teams CPNs, social workers and OTs are first and foremost Care Coordinators and all are offering a similar range of psychosocial interventions.

Reviewing and Monitoring the Care Plan

In an attempt to assist service providers and practitioners in providing the care service users need, standards are at last set for providing written care plans alongside a requirement that specific arrangements be put in place to integrate care management and the CPA (DH, 2008, p. 53). Review and monitoring arrangements are also likely to be governed by whether the service user is receiving section 117 aftercare under the 1983 Mental Health Act or is subject to a Community Treatment Order. Where the legislation influences the care planning process, reviews are required within specific timescales and the Mental Health Act 1983 Code of Practice sets our quite clearly the requirement for these to be 'interdisciplinary' in their approach, embracing the contributions of a range of stakeholders.

Where service users are receiving care in hospital a review should be held in readiness for discharge to reassess their needs which require ongoing intervention in the community. This is where an interdisciplinary model of working that spans the service interface can be instrumental in ensuring continuity of care. This may also require an integrated inter-agency response particularly where issues of funding come into play.

Summary

The CPA is a framework for care planning that should underpin rather than undermine interdisciplinary working. It should be used as the framework for care planning for all people in contact with specialist mental health services spanning the interface of hospital and community provision. Hospital admission can be part of the CPA as it is simply a change in location of the provision of care and the care plan should be flexibly enough to reflect this.

The Care Coordinator role should be allocated in full agreement with the professional concerned and the service user. A range of skills, knowledge and areas of influence are required for workers to be able to undertake the role effectively and leadership theory may help develop a partnership approach to its delivery.

The CPA provides a framework for discharge planning which currently links with statutory aftercare. It should provide the mechanism for making interdisciplinary decisions connected with discharge for anyone who has been in hospital.

A care plan should be needs led, have a clear aim and a set of objectives that are measurable such that at the point of review it can be seen whether the outcomes of the care plan have been met and if not then why not. Documenting the assessment and care plan should not be constrained by minimalist paperwork but must reflect the information needs of the interdisciplinary team involved with care provision for the individual.

5

Interdisciplinary Risk Assessment, Planning and Management

Key Issues:

- Risk assessment is a misleading term. It masks a process that involves the collection of information, judgements about whether risks are likely or not to occur and the severity of the consequences if they do.
- Whilst practitioners may be able to do little to reduce the elements of risk presented by a service user, they have greater control over how to monitor and influence the outcomes of these through risk management.
- Risk assessment and management should be a collaborative endeavour including working in partnership with service users and their families.
- Practitioners should be aware of biased thinking in making judgements about risk and effective interdisciplinary working is one way to challenge these biases.
- Interdisciplinary working that locates the accountability and responsibility for risk taking within interdisciplinary teams, supported by their organization, should lead to more robust strategies for risk assessment, planning and management.

If multidisciplinary working is being achieved successfully this should ensure that individuals with mental health needs are supported in coordinated work that is satisfying to the practitioners involved and guards against defensive practice in risk assessment planning and management. According to the Department of Health, *'dilemmas arise when practitioners of different disciplines cannot agree about what arrangements it would be best to support'* (DH, 2007). It is in these circumstances when delays in care delivery often occur and the likelihood of increased risk or inadequate safeguarding issues arise.

The concept of risk inevitably pervades every component of life. It is entailed in all courses of action and therefore cannot be eliminated. Although associated with conventionally negative outcomes such as loss, injury or harm, positive outcomes of taking risks include: a sense of achievement, mastery, affirmation and getting a buzz.

According to Stone and Taylor (2000) the concept of risk should replace that of dangerousness in mental health particularly to reflect the fact that 'dangerousness' is viewed as an inherent, static characteristic of an individual assessed through subjective means. By referring instead to 'risk' this invites further definition depending on the interaction between the individual and their environment. Risk is considered changeable over time and can be assessed more objectively.

The reality of risk is evident everyday in mental health practice and is described as 'the likelihood of an event happening with potentially harmful or beneficial outcomes for self and others' (Morgan, 2000, p. 1). As Foster (1998) points out, mental disturbance has the potential to render anyone emotionally and behaviourally unpredictable thus practitioners cannot rely on any one formula or policy that will eliminate risk or mental disorder. However, what often happens in the case of a mental health inquiry is that professionals are called to account and often persuaded that if they had more effectively monitored the behaviour of the individual then somehow they could have minimized or prevented the tragic consequences.

The mental health literature refers to this kind of approach as risk minimization or a 'safety first' approach which has several inherent problems (Titterton, 2005) and contradicts a recovery-oriented way of working.

Key concept 5.1:   Problems with a safety first approach to risk (Titterton, 2005, p. 15)

- Ignores the needs of vulnerable people
- Denies individuals the rights to choice and self-determination
- Leads to a loss of sense of self-esteem and respect
- It can lead to a form of institutionalization with the loss of individuality, volition and an increase in dependence
- At its worst it can lead to the abuse of vulnerable people

The alternative is to adopt a risk taking approach which Davis (1996) and Titterton (2005) assert is fundamental to working in partnership with mental health service users to promote autonomy, choice and social partnership. Such an approach, which is not the same as harm avoidance, embraces the importance of psychological and physical wellbeing whether individuals are in receipt of community or institutional care. It chimes with a more inclusive approach to mental health that considers individuals' rights to make decisions alongside those of their carers even when these may conflict. By accepting that there can be benefits to risk taking such an approach can challenge the paternalism and over-protectiveness of some mental health services.

The previous chapter explored the Care Programme Approach as the framework for interdisciplinary care planning. The most recent mental health legislation together with the updated guidance on the CPA (DH, 2008) consistently refer to the CPA as the mechanism for assessing and managing risk for people with severe and enduring mental health problems. Embodied within the statutory framework is the expectation that effective use of the CPA will lead to risk minimization. However where the CPA is aligned with a recovery approach to mental health and effective interdisciplinary working there is an opportunity to engage in a more inclusive, egalitarian approach to working with risk that can support, rather than undermine an individual's recovery.

Interdisciplinary Risk Assessment, Prediction and Management

Risk assessment is a misleading concept which is why according to Brearley (1982) practitioners need an organized and systematic approach for understanding and working with risk. Carson and Bain (2008, p. 19) provide a useful overview in which risk assessment is only part of an overall process.

According to Carson and Bain, risk assessment involves considering the risk elements and making judgments about which of these risks are more likely to be evident in certain circumstances (prediction). Risk management involves working with the dimensions of risk to establish which risks need to managed as part of the care plan either by the worker, service user and/or mental health team (risk management).

The extent to which the above process is evidence of interprofessional, multidisciplinary or interdisciplinary working will depend upon whether there is agreement reached about the values and models of mental distress that underpin the approach to risk assessment, prediction and management. Where service users and carers' conceptualizations of risk are considered alongside those of the professionals together with more holistic models of

Risk Assessment	Risk Management
– Collecting and assessing information about the risk elements	– Discovering and manipulating the dimensions of proposed risk into a plan

Risk Elements
 	
Features inherent in the risk proposed
 	
  – The outcomes (e.g. harm possible)
  – The likelihood of the outcome
	Risk Dimensions
	
	Features of the risk that may be influenced by the decision makers
	
	  – The resources available to manage the proposed risk including uncertainty
	
	  – Quality and quantity of knowledge about those resources and the risk elements

Figure 5.1 Carson and Bain's overview of risk (2008). Reprinted with permission of Jessica Kingsley Publishers

understanding mental distress as outlined in Chapter 3, the likelihood is that risk assessment and management will err on the side of being a more creative exercise. This is reinforced by guidance from the Department of Health in 2007 that advocates a person-centred planning approach to risk assessment and management (see Titterton, 2005 for a full description of PRAMS (Person centred, Risk Assessment and Management System)).

Risk Assessment

Key concept 5.2 below reveals that there is a general consensus that risk assessment involves gathering information. Often because workers are used to undertaking this task and are generally familiar with the concept of assessment there is a tendency to overemphasize this aspect of practice in risk situations. However, as Foster (1998, p. 84) explains, 'Part of the overall task of caring for the mentally ill in the community is to hold, to assess, to monitor and to manage risk and on the basis of this make informed decisions regarding the lives of our clients'. In accordance with a recovery model such decisions need to be reached in discussion and negotiation with the person using the service, their family and carers.

This requires that workers expand their repertoire of assessment and intervention skills to embrace approaches that can at times accommodate service users taking risks but on other occasions contain these where the service user is unable to act in the interests of their own health and safety. Workers' decision making also needs to be based upon best available evidence to promote interventions that are defensible (agreed in collaboration with the service user) rather than defensive (the best course of action as judged solely by the professionals) (O'Rourke and Bird, 2001, p. 11).

Key concept 5.2:   Definitions of risk assessment

- Risk assessment should be understood as collecting information about what might happen as a consequence of taking the proposed risk, how significant (good or bad) that might be and how likely it is that that will occur (Carson and Bain, 2008, p. 109).
- The systematic collection of information to determine the degree to which harm (to self or others) is likely at some point in time (O'Rourke and Bird (2001, p. 4).
- A gathering of information and analysis of the potential outcomes of identified behaviours. Identifying specific risk factors of relevance to an individual and the context in which they may occur. This process requires linking historical information to current circumstances, to anticipate possible future change. (Morgan, 2000, p. 2).
- The key principle of risk assessment is to use all available sources of information – a proper assessment cannot be made in the absence of information about the patient's background, present mental state and social functioning and also his or her past behaviour (DH, 1995).

Best practice in interdisciplinary working would therefore suggest that risk assessment cannot be performed in isolation as no one agency or professional can hold all the information about the needs of a person with mental health problems who is at risk. There may be a need to seek out more comprehensive information from several sources or better quality information based on evidence of behaviour in certain situations. This requires that inter-agency information and that held by members of the mental health teamworking directly with the service user is pooled. During this stage it is important to be clear about the principles that will guide the risk assessment process and these can support or undermine interdisciplinarity.

For example the principle that risk taking hinges on all team members sharing and debating openly information relating to the assessment of an individual's risk behaviours will strengthen the likelihood of an interdisciplinary approach. Agreement needs to be reached at the outset of the assessment about what kind of information should be collected from whom, using which methods and how this will be updated. Very rarely do mental health teams take the time to explore these issues in-depth especially where 'tick box' risk assessment schedules encourage a procedural rather than process oriented approach.

Interdisciplinary information collection and dissemination pertaining to risk behaviours is particularly important in the light of the functionalization of mental health teams especially as a service user may be receiving a service from one or more teams including an inpatient service at a time of crisis. Understandably each team will have slightly different priorities in respect of the information they require about risk although there are likely to be areas of overlap which need to be explored and acknowledged openly. The fact that shared information also needs to be detailed and accurate has been highlighted by a number of mental health inquiries, including the inquiry into the death of Jonathon Zito at the hands of Christopher Clunis in 1994. This inquiry made three specific recommendations in respect of risk assessment (Reith, 1998, pp. 32–41).

Key concept 5.3:   Recommendations for risk assessment from the Clunis Inquiry

An accurate record should be made of any incident of violence and the details should be included in the patient's discharge summary.

An assessment of the risk of dangerousness should be included in the discharge summary whenever the patient has acted with violence.

Everyone who has contact in his professional or service work with mentally ill people who pose a risk of violence should have training in the assessment of dangerousness and understand when to refer a patient for expert guidance.

An interdisciplinary approach will also be difficult to achieve where there is a gap in inter-agency procedures for sharing information with others such as the police or voluntary sector workers who may be involved more peripherally in an individual's care plan. Reaching agreements about the boundaries of confidentiality are complex as they are influenced by the professional bodies with their associated codes of conduct, specific agency requirements and national legislation. Thus, in accordance with Article 8 of the Human Rights Act, mental health service users have a legal right to expect confidentiality and mental health workers have a duty to protect service users' civil liberties as far as possible. As O'Rourke and Bird (2001, p. 4) point out, the information or confidence belongs to the service user and professionals must negotiate information sharing except where it can be argued a breach of such confidentiality is necessary to preserve public interest. They assert that where mental health workers break confidentiality they must be able to: explain their reasoning, have evidence to support their decision and have consulted others about the issues. All of these factors hinge on effective communication with other members of the interdisciplinary team including the service user and their carer.

Effective systems for interdisciplinary and inter-agency communication are fundamental to the process of risk assessment. As Reith points out it is now a familiar finding that such communication is identified as a systematic failing in a number of mental health inquiries. For example, the Boland inquiry (1995) (Reith, 1998, pp. 53–56) identified the following factors as contributory to the death of Ellen Boland at the hands of her son who received input from the specialist mental health services over a nine year period.

- Lack of continuity of information passed between junior doctors and the GP;
- No referral to social services which hindered the collection of sufficient information;
- No multidisciplinary team operating;
- No liaison with other agencies including the police or probation service.

If the information gathered for the assessment of risk reflects level 1 multidisciplinary working (Chapter 1) this will constrain the robustness of the approach as evidenced by at least three mental health inquiry reports. First, the Stoker inquiry (Northumberland Health Authority, 1996) asserted that although each discipline had considered the risks from their own perspective the information and individual assessments of risk were not shared.

Similarly the Viner Report (1995) concluded that 'the professional work undertaken with Robert Viner was sometimes impeded by ineffective multidisciplinary teamworking...there was...little evidence that teams actually functioned as teams' and 'multidisciplinary working can be problematic, particularly where the team formation takes place in the context of professional rather than functional management' (Reith, 1998, p. 82–88).

Finally Smith (1996) alludes to a holistic model for understanding mental distress as underpinning an effective collaborative risk assessment: 'Given the psycho-social nature of the impact of schizophrenia, and other severe psychiatric illness, on the patient, relatives and carers, it is important to ensure that a multi disciplinary and multi-agency approach is always adopted'.

A useful framework to assist an interdisciplinary approach to the collection of information is given by Morgan (1998), who suggests that a range of methods should be employed to collect information in respect of:

- Individual risks to self and others;
- Those risks which relate to given situations, and;
- Risks that arise as a consequence of the systems that impact upon the service user and their care.

Similarly, guidelines on risk assessment issued by the Department of Health and Social Security (DH, 1990), suggests that information relating to past behaviour, present mental state and social functioning, together with defining situations and circumstances known to present increased risk are necessary to make an accurate assessment. The guidelines are informed by the case of Kim Kirkman (West Midlands Regional Health Authority, 1991) highlighting the sources of information that should be considered in order to achieve an accurate assessment of risk pertaining to the above. These include:

- Past history;
- Self reports from the service user and observations of their behaviour;
- Discrepancies between what is reported and what is observed;
- Psychological and, if appropriate, physical tests;
- Statistics from studies of related cases;
- Predictive indicators derived from research.

Where mental health teams are committed to implementing an interdisciplinary approach to the assessment of risk, time should be given to considering what is a growing body of available guidance to arrive at a decision about the type and sources of information that the team needs to share at relevant stages of the risk assessment process.

Risk Prediction

The purpose of collecting information is to be able to make a prediction about the likelihood of a risk behaviour occurring in the future. As Mullen (1984) suggests, 'the question to be posed in clinical practice is not "is this person dangerous?" but rather "might this person in certain circumstances behave in a dangerous way?"' This approach leads into a more clearly delineated formulation of risk that considers whether the level of risk is high, medium or low and whether the risks posed are general or specific to individuals or given sets of circumstances. A formulation of risk should also consider over what timescale the risks might be evident (Carson and Bain, 2008, refer to this as the risk period), alongside a consideration of the individuals' coping strategies to arrive at a more in-depth understanding of when they might need help to implement such strategies effectively.

Risk prediction, or risk decision making as it sometimes described, links the collection of information from the assessment with the management plan. Writers differ in the detail of the definitions although there is some agreement that this stage in the process involves weighing the available evidence gained during the assessment in order to make an informed judgement on the likelihood of the risk behaviours identified in the past presenting themselves again in the future (see key concept 5.4 below).

Key concept 5.4:   Definitions of risk prediction or decision making

- The method and procedure by which the risks perceived to attend a given situation, a given set of facts, or some proposed course of conduct in connection with these are considered, measured, assessed and recorded so that the appropriateness of a present situation or a proposed course of conduct can be better measured and determined (Northumberland Health Authority, 1996, p. 28).
- 'The assigning of probability to a person, indexing the likelihood of that person to cause harm to self or others within or outside hospital' (O'Rourke and Bird, 2001, p. 4).
- The link between risk assessment and risk management. It uses the element of prediction as a basis for identifying the balance between the benefits and harms of risk behaviours. Risk decisions will form the basis for the subsequent planning process (Morgan, 1998, p. 10).

The difficulty with this aspect of the approach is that risk prediction is not an exact science. According to Morgan, linking risk assessment with prediction in mental health has limited value not least because people are inconsistent in their behaviour even without the experience of mental health problems.

Carson and Bain (2008) recommend adopting the cognitive continuum model initiated by Hammond (1978) which consists of six levels of knowledge to support a risk decision. These range from intuition through to peer-aided and system-aided judgement to quasi-experiment, controlled trial and scientific experiment. Different levels of knowledge will exist for different risk situations and practitioners should aim for the highest level of knowledge available. This may seem fine in principle but it is unethical to subject people with mental health problems to scientific experiment to ascertain whether they will demonstrate the risk behaviour in question. Interdisciplinary working can strengthen peer and system-aided judgement where information about an individual is shared effectively. This can be augmented by higher level information from research studies which might suggest how groups of people with given mental health problems may act in certain circumstances.

Moore (1996) points out that predicting risks can lead to four possible outcomes shown in Table 5.1. This reveals a fifty per cent likelihood of the outcome being accurately predicted even when assisted by the use of valid models and instruments and best available information about how people with mental health problems behave in certain circumstances. Reed (1997) emphasizes this weakness by suggesting that although mental health workers may have a good understanding of the general picture of risk factors it is bridging the gap between the general to an individual's particular situation that presents the greatest difficulty. This is where effective interdisciplinary communication can be of great value.

Predicting risk therefore has particular implications for working in partnership with service users. Both Moore (1996) and Duggan (1997) question the ethical dilemmas surrounding the false positives and negatives of prediction. Where an individual's behaviour is perceived as risky they maybe subject to sanctions which impact upon their civil liberties even though the risk behaviour would not have materialized anyway (Bacon, 1997). Similarly the sanctions imposed may themselves create a higher risk or another outcome occurring, which has not previously been considered as part of the risk assessment. For example Ryan

Table 5.1 Outcomes from risk prediction

	Positive prediction that risk behaviour will occur	Not predicted that risk behaviour will occur
Risk behaviour occurs	Successful prediction of outcome (risk behaviour was predicted and occurred)	Type 2 Error (false negative), risk behaviour not predicted but occurred anyway
Risk behaviour does not occur	Type 1 error (false positive, predicted that risk behaviour will occur but it didn't)	Successful prediction of outcome (risk behaviour was not predicted and did not occur)

(1997) draws attention to the iatrogenic risks inherent in the mental health system such as the long-term, insidious side effects of medication or electro convulsive therapy. The service user may consider these more risky and detrimental to their lifestyle in the longer-term than complying with prescribed medical treatment for controlling acute symptoms. In order to guard against such errors an interdisciplinary approach can promote reflexivity in respect of biased thinking that impacts upon the prediction of risk behaviours occurring.

Attribution bias occurs when the mental health professional over identifies with the person with whom they are working because of similarities in demographic characteristics such as age, gender or class. The more the worker identifies the more they are likely to attribute the individual's behaviour to an external rather than an internal cause.

Given that the majority of practitioners will not have direct experience of using mental health services there already exists an implicit risk of judging peoples' behaviour as internally driven. For example, consider a mental health service user who is found to be agitated and angry in their GP's surgery. A worker from the Primary Care Mental Health Team may be more likely to attribute this distress to a worsening psychosis than the fact that the service user may have been verbally taunted by some youths during the bus journey to the surgery. Personal characteristics contribute to the attribution bias by adding to the likelihood that an individual is perceived as different. This compounds the discrimination individuals may experience in the way that mental health professionals seek to explain their behaviour. By obtaining a range of perspectives on the individual's presentation from different members of the interdisciplinary team including the service user and their family the chances of challenging an attribution bias are strengthened.

Selectivity bias occurs when an event is judged more likely to happen because it can be pictured mentally or recalled relatively easily. Because of their increased exposure to people with severe and enduring mental health problems, mental health workers may be more likely to predict that people in a psychotic episode will become violent and aggressive compared with members of the public who have never witnessed a person with a disorder such as schizophrenia or manic depression. Similarly a confirmation bias results in more weight being given to information that supports a hypothesis rather than information that is likely to refute it. Thus mental health workers may regard more significant, an individual's violent outburst five years ago as indicative of future violence, than subsequent reports that the same individual has coped well with psychotic episodes by drawing on support from fellow service users in a self-help group. The availability hypothesis suggests that the more information that is available on a potential risk event, the more likely it will be predicted to occur (Tversky and Kahneman, 1973; Combs and Slovic, 1979; Kahneman et al., 1982).

By using interdisciplinary fora, such as team briefings, care plan reviews, allocation and referral meetings, to pool available information and consider evidence collectively, the influence of the above biases on the team's risk decision making process should become more explicit and thus more readily subject to challenge and debate. This is particularly important as mental health professionals and services have a duty of care not only towards service users but also to professionals.

However, where an approach to risk decision making is characterized by multi- as opposed to interdisciplinary working (see Chapter 1) this can have the opposite effect of colluding with some of the biases identified. For example, although information may be passed between team members if there is not an agreed philosophy of inclusive teamworking, information from colleagues considered to have less professional status may not be given equal weight. For example, in the Burton inquiry (1996) Mr Burton revealed to a student nurse that he had violent fantasies to harm his parents. This information was documented and shared with the supervising nurse but not the medical staff. Consequently when Mr Burton killed his landlady it was suggested that had such information been shared, whilst it might not have prevented the tragedy, without it the risk assessment was obviously incomplete.

Similarly Blom-Cooper (1996) highlights the critical value of information held by all team members irrespective of status in the Jason Mitchell inquiry. A detailed report compiled by an OT technician was undervalued by the clinical team because of the relatively low status of the worker. Such a phenomenon could equally apply where information held by those closest to the service user is discounted as part of the risk decision making process because of the perceived lay status of carers and close friends (Reith, 1998). An inclusive approach to interdisciplinary risk prediction would develop systems and policies to enable information to be considered from all available sources. This is highlighted by Titterton (2005) as the second element of the PRAMS model.

An interdisciplinary approach to risk prediction will also be influenced by the degree of control the team perceives they have over the risk decision making process. Where individual scapegoating and a culture of individual blame pervades, this will mitigate against collaborative, defensible practice. Thus if mental health organizations and teams are committed to supporting interdisciplinary risk prediction this needs to be underpinned by guidelines on good practice. Teams need to monitor and audit policies for making decisions about risk and tailor supervision and support structures to strengthen interdisciplinary working. This is particularly important in functionalized teams where different professions are 'merged' to deliver a particular service such as assertive community treatment. Morgan (2000) highlights that the following intrinsic tensions need to be addressed in order to assist such teams work effectively with risk issues that arise on a routine basis:

- Philosophies of working;
- Professional priorities;
- Caseloads/workloads;
- Methods of support/supervision;
- Access to risk training.

If a truly interdisciplinary approach is to be adopted it follows that people who use the service and their carers should be included in a consideration of all of the above as integral partners.

Risk Management

Once judgements have been made about which risks are more likely than others, and the circumstances identified in which they may occur, drawing up a risk management plan is the next stage of the process. Risk management relates to how the risk decisions are implemented. Ryan (1997) suggests that strategies to manage risks posed by people with mental health problems have evolved throughout the course of history from risk management by incarceration in the Victorian asylums, through decarceration to integration with care in the community. This shift mirrors the different stages of interdisciplinary working laid out in Chapter 2 and as the current approach to providing mental health services relies heavily upon the community as a whole, including short-term hospital provision for the minority, the need for an integrated interdisciplinary approach to risk management becomes central to the overall strategy.

Since its introduction in 1991 the Care Programme Approach has provided the systems and procedures for coordinating care in the community that has become synonymous with risk minimization as a management strategy. The integration of the CPA with section 117 of the 1983 Mental Health Act provides the framework for an interdisciplinary approach to risk management planning as part of the discharge process. According to Carson and Bain (2008) whilst the elements of risk are beyond the control of the risk takers the dimensions of risk are controllable to a greater extent. For example, a mental health service user may or may not continue to take their medication when discharged home, increasing the risk that their psychotic symptoms may resurface. The frequency of home visits by the Assertive Outreach Team will play a role in controlling relapse by monitoring to a greater or lesser extent how the individual is managing their medication,

---

Key concept 5.5: Definitions of risk management

- 'Implementation of a set of values and principles integrated with a set of operational procedures and supports surrounding an individual that enable a dynamic sensitivity to the individual's needs, vulnerabilities and evolving behaviours. The purpose of risk management procedures is to minimise risk and provide safe, sound and supportive services' (O' Rourke and Bird, 2001, p. 4).
- 'A statement of plans and an allocation of individual responsibilities for translating collective decisions into actions. The process should name all the relevant people involved in the treatment and support, including the individual service user and appropriate informal carers. It should also clearly identify the dates for reviewing the assessment plans' (Morgan, 2000, p. 2).
- 'The minimisation of dangers, both to and from the individual with the mental health problem' (Ryan, 1997, p. 93).

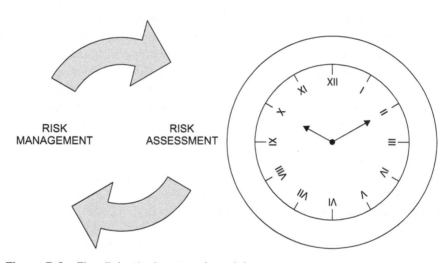

Figure 5.2 The dialectical approach to risk

Whilst risk minimization may be the objective of the mental health professionals responsible for implementing the risk management plan there is a danger that such a restrictive approach will undermine service users' and carers' coping strategies for dealing with risky situations on a daily basis. Carson and Bain (2008) assert that there is likely to be a sequence of key decision points spanning extensive control in hospital through to close supervision in the community to full autonomy as a citizen. This accords with a dialectical approach to risk assessment and management that continually inform and influence each other.

Timing is crucial in relation to the above as Carson and Bain (2008) point out. This relates to the time or risk period over which the assessment and plan will last, the amount of time available to make a risk decision and the time available to intervene in the risk management plan if the ongoing assessment suggests elements of risk are changing.

Davis advocates the risk taking approach to risk management that begins with a definition of risk that is positive and normalizing. It allows for the engagement with the stigma and socially exclusive policies and practices that people with mental health needs are likely to have experienced as part of their daily lives (Barham and Hayward, 1991).

Davis (1996, p. 114) asserts that the starting point for a risk management plan that allows for positive risk taking is a set of values committed to the notion that people with mental health problems are first and foremost people. Such values recognize the experience of living with a mental health problem as positive and valid in its own right thus linking with the interdisciplinary approach set out in Chapter 2. Interdisciplinary risk management becomes a balancing act conducted in negotiation with the service user and their carers about which risks the service user can take responsibility for managing and which must be managed in partnership with the mental health professionals and services.

Echoing this balance Morgan (1998) has identified different interpretations of risk management. This has been adapted to provide a checklist below and applied to a case example.

PRACTICE FOCUS 5.1

Teams Developing Risk Assessment and Management in Practice

As part of a research project to explore the impact of training on risk assessment planning and management on changes in practice, focus groups were conducted with seven out of nine Community Mental Health Teams and the two Assertive Outreach Teams in one Primary Care Trust. The focus groups focused specifically on collaborative working as an opportunity for working more effectively with risk issues, Questions that were used encouraged the team to think about and discuss:

How they engaged in creative thinking, to promote positive risk taking (supporting individual choice and decision making)

Then:

Whether all disciplines including service users and carers contributed to the collection of risk assessment information and known or potential interventions?

Whether each team had clear statements of anticipated risks that were agreed between professionals, the service user and their carers including how these risks can be managed in partnership?

Whether each team had a detailed knowledge of a person's history and early warning signs of risk?

Whether the team had agreed and made explicit the organizational policies and procedures for managing risk as they relate to the circumstances of a service user?

Practice Focus 5.1 – *continued*

Whether the team had a guide for monitoring progress in conducting interdisciplinary risk assessment, prediction and management planning together with service users' progress in managing individual risks in partnership with the team?

Whether the team could provide interdisciplinary crisis responses to real situations of clinical need and have an opportunity for an interdisciplinary team debrief where critical incidents occur?

The teams identified that in the main the way they worked reflected good practice in assessing and managing risk. There were processes in place for sharing information about risks which included team meetings, individual and team supervision and the recording of risk issues in individual service user's case notes.

The main concern in respect of managing risk was in relation to working with other teams in the mental health system such as inpatient teams and Crisis Resolution and Home Treatment. Three teams concurred that when these other teams became involved they felt they lost control or had to manage risks themselves if the other team could not take the referral. Sharing information was also reported to be very 'hit and miss' at an organizational level and recording systems were deemed inadequate leading to paper work going amiss especially between inpatient and community services.

In order to improve standards all teams were using an audit process to consider three risk assessments per month, the issues arising from these in respect of collaborative practice and how this was being dealt with. Five teams had developed an action plan as a result of the training they had received and all the teams could identify what steps they were taking to develop their practice.

Accountability

For an interdisciplinary approach to risk management as outlined above to work effectively the issues of accountability as they impact at the individual, team and organizational level also require consideration in order that they support rather than undermine an interdisciplinary approach. To assist this process, and guard against defensive practice and a pervasive blame culture, teams need to clarify their position in respect of accountability and responsibility. It may be helpful to consider that if a team is adopting a truly interdisciplinary approach that involves the service users and their carers then the team as a whole will be accountable for the implementation of the risk management plan and thus collectively accountable to the mental health organization. As a consequence individual workers, service users and their carers will be responsible for managing different risk dilemmas either individually or in partnership and thus be collectively responsible for keeping each other informed about progress or any difficulties that emerge.

In an interdisciplinary approach to risk management no single individual can be solely accountable for the implementation of the risk management plan. Whilst a mental health worker can be responsible to a service user for their professional contribution they are unlikely to assume total responsibility for that service user's wellbeing, except in a crisis situation of extensive control where necessary interventions to contain risks have been agreed with the service user or their carer in advance.

The interdisciplinary team will thus need to arrive at precise statements for the accountabilities of specific people in particular the Care Coordinator if the service user is subject to the CPA. In addition the accountabilities of key players in the team such as the team leader and Approved Clinician will also need to be made explicit to avoid confusion and buck passing. Decision making will need to be collective and based on all available information and supported at an organizational level by policy guidelines on risk together with explicit mechanisms for supervision and support. Where mental health agencies are able to become learning organizations where serious critical incidents are tackled so that lessons are learned to improve interdisciplinary working rather than undermine it this will increase the likelihood that teams continue to adopt a defensible and creative approach to risk management even in the most complex of cases.

Summary

Risk assessment is a misleading term. It masks a process that involves the collection of information, judgements about whether risks are likely or not to occur and the severity of the consequences if they do. Risk assessment requires collection of information specific to individuals alongside more general information about how different types of mental health problems present and should be effectively managed. Effective interdisciplinary working is necessary to underpin risk assessment, prediction and management. It will ensure that information between team members is shared and considered seriously regardless of the status of the team member. By adopting an inclusive approach to information gathering; including relevant details from service users and carers it will also help to guard against the influence of biased thinking in the interdisciplinary decision making process. Finally by clarifying issues of accountability and responsibility interdisciplinary teams, if supported by their organization, should be able to adopt a collective accountability for risk management. This will include a greater emphasis on risk taking management strategies where responsibility for aspects of the plan is shared between the service user and the professionals. Values which recognize the valid and positive experience of service users living with mental health problems and a holistic model of mental distress will help to support interdisciplinary working arrangements for risk assessment, prediction and management.

Interdisciplinary Working in Practice

6

Involving People Who Use Services in Interdisciplinary Working in Mental Health

---

Key Issues:

- Service user involvement in mental health is embedded in societal changes, influenced by top down government policies and bottom up lobbying from service user groups and the survivor movement in psychiatry.
- Service user involvement can be understood on a continuum from the giving of information and explanation to service user control. The latter accords with a democratic model of service user involvement and lends itself to interdisciplinary working.
- Choices regarding the level and type of involvement are fundamental to an interdisciplinary approach and service users should be in a position to influence this individually or collectively.
- Partnership working with service users is integral to interdisciplinary mental health care and occurs where leadership is co-created to develop a shared vision of service provision and care delivery.

Chapters 1 and 2 have outlined a framework for interdisciplinary working that hinges upon a contribution from service users born out of their first hand experience, often over a significant time period, of living with mental distress and receiving interventions from mental health services. These earlier chapters have suggested that the recovery model for understanding mental distress, allows for a combination of perspectives, skills and expertise from professionals and service users which together can facilitate a more collaborative approach to recovery that is synonymous with interdisciplinarity. As Gosling (2010) notes:

> Involvement is a two-way street – involvement is not just about us being involved in your (mental health professionals') lives – it is about you being involved in ours Gosling (2010, p. 38).

This approach needs to be underpinned by a healthy respect for the different values individuals bring to interdisciplinary working whilst achieving a shared goal of improving service users' experiences of care delivery and health and social care outcomes. Achieving the above is a complex task that like any culture change will take time to embed. This chapter aims to establish how the changing political agenda in recent years has created a climate whereby service user participation can have a more direct influence over mental health care delivery. The benefits such involvement can bring are becoming more widely acknowledged alongside the issues that need to be tackled in order for such involvement to make a more effective contribution.

Service User Involvement: The Political Agenda

According to Kemp (2010, p. 15) service user involvement can no longer be considered a transient phenomenon because 'it is embedded in and arises from, fundamental changes within wider society that have taken place in recent decades'.

In a recent review of the literature Smith and Bailey (2010) identified themes that echo with those of Kemp (2010) and suggest that service user involvement in mental health care has been influenced by: wider social changes impacting upon the concepts of participation and citizenship, top down government policies that have sought to create a socially inclusive climate for involvement and the growth of the service user or 'survivor' movement in mental health that has in turn influenced the response from the politicians and the professionals.

Concepts of Participation and Citizenship

Since the 1980s the thrust of the political agenda has been to reconstruct the boundaries of the state through the processes of regeneration and social inclusion. In the UK, the White Paper, *Working for Patients* (DH, 1989b) was the government's first overt attempt to 'redefine the relationship between the NHS and the public, framing it in free market terms of competition, choice and consumerism' (Rowe and Shepherd, 2002, p. 276). In the 1990s the requirements for the developing Primary Care Groups (PCGs) and Trusts (PCTs) explicitly set out the need to involve members of the public and work with local groups to develop shared aims and priorities for improving the health and wellbeing of local communities (DH, 1998c).

Community involvement was promoted more generally by a raft of initiatives such as the City Challenge introduced in 1991 followed by the Single Regeneration Budget, along with the Home Office's Connecting Communities Fund, the New Opportunities Fund, and the Neighbourhood Renewal Fund.

All these financial initiatives were designed to establish incentives for multi-sector partnerships to improve health and wellbeing. According to Smith and Beazley (2000, p. 862) such partnerships are 'promoted as the solution to difficult problems, and they have the potential to: enable local needs to be identified and addressed, give local people a voice and empower local communities leading to greater social justice'.

This concept of 'local responsiveness' was officially launched by New Labour in 1997 alongside a political shift to view service users as 'active citizens' who should have direct involvement in decisions that affect their neighbourhoods and services. This increasingly democratic model of participation that seeks to value involvement as an end in itself, and as an enriching and empowering experience, has become manifest in what Kemp (2010, p. 16) refers to as a more 'participative form of governance' that emphasizes collaboration over control.

Subsequent policies, such as Our Health, Our Care, Our Say (DH, 2006), have reinforced the view that 'the previous paternalistic model of service delivery that cast the patient in a passive role, grateful and dependent on the wisdom and expertise of the health professional is increasingly seen as inappropriate, undesirable and unachievable in today's National Health Service (NHS)' (McAndrew and Samociuk, 2003, p. 616). Milewa et al. (2002, p. 798) identify this shift as an 'explicit expansion of health policy beyond the medical model of physiological diagnosis and intervention'.

Growth of the Service User and Survivor Movements in Mental Health

The aim of the NHS Plan (DH, 2000) was to set out the top down agenda for the overall redesign of more responsive services even though mental health service user organizations had been lobbying for change through a more bottom up approach over a much longer time frame. The NHS plan set out to provide better information about health services generally, resolve complaints efficiently and facilitate the representation of service users on decision making bodies through the establishment of Patients' Forums and a Patient Advocacy and Liaison Service in every hospital and PCT.

However, since the 1970s people with mental health problems have pursued collective action to develop alternative thinking about their lives and experiences explicitly within the psychiatric system. This led to the emergence of groups such as the 'British Network for Alternatives to Psychiatry' and the 'Campaign against Psychiatric Oppression' in the 1980s (Peck et al., 2002). Some would argue that it was this growing profile of influence on statutory mental health service developments through less formalized patient councils and advocacy groups that pre-empted the direction of the NHS plan.

Service users are now represented on the management committees of mental health Trusts, involved in the training and assessment of mental health professionals, in mental health research and in the evaluation of services. Indeed such involvement has become increasingly expected and required by service providers, policy makers and service users themselves. The development of this growing social movement over the last 30 years has led Stickley (2006, p. 570) to conclude that 'In no other arena in health care has there been the equivalent of what we now call the user/survivor movement in psychiatry'.

Power Dynamics and the Political and Professional Response

Despite the political support for service user involvement from the policy makers, that in theory should fit with an increasingly interdisciplinary approach to mental health care, there is scant evidence of involvement being translated into actual collaborative practice (NIMHE, 2003; Peck et al., 2002).

A prime example of this has been the CPA, which from its introduction in 1991 was geared to include service users in the process of care planning. Little changed during the next decade and despite the subsequent reinforcement of the involvement message in the NSF in 1999 routine service user involvement has remained patchy (Rose et al., 1998; Simpson, 1999; Warne and Starke, 2004). Reasons for the relative absence of service user involvement at a practice level generally are complex and include issues such as a lack of resources, limited commitment and resistance from professionals. A common factor is also an over reliance on a small number of individuals who aren't considered to be representative of the service user community as a whole. This reflects a key tension in interdisciplinary working – notably the relative lack of power vested in service users compared with professionals.

In an attempt to redress the power imbalance the Ten Essential Shared Capabilities (DH, 2004) set out a value base to underpin service delivery that places service users at the centre of their care, and reinforces the recovery model of mental ill health. Whilst in terms of philosophy these developments should facilitate a shift in relationships between service users and professionals, there remains a difference between 'involvement in' and service users leading the decision making process about their care plans or service development. In part this can be attributed to more widespread confusion about the meaning and purpose of service user involvement.

Defining Service User Involvement

In a similar way to multidisciplinary, interprofessional and interdisciplinary, the terms service user involvement, service user empowerment or service user participation have become common parlance, often used interchange-ably, largely as a result of the political developments described above. There seems to be some consensus at a relatively simplistic level that all these terms refer to people who use mental health services participating in a process of decision making. This has been demonstrated in relation to:

- Individual care issues (Felton and Stickley, 2004);
- Service planning and evaluation (Robert et al., 2003);
- Interviewing and selecting staff (Newnes et al., 2001);
- Training and education (McAndrew and Samocuik, 2003; Bailey, 2005) and;
- Research (Thornicroft et al., 2002; Telford et al., 2004).

Beeforth (1993) suggests that such decision making can take place in relation to the purchasing and providing of services and at a number of levels of care spanning the immediate care environment of a hospital, day centre or group home through to locality services, national and international care provision.

Service User Involvement

Being involved in decision making per se does not however equate with, an interdisciplinary approach. Such involvement can be tokenistic, more about obtaining service users' perspectives as part of a multidisciplinary consulta-tion exercise with the primary aim of adding legitimacy to stakeholders' plans (Allott and Holmes, 1993; Repper et al., 2001). Indeed, Gordon (2005, p. 362) makes a distinction between involvement at a micro level which she describes as 'being a partner in the clinical process rather than being compli-ant with the clinical decisions made by experts' and that at the macro level which 'means contributing to decision making about the way services oper-ate, including planning and reform processes'.

As with professional involvement in interdisciplinary working the issue of power seems to play a key role in determining the extent to which participa-tion occurs at either level. Gordon (2005, p. 363) suggests that service user involvement is most often witnessed in relation to trivial issues while 'real' participation is questionable, particularly in power influencing positions at leadership and management levels. Stickley (2006, p. 571) asserts that 'serv-ice user involvement is a concept created by the dominant discourse' (in men-tal health psychiatry) 'that reinforces the power/knowledge position of that discourse and it is only by applying theories of emancipation and liberation that change may be wrought for the position of the service user in relation to psychiatry'. Stickley goes on to suggest that 'Service users have sought power by learning the language of the dominant discourse and becoming involved in their decision making committees' (p. 573). This suggests compliance with an overriding multiprofessional approach, a view shared by Barnes and Bowl

(2001) who claim that service users themselves continue to be disempowered by such a system while professional power is protected.

Service User Empowerment

According to Lloyd (2007, p. 485) 'empowerment is described in policy documents as involving service users in all levels of their care from planning to provision'. Empowerment in mental health has therefore been largely to do with service users having their say in service developments. Within a multiprofessional approach this implies a degree of circularity as in order to be involved service users first need to be assured that they can question the professional status quo although believing they have the power to do so can be difficult if they are excluded from involvement at the outset. Stickley (2006) thus claims that the concept of service user empowerment gets us little further than that of involvement for as long as statutory workers empower their clients the actual power is retained within the existing system.

Barriers to service user empowerment exist because at different levels of decision making there are a number of strategies professionals can use to ensure the existing hierarchies of power inherent within the psychiatric system remain. Nettle (1993) suggests that service providers will simply search for service users who fit their structures. Often professionals argue that service users' contributions must be discounted on the grounds that they are unrepresentative. This supposes, of course, that by contrast all professionals' contributions are always representative of the wider collective and supports Campbell's view (2002, p. 30) that professionals will use representativeness as a 'suffocating blanket' to drown out service users' influence.

Another empowering strategy is to develop the role of so-called 'lay professionals' (Boote et al., 2002) who are then included in decision making as a defacto service user voice. The danger here is that the increasing 'professionalization of the role' results in the individual fulfilling it being socialized away from the lay perspective to take on that of a quasi professional. The introduction of STR workers and Carers Support Workers into the mental health workforce is an example of this in practice. Although these roles were originally intended to support employment options for individuals with lived experience of the mental health system many of these workers do not have such a background. Data shows that they are also taking on the role in very varied and different ways in across the statutory and voluntary sectors (Dickinson et al., 2008).

In order to progress the involvement of service users in an increasingly interdisciplinary approach Hawker and Hawkins (1995) helpfully suggest that empowerment can include an element of authorizing and enabling that brings with it a degree of control and influence. Askheim (2003) explains that empowerment is not therefore the simple transfer of power from one individual or organization to another, but it is a process of consciousness rais-ing and working in partnership to address the balance. This reflects Lloyd's idea that service user empowerment is about collaboration with professionals that through a shared approach to recovery interventions seeks to:

- Improve service user outcomes and recovery *(service user empowerment)*;
- Develop political knowledge and skills to challenge the system and take a broader view of practice to incorporate political and social theory in a search for meaning and influence *(organizational empowerment)* and;
- Locate practice within an inclusive 'lifeworlds' approach of everyone in the organization *(professional empowerment)*.

Stickley (2006) would consider the above as ingredients of service user eman-cipation which allows for individuals to take power from the professionals rather than have it given. This is more synonymous with an interdisciplinary approach as it suggests interaction to reach a more inclusive approach to care delivery. Stickley gives examples of projects such as the Service Users Research Group England (SURGE), User Focused Monitoring Schemes and the Strategies for Living project at the Mental Health Foundation as providing services to mainstream statutory mental health services but not being managed by them. This then places service user groups and organi-zations in a different position from which to negotiate collaboration and involvement.

Service User Participation

It is from this position that meaningful participation occurs that chimes with the emphasis on service users as citizens who have a right to information, access, redress and choice. The democratic model values the actual proc-ess of participation as intrinsically valuable for broadening citizens' experi-ences and perspectives giving them a greater say in the pattern and delivery of services. While this can still be considered a process of legitimizing decision making it is also about giving service users the opportunity to challenge and force those in power to consider and justify their practices from a different perspective.

Choice as a Fundamental Principle for an Interdisciplinary Approach

A common purpose of both interdisciplinary working and service user involve-ment is therefore to promote increased choice within an ever increasingly complex mental health care system. This may relate to a choice of worker or intervention, or choice as in a range of service models such as Assertive Community Treatment or Early Intervention to meet the diversity of need.

This is mirrored in government policy that considers choice to be a good thing, necessary to underpin current reform in health and social care.

According to the Sainsbury Centre for Mental Health (2006, p. 1) 'The expectation is that giving patients increased choice over the care they receive will empower them, diversify the range of available services and providers of services and improve standards through competition'. These expectations are supported by evidence from a systematic review conducted by Crawford et al. in 2002. The review included 42 studies that described the outcomes of involving service users and revealed that although some people were dissatisfied with the process of involvement others welcomed the opportunity to participate and their self-esteem improved as a result. In several studies staff also found the experience of involving those who used the service rewarding. Changes to services most frequently reported as a result of participation concerned the production of new or improved information for individuals about their care, alongside efforts to make services more accessible through improved appointment procedures, opening times or transport arrangements. Some studies provided examples of new services being commissioned at the request of service users. Other effects of involvement included more favourable staff attitudes and organizations becoming more 'open' to the concept of involvement.

Based upon the range of involvement detailed in the studies it seems that it is having the *choice* about whether or not to participate at a range of levels that makes service user involvement more meaningful and intrinsically valuable to interdisciplinary working. There will be times when involvement is constrained either at an individual or collective level because of factors such as legal requirements where it becomes necessary to manage issues of risk and protection or because resources and information are limited. It may be that at times service users will lack the capacity to be involved in making choices about their care and treatment or their contribution will be minimized because staff are unresponsive or harbour negative attitudes to involvement generally. In order to choose whether or how to contribute most effectively service users need to know whether they are dealing with a team that is predominantly multiprofessional in its outlook or one that seeks to be more responsive and interdisciplinary.

The extent to which interdisciplinarity is fostered will influence the options open to service users to contribute. Hickey and Kipping (1998) identify a continuum of participation that links the consumerist and democratic models of involvement at either end. Where a uni or multiprofessional approach to mental health care delivery is being adopted the choice of involvement is likely to be limited to service users being given information and explanation. Consultation becomes more of an option with a multidisciplinary approach and partnership/service user control with interdisciplinary and inter-agency

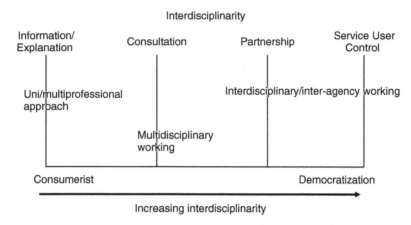

Figure 6.1 Hickey and Kipping's participation continuum and degrees of interdisciplinarity

working where people with direct experience are providing an independent service or contributing from their distinct perspective of being on the receiving end of care delivery.

Where service users are in receipt of care on a one-to-one basis studies by Canvin et al. (2002) and Warne and Starke (2004) reveal how the centrality of choice influences the kinds of interactions service users will engage in with mental health staff. Canvin et al. found that service users are seemingly capable of contradictory responses to compulsory mental health care in the community. In the study service users were subject either to a Guardianship or Supervised Discharge order under the 1983 Mental Health Act. Simultaneously they reacted with acceptance and resistance to the conditions imposed such that Canvin et al. were able to differentiate between active and passive responses. The latter involved service users resigning themselves to their situation in a rather fatalistic manner and demonstrating feelings of dependency as the orders were seen as providing safety and security with service users enjoying the professional contact.

More active responses included ownership where service users saw the benefits of the orders and wanted to maximize these. Some service users used the legislative contraints as a bargaining tool to achieve personal goals such as living in their own home or leaving hospital. The range of strategies the service users chose to employ suggests that by virtue of their own actions they can influence the extent to which they elicit a multiprofessional or an interdisciplinary response from mental health professionals.

This suggestion is supported by Warne and Starke's study that considered the perceptions a group of service users held about their experiences and contact with a multiprofessional team. This was part of a two year evaluation for the English National Board for Nursing, Midwifery and Health Visiting. Warne and Starke found that service users would construe professional involvement in their care as more or less 'useful', which encapsulated their experiences of having things done for them and being with others at times when they were experiencing particular difficulties.

The professionals were deemed to serve different purposes for the service users with the psychiatrist being seen as a diagnoser and fixer while the Occupational Therapist (OT) and social workers were judged to take on a more educative role. Where staff, usually in managerial roles, were seen to fulfil a more administrative function, service users' views of their usefulness were more mixed. What was important to the service users was the availability of people around them who could help them to get better when they needed to and who had the skills and knowledge that they did not possess to help improve their situation.

This links back to the recovery model in Chapter 2 suggesting that it is the sharing of interdisciplinary skills and knowledge that becomes important to optimize service users' mental health that in turn results in them being able to make a more active contribution to staying well and taking control of their day to day lives. Valimaki (1998, p. 60) identifies the latter as self-determination which she describes as 'as being able to participate in decisions that affect your life without constraints being imposed by others'. Where service users' choices are constrained (as in the examples above) Valimaki identifies shared self-determination as one way to counter this. It involves service users working together and being supported by professional staff, being valued and respected as human beings in a relationship that promotes teamwork and mutual support. This is summarized by some of the service users that Valimaki (1998, p. 64) interviewed in her study:

- 'It's good that we talk [with staff] about things, that we don't get to decide everything ourselves just like that'.
- 'I can go to the canteen and go for a walk in the garden with a nurse. There's often coffee out in the garden and we spend a lot of time out there. I like that'.
- 'I think it's important that you're respected, valued as a human being'.

Such comments reinforce the value service users place on the 'being with' aspects of care that requires staff to listen, be patient and non-judgemental as opposed to the more professionalized 'doing to' aspects such as assessment (Hinshelwood, 1998). In Warne and Starke's study the 'being with' role was mostly undertaken by Health Care Assistants and student nurses although community nurses were valued for the balance they achieved between the 'being with' and 'doing to' elements suggesting support for an approach that promotes shared self-determination.

Partnership Working and Interdisciplinarity

Interdisciplinary working therefore hinges on partnership working with service users whether at an individual or more collective level. Anderson et al. (2006) studied public involvement in planning primary care services and found three interlocking themes of partnership, process and power that affected how partnership working was experienced. These can be applied to interdisciplinary working in mental health as follows.

Partnership

In Anderson's study relationships and partnerships evolved as people learned to communicate across traditional boundaries. From the studies by Warne and Starke (2004) and Canvin et al. (2002) findings support the importance of effective communication across the traditional professional/service user boundary if service users are to feel they have a genuine contribution to make to decisions regarding their care. Anderson claims this entails a process of adaptation that symbolically reflects a need to do things differently. One of the professionals in her study described this as 'taking off the suit' (Canvin et al., 2002, p. 74).

At a strategic level the Anderson et al. (2006, p. 77) findings stressed the importance of achieving a balance between the views of local people and health professionals and to be clear about the purposes of involvement. This relates to inter-agency working in mental health where service user groups and organizations are working collaboratively with mainstream statutory services to provide more choice in care provision. Anderson identifies this as the 'third way' approach to reflect the government's promised shift in the relationship between the individual and the state.

Process

People got involved in planning primary care in Anderson's study at two levels; some by keeping in touch with projects through newsletters and events, while others became more deeply involved, often as a result of personal motivation to see changes occur. This resonates with the author's experience of involving service users in mental health service developments where there are differing levels of interest and service users bring a range of skills and expertise. Not all people who use mental health services wish to be involved in decision making at board level. Some may prefer to contribute to the education and training of the workforce while others may wish to support fellow service users on a one-to-one voluntary basis or through a mutual self-help group. What is central to involvement at any level is being supported by mental health workers and managers rather than feeling that service user involvement has to be about 'one size fits all' otherwise there is no opportunity to contribute.

Power

In Anderson's study people still felt that the traditional power held by the statutory agencies was upheld despite the rhetoric of involvement in the planning process. This is supported by some of the other studies referred to in this chapter and is not surprising given that the statutory power base in mental health has resided with psychiatry for well over a century. The New Ways of Working initiative recognizes that this is not about to change overnight as studies in this chapter have shown. There will be some situations when service users want mental health professionals to use their power in ways that help them to stay feeling safe and protected. In an interdisciplinary approach it is about being open about the power dynamics that exist so that service users can become attuned to the prevailing culture. This was particularly evident from Anderson's study reinforcing that if individuals understood the power relations then they could choose when and how to leave power in the hands of professionals and when to pursue opportunities to challenge.

Service User Involvement and Leadership as Partnership

Power, therefore is a prevailing theme that influences professionals' and service users' contributions to interdisciplinarity and is usually associated with the role of leader. Leadership is typically understood as a function provided by a mental health professional, often the psychiatrist or the team manager. Rarely is the role of leadership ever considered in relation to service users (Gordon, 2005).

However, there is a growing body of literature that documents service users' experiences in relation to a range of factors salient to contemporary mental health care. It is this first hand experience gained as a direct result of using services that places service users in a position of expertise that is different but complimentary to the expertise of professionals who provide the service. It is from this position that service users are able to make a collective 'disciplinary' contribution to mental health care delivery.

From research studies that have harnessed service users' experience we now know more about their satisfaction with and views of services as well as their personal perspectives about why and how some community programmes are effective. Service users have provided evidence about what impacts upon their quality of life, and their experiences of social support. They have shared their experiences of Mental Health Act assessments and coercion, discharge planning and living with mental health problems in the community. This body of expertise need to be considered as equally valid alongside research into the issues professionals experience as pertinent to the provision of care.

In working with the change agenda in mental health and social care professionals could be considered remiss to discount this growing evidence base together with the power and influence of the service user movement that has attracted increasing political recognition. If organizations are going to provide responsive and effective contemporary mental health services professionals need to be able to work in a different way with service users to combine the being and doing aspects of care that, if balanced, service users find of value. Ramon and Williams (2005, p. 15) suggest this involves replacing a less distanced 'hands off' with a more 'hands on' approach that demonstrates emotional closeness to the service user and an interest in the everyday affairs that matter to them. In order to work collaboratively with service users to develop shared goals and aspirations it is the emotional availability of the worker that Ramon and Williams claim 'marks good psychosocial professionalism from the traditional model of psychiatry'.

Moxley (2001) identifies joining power and forces in the accomplishment of such a shared goal as an essential ingredient of leadership as partnership. He claims that leadership becomes co-created when individuals share their experiences and perspectives to 'develop a shared vision, set a direction, solve problems and make meaning of the work' (Moxley, 2001, p. 47). Such an approach would sit comfortably with the delivery of interdisciplinary and inter-agency mental health care as it relies upon:

- Each individual claiming personal power to co-create win-win solutions and reach a shared goal.

This would harness the individual and collective experience service users are able to bring to their encounters with mental health professionals and seek to promote a common agenda for interdisciplinarity where there is openness about the power dynamics involved.

- A sense of shared responsibility and accountability.

This was discussed in Chapter 5 specifically in relation to risk assessment, planning and management and links to the earlier discussion in this chapter about shared self-determination.

- Respect for the person which applies to both service users and professionals.

This links to Lloyd's (2007) concept of professional empowerment that hinges upon a value base of inclusivity that locates the practice 'lifeworlds' of everyone in the organization. Respect has also been a recurring message in this chapter as a fundamental factor in promoting choice regarding involvement. Where situations arise where shared goals aren't possible, such as in situations of care and protection sharing, values of mutual respect become increasingly important.

- Partnership working that needs to be applied to all aspects of decision making not just the trivial.

This has perhaps been more difficult to achieve in relation to service user involvement in mental health and requires real commitment through both top down and bottom up support within mental health organizations.

Wheel of Involvement

Smith and Beazley's wheel of involvement (2000) provides a helpful model that depicts how the issues, of power, values, participation and partnerships interconnect. Although this model was originally developed to evaluate the effectiveness of community involvement, it is adapted in Figure 6.2 to relate to interdisciplinary working in mental health and the promotion of leadership as partnership described above.

Interdisciplinary working which includes a leadership contribution from service users as partners at an individual or collective level will be promoted where there is evidence of a shared power structure and strong participation

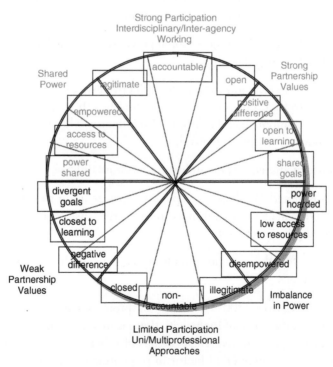

Figure 6.2   Smith and Beazley's wheel of involvement (2000)

reflecting a shared sense of accountability and responsibility. Also where there are strong partnership values that promote shared goals and openness about power relations thereby facilitating the inclusion of service users and their agendas.

Uni or multiprofessional approaches are, in contrast, likely to feature at the bottom half of the wheel where service users are disempowered and excluded by imbalanced and closed power relations and the values attached to partnership working are weak. This is illustrated by the following case example.

PRACTICE FOCUS 6.1

Service User Led Research

In 2005, based upon previous initiatives to involve service users in improving care standards, a North East mental health Trust commissioned a service user led research project to design an evaluation tool to measure the quality of care received from the Trust as part of the Care Programme Approach (CPA). An interdisciplinary approach to the project was marshalled from the outset with service users working together with Trust managers and university academics to draw up the specification for the study. An interdisciplinary Steering Group was established to lead the project ensuring that power in relation to the decision making process would be shared. This group was chaired by a service user who worked in a paid capacity for the organization. The project was funded as a partnership between the Trust and a local university in order that support and supervision could be provided to: guide the research process, assist in the training of service user researchers and ensure degree of objectivity in the way the project was conducted within the organization.

The Steering Group designed the job description and person specification for the appointment of a research associate to lead the project with the explicit aim that this person would train service user researchers within the Trust. This would, in turn, build research capacity such that when the project reached completion there would be a body of service users who had the power and influence to continue to take the research agenda forward. In accordance with the democratic model of participation it was intended that taking part in the project as a service user researcher would be intrinsically valuable and broaden an individual's experience and skills.

Interviews for the research associate were conducted by a panel of service users and professionals, chaired by the service user who was also Chair of the steering group. A key focus of the interview panel was the values candidates were bringing to the role and their willingness and ability to lead the project whilst also being supportive to the service user researchers and helping them to develop their skills and expertise. A secondary aim of the project was to explore, describe and document the extent to which Trust systems and structures were supportive of service user led research and make recommendations for how this could be further enhanced in future. This was to ensure that if there were organizational constraints on service user participation in interdisciplinary services these could be identified and acted upon.

Summary

People with first hand experience of using mental health services are key partners in interdisciplinary mental health care. In order for their contribution to be effective and meaningful they need to be able to engage in shared decision making with professionals and have real choices about how and whether to be involved. Involvement in interdisciplinary working can be intrinsically valuable for individuals who use services by enhancing their self-esteem and broadening their experience and skills. Service users can take an increasing leadership role in a collaborative approach to improved mental health care if their involvement is underpinned by strong partnership values and a shared power base with professionals.

7

Interdisciplinary Working with People with Mental Health Problems in Primary Care

Since April 2004 all primary care services in England have been provided by Primary Care Trusts (PCTs). Serving an average population of 100,000 PCTs constitute the basic organizational units of the NHS in England. Their function is to manage, commission, and, in some areas, provide primary care services that were typically offered by GP fund holding practices. In 2002 the Department of Health gave PCTs the additional remit of commissioning all mental health services resulting in some organizations amalgamating community and mental health trusts, serving populations in excess of 350,000. Some of these organizations are now in the throes of converting to Foundation Trust Status, a requirement for all NHS Trusts by 2013 (DH, 2010).

The delivery of mental health services by PCTs has featured to a greater or lesser degree depending on their size, particular health care interests and relationships with specialist mental health trusts. As about 90 per cent of mental health care is delivered solely by primary care the government's continued journey to a primary care led NHS looks likely to become much more of a reality for people with mental health problems in the future. In the latest update on High Quality Care for All (DH, 2008) 50 new GP led health centres are launched as the health service overhaul continues.

Compared with specialist care, primary care mental health services delivered in general practice are found to be more accessible for service users, less stigmatizing and allow the opportunity to treat physical and mental health problems concurrently (Rothmann and Wagner, 2003). Yet the assessment and management of mental health problems by primary care teams has not been without difficulty. This has implications for interdisciplinary working within primary care and between primary and specialist services. According to the National Institute for Mental Health England (NIMHE, 2004) and Northern Centre for Mental Health in 2001 PCTs regard specialist mental health services with scepticism and argue that better use could be made of this provision if continuity of care were improved.

The Evolution of Multidisciplinary Working in Primary Health Care Teams

People with mental health issues present to primary care teams in different ways. As the main point of entry into the NHS, GPs typically encounter the whole range of mental health problems and are involved in screening, diagnosing and treating mental health ill health (Bambling, 2007). People with common mental disorders such as anxiety and depression form a large group of those presenting to GPs, accounting for about 300–400 patients per partner, (Paykel and Priest, 1992). These individuals may have interrelated physical health concerns and generally speaking can be managed effectively in primary care with little need for recourse to specialist mental health services.

In addition, there are people with severe and enduring mental health problems who constitute a much smaller group varying from 4–12 per GP (Strathdee and Jenkins, 1996). For these individuals care coordination is especially important (Freeman et al., 2002). As specialist mental health services have continued to evolve since the introduction of the Policy Implementation Guide in 2001 collaborative working with primary health care teams continues to ebb and flow depending on the reconfiguration of these teams vis-a-vis Community Mental Health Teams and hospital-based services. Although primary care teams have greater collective responsibility; together with service users and carers for promoting the health and wellbeing of the local population through partnership approaches (West and Poulton, 1997) their typical multiprofessional configuration is difficult to describe as a spectrum of involvement of different disciplines has developed.

At one extreme, and in an increasing minority, are small GP practices who employ a core team including practice nurses and reception staff. In these teams input from health visitors and district nurses is usually shared with other practices. In contrast large practices with several GP partners are more like GP led health-centres often engaging the services of more than 40 primary care workers including administrative and clinical staff. In these settings several teams are likely to emerge within the organization as a whole providing services to particular client groups or centred around specific areas of professional expertise (West and Poulton, 1997). This diversification of the makeup of primary health care teams was assisted by the introduction of the 1990 GP contract and fund holding in 1991. As a consequence of the latter GPs could purchase the services of district nurses and health visitors and some practices saw this as an opportunity to use money derived from health promotion activities to employ practice-based counsellors. In some areas school nurses are also embraced as part of the primary health care team.

The attachment of social workers to general practice is now virtually non-existent compared with the 1970s and early 80s (Close and Corney, 1982). A large number of these schemes were discontinued as a result of funding difficulties and the significant reforms of the social work profession that arose as a result of the NHS and Community Care Act (CCA) (1990) and the Children Act (1989) also played a part in their demise. In some areas similar attachment schemes have since been reintroduced to link with specialist mental health teams and have sparked the debate about integrated mental health care with the co-location of psychologists and psychiatrists in primary care settings.

Standards 2 and 3 of the National Service Framework for Mental Health (DH, 1999a) are identified as core business for primary care professionals requiring effective assessment and management of common mental disorders together with efficient referral pathways to specialist services where necessary.

Key concept 7.1: National Service Framework standards for primary care

Standard 2
Any service user who contacts their primary health care team with a common mental health problem should:

- Have their mental health needs identified and assessed.
- Be offered effective treatments, including referral to specialist services for further assessment, treatment, and care if they require it.

Standard 3
Any individual with a common mental health problem should:

- Be able to make contact round the clock with the local services necessary to meet their needs and receive adequate care.
- Be able to use NHS direct, as it develops for first level advice and referral on to specialist help lines or local services.

To assist with the achievement of the NSF standards a new role for graduate Primary Care Mental Health Workers (PCMHWs) was created with government funding to appoint and train 1,000 of these new workers (DH, 2000c). It was envisaged that this extra resource would help primary care to manage and treat people with common mental health problems and that the workers would be trained to undertake roles and responsibilities in three main areas (DH, 2001 and DH, 2003a) as follows:

Key concept 7.2: Roles and responsibilities for primary care mental health workers: National Institute of Mental Health in England, North West (2004, p. 9)

Client work – for example clinically brief psychological therapies; facilitating referral pathways; providing information for patients and families, facilitating self-help programmes, using computerized Cognitive Behavioural Therapy (CBT) programmes.

Practice teamwork – e.g. audit; improving information and communication; developing information infrastructures such as care management systems, review systems etc, facilitating service user involvement etc.

Work in the wider community – linking with the Local Authority, community and voluntary sector agencies.

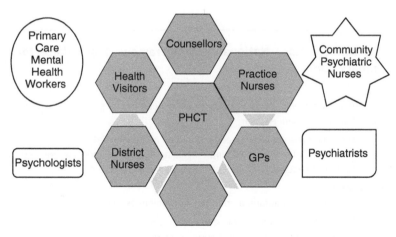

Figure 7.1 Multiprofessional makeup of Primary Health Care Team

Given the widening involvement of these new workers in primary care arriving at a definitive description of the multiprofessional primary health care team is problematic. Figure 7.1 attempts to depict the likely core members of a multidisciplinary Primary Health Care Team (PHCT) and the groups who tend to be more or less 'attached' depending on the size of the practice. The extent of community mental health nurses and psychiatrists' involvement will vary depending on whether the team has a particular interest in mental health care and how services are currently commissioned by the PCTs.

Roles and Responsibilities of the Primary Health Care Team (PHCT)

Because of the generic responsibilities of PHCTs providing primary mental health care is only one of a number of competing priorities. For example, Practice Nurses provide a range of health care including: cervical cytology, immunizations and chronic disease management associated with asthma, diabetes and coronary heart disease. There is some evidence to suggest that they provide these interventions less readily to people with a known history of mental health problems. There is also conflicting evidence regarding the specific role of Practice Nurses with people with severe and enduring mental illness. Several studies have identified that practice nurses play a key role in giving depot injections (Shia and Marriott, 2002; Burns et al., 1998; and Hamilton, 1996) and monitoring medication despite a general lack of mental health training (Gray et al., 1999; Atkin et al., 1993). Other studies suggest that they do not undertake these tasks and are more often dealing with 'less serious' mental health problems in people who present for the range of general nursing interventions on offer (Secker et al., 2000).

By comparison district nurses are in contact with large numbers of elderly people or people where intervention is targeted primarily at physical health problems. Not surprisingly Secker et al. (2000) report that district nurses identified dementia as the most frequently mentioned mental health problem they encountered in older people. Interestingly, district nurses were of the view that other mental health problems were outside their remit.

The predominance of people with dementia on districts nurses' caseloads is likely to be sustained as the numbers of elderly people in the population increase (Chambers et al., 2001). Armstrong (2000) highlights that the district nurse may be the only member of the primary health care team with whom a persons' carer has contact. As revealed in several studies the caring role is likely to come with its own increased risk of developing mental distress (Pearsall and Yates, 2004) thus district nurses may be able to play a key role in early detection and referral for treatment.

Several studies identify the important role Health Visitors play in the recognition of post-natal depression (Secker et al., 2000). They are also the professional group more likely to encounter other mental health problems in the post-partum period and more general mental health problems in families (Armstrong, 2000). Secker et al. (2000) also found that health visitors in particular were supporting women with mental health needs that stemmed from abusive experiences in childhood, social isolation and domestic violence.

For GPs dealing with the whole range of mental health problems, evidence suggests that the biggest issue is the difficulty surrounding recognition and diagnosis. As Docherty (1997) has outlined, these barriers can be divided into 'physician' and 'patient' barriers. GPs' ability to recognize mental ill health will be dependent upon their self-confidence in dealing with mental health issues, their knowledge of mood disturbance, and their skills in eliciting relevant information from their patients. In addition, they will be influenced by their own beliefs and attitudes towards mental distress and those who experience it. The patient barriers include the degree of awareness the individual has regarding their depression and the extent to which psychological symptoms coexist with symptoms of other disorders, both mental and physical.

According to Fleury et al. (2009) three sets of variables are associated with GPs taking on service users with severe and enduring mental health needs. As well as expertise, the profile of their clinical practice and the interprofessional relationships with specialized services will determine whether GPs will play a role in treating severe mental illness. This suggests the need for more integrated models of treatment such as shared-care or case management (Craven and Bland, 2006).

The contrasting perspectives and exposure to the diversity of mental distress among team members makes agreeing a collective responsibility and a coordinated primary mental health care response a significant challenge. In responding to such a diverse patient population a complex set of issues surface with regard to professional barriers, inequalities in status and separate lines of accountability. All these factors have the potential to hamper effective interdisciplinary teamworking. One possible first step towards overcoming these hurdles involves developing a more coherent team that integrates rather than fragments the contributions from core team members and attached staff.

Developing a Team Approach

Developing a team approach in primary care as a means of improving health outcomes has commanded significant attention (Wood et al., 1994; NHSME, 1993; Jones, 1992 and Adorian et al., 1990). The value of facilitation as an aid to developing a teamworking and thereby improving care quality is also widely recognized (Byng and Single, 1999; Thomas, 1994; Wilson, 1994; Armstrong, 1992). West and Poulton (1997) identify the general characteristics of a team approach, some of which are echoed in respect of primary mental health care by Chambers et al. (2001). Key concept 7.3 outlines these elements, which underpin interdisciplinary teamworking.

> **Key concept 7.3: Elements of an interdisciplinary team approach in primary mental health care**
>
> An identity as a work team with a defined organizational function and shared ownership of a common purpose.
>
> A collective responsibility between team members, which extends to patients and carers for promoting the health and wellbeing of the local population and achieving shared aims and objectives.
>
> Well-defined roles with clear areas of overlap and differentiation.
>
> Open communication and effective interaction between team members.
>
> Opportunities for all team members to enhance their skills in accordance with frameworks for clinical governance.

Barriers to realizing the above stem from the stereotypical assumptions and lack of clarity that primary care workers report regarding the roles and responsibilities of colleagues. GPs are understood to have a poorer understanding of what health visitors do compared with their appreciation of the role of district nurses (Bond et al., 1985). Robinson et al. (1993) and Ross (1992) also reveal that some GPs don't recognize that training opportunities play an important part in the development of the practice nursing role and there has been resistance from GPs to the role of nurse prescribing. GPs also appear to hold conflicting views on the extent to which community mental health nurses should be involved in medication management despite an overwhelming consensus that they ought to be an integral team member of the primary health care team (Badger and Nolan, 1999). In a later study, which focused on practice nurses and community mental health nurses, Badger and Nolan (2001) found that joint workshops, which explored previous perceptions and respective roles shifted some of the unhelpful assumptions each profession held of the other.

In a review of the literature several studies that focused upon collaborative working between primary and specialist mental health services revealed a general agreement that some form of liaison role between GPs and specialist services was required and is beneficial (Bailey et al., 2012). However, studies varied in the types of outcome measures used to evaluate this. Most common measures included consultation rates and referral/response times together with qualitative measures to assess GPs and service users' satisfaction with the care delivered. According to Lester (2005) the benefits of the pooling of expertise and holistic care are offset by barriers over roles and responsibilities, stereotyping and poor communication between team members. This reflects similar tensions in specialist mental health services as outlined in Chapter 2.

The introduction of graduate primary care mental health workers (PCMHWs) to assist in liaison between primary and specialist mental health services has not been without its tensions. Dym and Berman (1986) point out that unless these workers are also familiar with anatomy, physiology and pharmacology there is a danger that their input will be limited to discussions of psychosocial phenomena. Bailey (2007) highlights the issues surrounding the supervision of PCMHWs and the resistance to their role by other professions, notably psychologists who have expressed concerns about role overlap and inadequate training of PCMHWs for them to be dealing with individuals with mental health problems.

There is also the danger that as these workers become embedded in primary care this will allow other members of the primary care team to abdicate responsibility for individuals with common mental health problems solely to these specialist workers. This could result in other team members becoming deskilled in the area of mental health perpetuating rather than facilitating continuity of care that addresses psychological as well as physiological health issues.

A truly interdisciplinary team approach must also include as integral partners people who are using primary mental health services and their carers. Although patchy, the current involvement of users is being achieved on two levels. In some areas, service user workers have been recruited to some of the newly created posts although these are still small in number and where they do exist service users are unsure of themselves and their role within the primary health care team. At the PCT level, service users and carers' opinion on service planning and development is being sought in accordance with government policies for involvement (DH, 2006) although little evidence exists of the influence of involvement in practice at 'grass roots' level.

Taken together, the issues that beset teamwork in primary care mental health services suggest that an interdisciplinary approach as outlined in Chapter 2 can only be achieved with targeted facilitation and personal and professional development planning. A resource to assist with the latter has been produced by Chambers et al. (2001) with useful exercises for encouraging collaboration at the end of each chapter. However, primary health care teams will need to explore creatively opportunities for the participation of service users and carers as this is still omitted as a central issue in the development planning process.

Core Components of Integrated Working in Primary Care: Coordination and Co-location

Developing a team approach is only one component of an interdisciplinary response in primary mental health care because, as Shiers (2001, p. viii) points out, what is needed is 'a model of mental health therapy that is consistent with the goals, strategies and culture of primary care not imported from translocated models of specialist mental health care'. Such a model will need to be underpinned by an agreed philosophy and set of values that encompass:

- The 'meaningful involvement of patients and the public, including those with mental health problems, those who care for them and the general population' (Chambers et al., 2001, p. 3).
- A real commitment to treating patients in accessible and non-stigmatizing settings.
- A holistic mind/body perspective that views mental distress and physical health as undifferentiated.

These elements are suggestive of an integrated model of primary mental health, which involves 'increased collaboration of mental health professionals within primary care settings' (Aitken and Curtis, 2004, p. 322) and is advocated by a growing body of research in several countries. According to research, integrated care has demonstrated positive outcomes for a range of mental health problems including: depression, anxiety and panic disorders (Aitken and Curtis, 2004). Blount (2003) found that integrated care not only improved clinical outcomes but was also more cost-effective and increased both service user and provider satisfaction with care delivery.

Models of primary care mental health vary in the level of integration. These can be conceptualized in respect of horizontal integration where professions and services that operate at similar levels in the care hierarchy are brought together compared with vertical integration which brings together different levels of care into one hierarchy (England and Lester, 2005). Blount (2003) contends that in the US a continuum of care exists in respect of the location and nature of the relationship between providers. At one end of the continuum behavioural health providers are located in different settings to the primary care team, use separate treatment plans and rarely communicate with each other. At the other end they are co-located services, in shared premises with the same administrative staff and systems and collaborative treatment plans. This continuum of care reflects the debate about multidisciplinary compared with interdisciplinary approaches to mental health care generally and in the US this has led to a growing body of literature on coordination versus co-location of services for optimizing mental health outcomes (Guck et al., 2007).

According to Blount integrated care can also be characterized as targeted at service users experiencing specific concerns such as people with mental health issues and substance misuse problems or non-targeted where a broad array of services are provided to service users with diverse health needs. In a non-targeted model practice hinges on close collaboration between GPs and mental health professionals who consult regularly throughout the day, often informally, utilizing an overarching case management approach to mental health care. GPs remain responsible for the service user's physical health needs while the mental health professional undertakes appropriate assessment for mental distress, provides short-term interventions and links the service user with appropriate support services. Non-targeted integration usually operates from the biopsychosocial model of health care where service users are offered mental health services within the same practice as their GP. Targeted services include multiprofessional treatment teams including nurses, social workers, counsellors and psychologists. Colleagues collaborate with the primary health care team but offer a specialized service and retain responsibility for service users who have specific needs in respect of mental health interventions.

In order for integrated models to succeed the literature suggests there are a number of factors that need to be addressed to ensure integration does not simply add to the workload of primary health care workers and overburden them. These are summarized below (see Aitken and Curtis, 2004; WHO, 2001 and Petersen, 2000).

Key concept 7.4: Factors underpinning an integrated approach to primary care mental health

- A comprehensive discourse of care which understands illness as emerging out of an interaction of biological, cultural, psychological and social imperatives (Petersen, 2000, p. 322).
- Staff must be comfortable working with a biopsychosocial model of care which includes medication.
- Sufficient numbers of adequately trained specialist and primary care staff.
- Regular supplies of essential psychotropic drugs.
- Referral criteria.
- Information and communication systems.
- Appropriate links with other community and social services and with specialist care services through a case management approach.
- Mental health professionals should find ways to network with GPs.
- Staff skilled in assessment techniques and the use of brief standardized screening instruments to respond to the fast paced treatment environment.
- Staff skilled in time-limited group interventions, relaxation training, psycho education.

As suggested by the above, 'health' needs to be conceptualized more widely in this context than being merely symptom free. Primary care has a long history of health promotion in areas such as coronary heart disease, which has not readily transferred to mental health yet standard 1 of the National Service Framework for Mental Heath emphasizes such promotion and prevention. Fundamental to the health promotion approach is the promotion of choice, options and information for service users to enable them to change their lifestyle. All these elements when used in respect of mental health facilitate an individual becoming an active participant in their own recovery process (Deegan, 1996). However, ethical issues can arise with integrated approaches as practitioners may conflict in their views about what is best for the service user (Lesser, 2000). For interdisciplinary working to succeed professionals need to be able to discuss and debate their ethical standpoints in order to acknowledge where conflicts may occur and to arrive at strategies for negotiating differences whilst maintaining ethical integrity.

One way in which ethical dilemmas can be managed in integrated care is by the use of Integrated Care Pathways which are typically implemented for homogenous service user groups with common predictable illnesses. The latter, in particular, has limited their application to mental health issues. However, in a study conducted by Rees et al. (2004) ICPs in mental health were useful for helping team members clarify their roles and responsibilities and supported an approach underpinned by shared accountability for the service user's care. However, ICPs were thwarted because of differences in team members' workload, a lack of integration at management level above the CMHT and lack of understanding of how integration was supposed to work in practice.

Interdisciplinary Working Across the Interface of Primary and Specialist Mental Health Care

Implementing standard 2 of the National Service Framework affords a real opportunity for interdisciplinary working that spans primary care and specialist mental health services. In some areas in England, CMHTs have been reconfigured into primary care liaison teams to support Assertive Outreach, Early Intervention and Crisis Resolution and Home Treatment teams. In accordance with the models of integrated care discussed above the aim of primary care liaison is to provide better access to assessment and short-term targeted interventions particularly for people with less severe and enduring mental health problems.

Chapter 3 set out the dimensions of interdisciplinary working spanning the individual, team and organizational levels of practice. For primary care liaison to work effectively it needs to be embedded in a whole system approach to mental health provision (Bailey et al., 2011) that embraces change across these three levels. Byng et al. (1999) and Mauksch and Leahy (1993) provide some useful service development outcomes for primary care mental health that can form the basis for service development plans as primary care aligns itself with the specialist mental health teams to provide care continuity synonymous with interdisciplinary working. These outcomes have been adapted and grouped together below into the respective levels for development.

Key concept 7.5: Service development outcomes for promoting an interdisciplinary approach spanning primary and specialist mental health services

Strategic/Organizational Dimension Service Features

- Action plans need to be in place to 'improve physical proximity' between primary and specialist services. This could be achieved by either locating primary care liaison teams in primary care where possible or if space does not allow for this, having a mental health liaison practitioner on site at least one day per week.
- Mental health specialists need to be comfortable and effective in the role of consultant as for many service users the majority of mental health treatment will continue to be delivered by GPs and practice nurses even in integrated settings. As PCTs commission mental health services new ways of working needs to feature in the way that services are commissioned and continuity of care supported between primary and secondary care services.
- Organizational policies should be created that integrate primary and specialist mental health care rather then promote an adversarial relationship between providers and between providers and service users. As these policies are designed and implemented they need to address standards of equity between psychological, social and medical contributions to recovery.
- Effective communication is a key element of an interdisciplinary approach which relies upon:

  - Agreement about the core information required by the primary health care team in assessment, follow-up and discharge letters and by the CMHT in referral letters.
  - Specification of a time period for receiving and sending letters, and the use of shared records.
  - Agreement on criteria for referral and discharge.

- Where new services are to be developed or existing ones maintained this provides an opportunity for the:

  - Establishment of a shared case/care register. The criteria for inclusion and a mechanism for updating this needs to be agreed with service users.
  - A recall system for review, depot injections and repeat medication given by the general practice.

Key Concept 7.5 – *continued*

    – Joint team meetings that take place attended by both primary and secondary care colleagues together with service users and carers.
    – Shared care guidelines that are devised jointly and include input from service users and carers.

- Agreement on the training required by staff, availability of work placements and personal learning plans to support an interdisciplinary approach. Where possible there should be opportunities for people with direct experiences of using services to contribute to staff training and development.
- An approach to care continuity that views patients as people with a commitment to working with individuals over time, rather than through a series of isolated treatment episodes.

Team Dimension: Service Features

- At a team level it is important that colleagues know how to contact each other and the following contact details need to be made available to members of the PHCT and CMHT:

    – Names, contact numbers and professional mix of CMHT and PHCT.
    – Details of service provision for routine, urgent and emergency assessment.
    – Practices' out of hours and crisis service provision.
    – Bypass telephone and fax numbers.

- In order to prevent role overlap, confusion and territoriality there is a need for a clear definition of roles and responsibilities in both primary and secondary services including the roles of the psychiatrist, attached/linked community mental health workers, GP, practice nurses, and professionally affiliated workers such as graduate PCMHWs. Each role needs to be clarified sufficiently to promote an integrated response. This means that team members and service users know who has responsibility for the overall needs assessment, mental state monitoring, medication review, changes and repeat prescribing, including any depot administration.
- The PHCT should be clear and in agreement with the specialist mental health teams about their involvement in the Care Programme Approach (CPA) process (see Chapter 5).
- As a means of improving care coordination, joint medical records should be in place and in complex cases there should be a designated Care Coordinator whose functions and remit are understood by all.

Individual Practice Dimension: Service Features

- In line with contemporary service development and evidence-based interventions, mental health practitioners need to try more episodic models of care and shorter treatment sessions.
- Where the PHCT is providing the main interventions to a service user there needs to be mechanisms in place to include a mental health consultation

Key Concept 7.5 – *continued*

> earlier in the course of an individual's treatment plan to minimize delay and promote care continuity.
>
> • Individual practitioners should have access to each other for consultancy where mental and physical health care issues interrelate.
>
> • The service user should be central to the interdisciplinary care planning process and where interdisciplinary care is necessary the care plan should be agreed with all contributors from the PHCT and specialist mental health services.

Whilst all of these outcomes seem worthwhile their realization is a daunting task and service innovation, whilst evident at one level may be hindered at another as demonstrated by a multiprofessional approach to post-natal depression, established in Oxford. This was achieved through the use of guidelines for shared care at a service level between health visitors and the CMHT. A multidisciplinary protocol for intervening with individuals with depressive symptoms at team level contributed to effective team management. However, the tension between the roles of CMHT workers and their need to prioritize people with severe and enduring mental health problems impacted at a service and individual practice level and meant that their availability was constrained. This together with a service level decision to withdraw social work colleagues from the primary health care team, left health visitors feeling sceptical about the extent to which this multiprofessional initiative could be developed into a more integrated way of teamworking (Secker et al., 2000).

If primary care mental health seeks to develop an interdisciplinary approach in accordance with the service features identified above, then considerable attention needs to be paid to how integration at all levels is established and supported. This can be illustrated with reference to a case example, which is presented below.

PRACTICE FOCUS 7.1

Integrated Working Across the Primary and Specialist Mental Health Service Interface

Aled is 48 years of age and has worked as a prison officer for the past 20 years. He is married to Janine and they have a three year-old son, Dillon. Aled reports playing a very active role in his son's upbringing but over the past 12 months, has experienced particularly high levels of stress at work. Due to the implementation of new procedures his normal shift pattern has changed and he is dealing with more dangerous prisoners. Aled is finding is increasingly difficult to concentrate and has little enthusiasm for his work. He presented to his GP with sleep problems and was prescribed tranquillizers, which he has continued to take on a long-term basis. Subsequently he has developed pronounced symptoms of anxiety including palpitations, headaches and

Practice Focus 7.1 – *continued*

nausea, together with symptoms of depression, including tearfulness and lethargy. He admits to feeling bleak about his future and is trapped in a vicious circle of negative thoughts that only serve to catastrophize and personalize his perception of a desperate situation. He feels he has somehow brought these problems on himself by being weak-willed. He considers himself a failure at work and at home, particularly as he has spent less and less time with Dillon. He repeatedly blames himself for placing what he sees as an unreasonable burden of child care on his wife.

Things came to a head recently when he persuaded Janine to go and stay with her parents for a week's break. During her absence, Aled started drinking heavily. During telephone conversations his wife and in-laws became concerned about his increasing intoxication, despondency and continued mutterings about ending his life. Janine contacted Aled's GP who arranged for a Mental Health Act assessment to be undertaken by the Crisis Resolution and Home Treatment Team. The Approved Mental Health professional who assessed Aled concluded he was experiencing an acute stress reaction coupled with severe symptoms of depression. The suggestion of some short-term intervention from a Community Psychiatric Nurse was made but Aled was reluctant to engage as he believes this will confirm he is mentally unstable and thus incapable of returning to work.

Aled would prefer his GP to respond to his difficulties yet the complexities of his needs suggest that this will need to incorporate:

- Immediate interventions to help him deal with the abuse of alcohol and the severe symptoms of depression.
- Support and guidance to help him withdraw from tranquillizers.
- Structured discussion with his wife and possibly other family members about how the stressful situation at work has impacted significantly on his home life and close personal relationships.
- Coping strategies for the future that will enable him to deal with working in an increasingly stressful environment.

By understanding Aled's needs in respect of the biopsychosocial model, decisions can be reached regarding an integrated approach between primary and specialist mental health services that can in turn form the basis for an interdisciplinary care plan.

In respect of the biological element, Aled can be offered antidepressant medication to address his symptoms of anxiety and depression and improve his sleep pattern. If Alec accepts medication, this will need to be prescribed to accommodate a planned withdrawal from the tranquillizers and alcohol.

The withdrawal process should be overseen by a psychiatrist acting in a consultancy capacity with either Aled's GP or a CPN preferably 'attached' to the primary care team, to promote sharing of information. A withdrawal programme is more likely to be effective if agreement is reached at the team level about roles and responsibilities vis-a-vis prescribing and monitoring and supported by a protocol or shared care guidelines that integrate respective inputs and sign post referral routes if the primary care response is proving of limited success within a given timeframe.

Psychologically Aled needs to understand how depression can affect his thinking patterns and coping strategies and how symptoms of anxiety are created and maintained including the influence of prescribed medication and alcohol. In addition, given the significant work pressures Aled has identified, these need to be validated using a solution

Practice Focus 7.1 – *continued*

focused (Myers, 2008) or cognitive behavioural model (Cigno and Bourn, 1998) such that Aled can see the stress reaction in part as a natural response to a turbulent work experience rather than as a personal failure. Helping Aled to explore his coping strategies more generally, including his recent drinking behaviour can be conducted by the CPN or by a member of the PHCT if suitably trained and should be offered concurrently with the medical intervention. Where interventions are being provided concurrently joint medical records can be especially useful and Aled needs to be integrally involved in deciding the nature and extent of the information being shared between professionals in order to optimize his ownership of the interventions and continued engagement with services.

In respect of the social context there are a number of issues to be addressed; some relating to personal and family relationships but others involving employment practices. Whilst some family sessions facilitated by a worker with skills in family work might help resolve expectations around child care and parenting responsibilities, an opportunity for Aled to explore with his wife how he might try coping differently under pressure from work in the future, would also be helpful. With regard to Aled's employment, it would be helpful to explore if staff sickness is increasing generally and whether any stress management opportunities are available in the work setting to prison staff to encourage mutual support.

All of these elements will need to be formulated into a coherent care plan that is negotiated with Aled and his family who are continually involved in the ongoing process of review and revision as his needs change.

Summary

Primary care is in a pivotal position to influence interdisciplinary working with specialist mental health services as the NHS in England reorientates to being primary care led. Integrated approaches in primary care may involve coordination and or co-location with mental health specialists that is underpinned by values, and a biopsychosocial model of mental distress. Interventions will need to be time-limited and targeted to fast paced primary care settings, underpinned by working protocols, guidelines and integrated care planning. Achieving effective integration is a time consuming process in a context of increasingly stretched resources and diversification of the primary care workforce. Key decision makers from the PCTs, primary health care teams and specialist mental health services will need to be identified to take this remit forward. However, an interdisciplinary approach in the long-term can prevent duplication of effort, ineffective communication and poor continuity of care. If delivered effectively, service user and clinician satisfaction levels can be expected to improve. The challenge is identified; the dilemma is how to achieve it.

8

Interdisciplinary Working with Children and Young People with Mental Health Problems

---

Key Issues:

- Children and adolescents may experience mental health issues directly with some mental health problems showing an increased prevalence in a younger age group.
- Indirectly parental mental health problems may affect young people's experience through child-rearing and attachment and/or as young carers looking after a parent with mental health needs.
- Young people need services that are integrated and responsive spanning needs which can be addressed by mental health promotion through to specialist child and adolescent mental health services.
- Statutory child care policies need to dovetail with the CPA for adults to underpin interprofessional working.
- A biopsychosocial model that addresses the needs of children and their parents in accordance with this framework can provide a useful starting point for an integrated assessment that takes into account the needs of children and their caregivers in a holistic way.

Adult mental health services are targeted at the 16 to 65 age group. Whilst interdisciplinary working with this population is fraught with challenges people with mental health problems falling outside this age range such as children and adolescents run an increased risk of receiving a service that falls short of interdisciplinarity and inter-agency working. In 2003 the Department for Education and Skills highlighted that children's mental health is everyone's business (Department for Education and Skills, 2003).

In respect of children and adolescents there are three main situations where their needs interconnect with mental health services. Some children and adolescents experience mental health issues and require a service before reaching the age of 16. Certain mental health problems are more prevalent in adolescence such as eating disorders and it is estimated that 80 per cent of first episode psychosis emerges in late adolescence/early adulthood. If these young peoples' mental health needs continue there will come a point at which a transition to adult mental health care is required.

Where an adult has a mental health problem this may impact on their parenting capacity resulting in their children being deemed at risk of significant harm and thus in need of services which are provided under the 1989 Children Act legislative framework.

Children and young people may find themselves in a situation where they are caring for an adult with mental or physical health needs who may or may not be in receipt of psychiatric services. Executing the caregiving role may render the young person vulnerable to emotional or educational difficulties and thus is need of additional support.

In addition to these particular needs of children and young people, there are a range of circumstances in which the above scenarios interconnect. Children with emotional and behavioural difficulties can precipitate or exacerbate mental health problems in adult caregivers. Where an adults' mental health difficulties contribute to an adolescent's mental health problem or where caregiving by the young person renders them at risk of impairment to their health or development this may occur to the extent that child protection procedures need to be instigated. As a consequence of these interrelationships the interface of adult mental health services with health and social care provision for young people is extremely complex rendering the need for interdisciplinary and inter-agency working ever more apparent.

Interdisciplinary Mental Health Services for Children and Adolescents

Statistics indicate that one in seven pre-school children has some kind of mental health problem and in addition, significant mental disorder has been identified in 10 per cent of young people between the ages of five and 15 years (Meltzer et al., 2000). Within this sample five per cent had clinically significant conduct disorders, four per cent had emotional disorders including anxiety and depression and one per cent were rated as hyperactive. Other studies have shown that the overall prevalence rates of mental health problems in young people increase with age (Petersen and Leffert, 1995) with late adolescent being a particularly vulnerable time for the onset of severe and enduring mental health problems, notably psychosis (McCurry, 2002). Suicide attempts in young men have increased by 118 per cent in the last ten years (Katz, 1999) and around half of young people with a severe mental health problem use street drugs which exacerbates their difficulties (Wellard, 2002).

Using the biopsychosocial model to understand the presentation of mental health problems in young people provides a first step towards interdisciplinary working as outlined in Chapter 1. According to Bownds (1999) socio biologi-cal research suggests a critical period extending into early adulthood during which a young person's self-image and social skills develop. Biologically this period of development is marked by the multiplication of nerve connections found in the frontal lobes of the brain indicating that physical maturation is not yet complete.

Biological contributions to mental health problems in young people may also arise through inheritance of a genetic predisposition to mental illness from family members or through some physical disabilities that are associated with an increased risk of developing mental health problems (Meltzer et al., 2000). There is a greater prevalence of mental health problems in young peo-ple with learning disabilities (3 out of 10) compared to 1 in 10 in the general population (Nixon et al., 2008). In the majority of cases these disabilities have a physiological component which affects a young person's neuro-biology.

During the transition from adolescence to adulthood young people experi-ence a range of developmental milestones. The extent to which they will be able to make a satisfactory psychological adjustment to these will depend upon their personal coping strategies, internalization of life events and their experiences of transitional periods and how this impacts on their self-esteem. Attachment in children and young people, as a psychological concept, fea-tures increasingly in understanding the presentation of mental health prob-lems in adulthood, in particular post-traumatic stress disorder and personality disorders (Barlow and Underdown, 2008).

Socially children and young people are particularly influenced by their peer group and where relationships with a boyfriend or girlfriend has bro-ken down this has been shown to have an adverse effect on mental health (Meltzer et al., 2000). Culture plays an important function of enabling young people to internalize social rules and routines. Bradshaw (2001) points to a relationship between older youths' own emerging socio-economic status and poor mental health. Young people are also affected by the social pressures of examinations and the need to find employment. Past and current family circumstances, educational experiences, employment and housing opportu-nities also contribute to young people's resilience and ability to cope with emotional distress.

The important interplay of the above factors should provide the starting point for any child and adolescent mental health service. As Walker (2001, p. 74) points out it is unrealistic 'to identify a linear sequence of causality from intervention through to outcome. There are just so many informal, psy-chosocial influences affecting children's emotional and behavioural develop-ment in the short term or cumulatively over the longer term'.

Children and Adolescent Mental Health Services (CAMHS) are serv-ices arranged in a four tier approach to providing care from primary care through to highly specialized forensic units (see Table 8.1). These services are thus provided not only by the NHS but also through collaboration with social services and youth justice departments, education and voluntary sector organizations.

The aim of CAMHS is to provide assessment and skilled interventions to young people with each Tier of service meant to address a different severity of need increasing from Tier 1 to Tier 4. Functions at Tier 1 include those delivered by the wider health and social care workforce who are in contact with children and young people on a daily basis such as teachers and primary care professionals. Their role is to identify and recognize mental distress and refer on to more specialist services where appropriate.

Services in Tiers 2–4 should be provided by staff working in professional CAMHS services although the extent of interdisciplinary working will vary. All Tier 4 services are expected to provide input from a multiprofessional perspective that includes Local Authority and education services as set out by the NHS Health Advisory Service (1995) in *Together We Stand*. Thus it can be seen in Table 8.1 that as the level of need increases so does the need for contributions from a range of different disciplines. The emphasis, primarily on the exclusive professional make-up of the different levels of services means that CAMHS cannot be considered truly interdisciplinary in respect of involving key contributions from children and young people themselves and their families or caregivers.

The vision for CAMHS set out in government guidance and consolidated through funding mechanisms (NHS Health Advisory Service, 1995) was for a service that hinged on joint working and improved liaison between primary care, specialist child and adolescent psychiatric services, social services and other agencies. The introduction of Primary Care Mental Health Workers into the CAMHS workforce was intended to improve interdisciplinary working across the primary/specialist care interface.

In reality as CAMHS services have developed they have varied dramatically across the country in terms of expenditure per health authority, mix of staff including the ratio of child and adolescent psychiatric consultants, and availability of the specialist Tier 4 service (Downey, 2002). There is a false assumption that Tier 3 services offering a multiprofessional approach are larger than they are with some areas lacking a specialist service and in others the first and second tiers being neglected in order to concentrate on providing a Tier 4 service. The older age cut off point for CAMHS also varies across the country (between 14, 16 and 19 years). Young Minds (2007) report that few services deal adequately with 16–21 year-olds despite the increased onset period of severe and enduring mental health problems coinciding with this age group. For young people with first episode psychosis, care should be provided through Early Intervention Teams (DH, 2001).

Table 8.1 The tiers of CAMHS services and level of interdisciplinary working

Tier 1	Tier 2	Tier 3	Tier 4
Non-specialist primary prevention	Uniprofessional groups offering specialist intervention	Multiprofessional Specialist Intervention	Highly specialist
Primary Health Care Team Social Services Schools Voluntary Agency Residential Care Juvenile Justice	Child Psychologists Paediatricians Educational Psychologists Child and Adolescent Psychiatrists Psychiatric Nurses Nurse Specialists	Child and Adolescent Psychiatrists Social Workers Psychiatric Nurses Occupational Therapists Drama Therapists Psychotherapists	In patient units and associated day and outreach services Secure units Forensic units Sexual abuse teams Specialist assessment for complex cases e.g. dual diagnosis Specialist neuropsychiatric services Gender identity services Residential family assessment for children with parents with a mental illness
Preventive services provided separately by individual agency concerned	Specialist services provided separately by each profession	Services provided collaboratively with contributions from different professional groups but in the main excludes young people and their caregivers and focus is on professional input	Services provided with contributions from different professional groups within a specialist setting

Increasing level of need →
Increasing level of interprofessionality

However, these are in different stages of development across the country and vary between geographical areas in how they operate and collaborate with CAMHS. Consequently getting help for young people with interrelated mental health and substance misuse needs can be even more problematic (see Chapter 10).

The development of, at best, an interprofessional CAMHS service has been beleaguered by a number of problems that similarly hinder interprofessional working in adult mental health care. At an organizational level these include a lack of multi-agency and partnership boards. Agencies are also interested in different outcomes reflected in a uniprofessional culture that leads to money not being spent because of inter-agency disagreements over shared priorities. At a team level many psychiatrists are not prepared to work on issues that affect young people such as family relationships, employment or training issues which can render treatment amongst team members inconsistent and lead to badly handled transitions between CAMHS and adult mental health services.

According to Rethink (2009), CAMHS services need to be improved significantly through a national strategic framework that includes better interagency working at every level together with locality-based youth services that address mental health issues appropriately.

At an organizational level, such an approach could be promoted through shared ownership of a strategy focusing on young peoples' mental health, with joint commissioning of services and an agreed agenda for action. This could be developed to enhance interdisciplinary working with involvement from young people themselves and agencies that reflect the needs of their families. Components of an integrated service would need to include assessments, with effective reporting and referral routes to courts, specialist services and family support services. Advice giving, early interventions and collaborative work across agencies would provide a range of different interventions to reflect an understanding of young peoples' mental health with reference to the biopsychosocial model.

In much the same way as the composition of adult mental health teams have been influenced by the historical development of hospital-based mental health care so too have CAMHS (Duncan, 2003).

In Scotland, there has been a proliferation of policy developments as teams have attempted to move away from the traditional composition of psychiatrist, psychologist and psychiatric social workers to workforce configurations that respond to the mental health needs of children in schools through to those requiring more specialist services (Scottish Executive, 2005; Public Health Institute for Scotland, 2003).

Consequently, difficulties with establishing a coordinated approach to providing CAMHS services have thus been well-documented and particular problems include: poor links with other service providers, a lack of real liaison or joint working with GPs (Audit Commission, 1999).

One example where a more interprofessional and inter-agency approach to CAMHS appears to be working well is in Norfolk.

PRACTICE FOCUS 8.1

Interdisciplinary Working in Family Support Teams in Norfolk

Initially funded as one of 24 pilot projects, Family Support Services in Norfolk were created to bridge the gap between primary and socialist care in child and adolescent mental health. Three multiprofessional teams were funded by health, education and social work, each coterminous with the PCTs and working together with one operational manager.

The Family Support Teams (FSTs) are governed by a collective multiprofessional policy with decisions made in team meetings. Staff are contracted or seconded from the three agencies to maintain the multiprofessional nature of the service. The integration of the teams is supported by a 60 hour core training programme for all staff that covers a range of topics including child mental health, attachment theory, child protection, anti-discriminatory practice and the Human Rights Act. The training programme was delivered to the whole countywide service promoting closer integration within the teams and across all three localities.

Core objectives for the service agreed at the outset are to provide:

- A school-age service responsive to children and their families;
- A service, which is local and accessible;
- Advice, information and consultation working together with professionals;
- A service offered in partnership with parents where the child's welfare is paramount;
- Intervention that respects the child's wishes and feelings;
- Help with emerging mental health problems.

An interprofessional approach is supported by establishing agreed client pathways through the service with clear eligibility criteria and stages of assessment, allocation and review. The maximum timescale for support is 12 weeks. The role of the teams to offer consultation advice, training and support to primary care staff was also clearly delineated at the outset.

An interprofessional approach is supported by a management structure in the teams that allows for appropriate professional autonomy whilst permitting the team coordinator to control the use of individual's time where need is most pressing. Staff report valuing the clear lines of accountability the coordinator role provides which assists with teams having a clear identity, streamlined communications and deemed a distinctive profile within a multi-agency service. The coordinator role was essential in enabling staff to manage caseloads and obtain regular supervision. A county coordinator for the service has also been appointed which is crucial in providing access to other resources and initiatives across Norfolk and embedding the FST in the County's wider repertoire of local resources and provision. In the first 18 months of operation a total of 694 requests for consultation have been received.

Practice Focus 8.1 – *continued*

> Each of the FSTs is located in a professional network of statutory and voluntary providers that enables a context of resource exchange and collaboration. There is evidence of good joint working with health visitors and other Tier 1 professionals. Teams have a focus within the CAMHS strategy to:
>
> Streamline the referral processes between each service;
> Exchange referrals and share in consultation; and
> Avoid families or referrers feeling passed around the system.
>
> At a strategic level team coordinators meet with divisional education welfare and educational psychology managers to maintain and improve integrated working.

The Impact of Adult Mental Health on Children and Adolescents

Between one in four and one in five adults will experience a mental health problem during their lifetime and at the time of their illness at least one quarter to one half of these adults will be parents (Falkov, 1998). However, it is worth stating from the outset that not all children whose parents have a mental health problem will experience difficulties themselves (Anthony and Cohler, 1987; Kauffman et al., 1979), and despite care in the community which means that parents with mental health problems and their children will be spending more time together not all parents with mental health problems will have an adverse impact on their children's development. Silverman's (1989) research suggests that between one and two-thirds of children who have difficulties have parents who are known to adult mental health services.

According to Falkov (1998, p. 12) the link between adult mental distress and child care difficulties can best be understood by reference to the biopsychosocial framework described above. He claims that 'it is the combination of bio-genetic inheritance and psychosocial adversities associated with mentally ill adults (impact of illness on parenting; family discord and disorganization; poverty and housing problems; disruption in child care and schooling) which increases the likelihood that children will experience difficulties'.

Falkov goes on to outline that within the population of families with mentally ill parents and dependent children there are several sub groups as shown below.

Particularly children who fall into categories C to E are in need of an interprofessional response that embodies a collaborative approach to tackling the impact of adult mental health on parents' child-rearing capacity.

A	B	C	D	E
Parents who have mental health problems but are mainly well	Parents whose children demonstrate resilience but are in need of support	Parents whose children are vulnerable and children in need of services	Parents whose behaviour means their children are in need of services and protection	Parents who kill, leading to child fatalities

Increasing needs of children ⟶ ⟶ ⟶ ⟶
Decreasing number of children ⟶ ⟶ ⟶ ⟶

Figure 8.1 A range of need among children of mentally ill parents

In order to begin to implement such a response practitioners in the mental health and child care arenas need to understand how the different presentations of mental distress in the adult caregiver are likely to impact upon the child. For example, Cleaver et al. (1999) summarize research into the effects of depression on mothers which can lead to them being insensitive to their children's needs, unresponsive to their cues and more angry and critical of their children. The presence of a personality disorder in a parent also affects their ability to control their emotions which can impact negatively at times of stress exacerbated by a difficult infant or a troublesome adolescent (Norton and Dolan, 1996).

A review of serious case reviews into incidents of abuse leading to child deaths (category E of Falkov's framework) (Falkov, 1996) indicated the presence of parental mental illness was a significant factor in the incidents that occurred. The study included 40 cases and compared these with two earlier studies (James, 1994, 30 cases and Owers et al., 1999, 10 cases).

The percentage of parents with mental health problems of the children affected were shown to be:

Table 8.2 Mental health problems in the parents of children subject to serious case reviews

	James %	Owers et al. %	DH Study %
Mental Health problems in parents	20	20	45

Of the 40 cases included in the DH study, 31 children died and seven of these were children murdered by a mentally ill parent. In one case, although there were 80 consultations with the mentally ill mother, the chair of the review concluded that 'no-one ever seemed to have added it all up' (Falkov, 1998, p. 54).

The DH review makes repeated references to the need for better inter-agency working including communication to safeguard children, improved sharing of information to promote more effective decision making and a planned coordinated response across professionals and the agencies they represent.

The challenge then in developing an interdisciplinary approach to caring for children whose parents are in contact with adult mental health services lies in ensuring that care planning provision (CPA) in adult mental health (see Chapter 4) dovetails with child protection procedures in Local Authorities. With the increasing domination of mental health teams (including Assertive Outreach, Crisis Resolution and Home Treatment) there is a danger that the social work contribution in respect of statutory child care and protection will be lost.

A Framework for Interdisciplinary Working

In the child care arena Working Together to Safeguard Children (DH, 1999c), the Framework for the Assessment of Children in Need and their Families (DH, 2000a) and Every Child Matters (DfES, 2004) provide the blueprint for an inter-agency approach. Children's Trusts were introduced to enable the pooling of resources, improve partnership and address the fragmentation of responsibilities between health; education and social care organizations following the 2003 Laming Report into the death of Victoria Climbiè (DH, 2003).

The legislative framework for child protection and the CPA for adults with mental health problems both emphasize interdisciplinary assessment which embraces an assessment of risk. It is usually the case that locally there will be agreed documentation for recording these assessments but each will reflect the services' respective focus. This means that assessments vary with regard to the level of detail about the impact of adult mental health difficulties on parents' ability to care and protect their children. Where a biopsychosocial model forms the basis for a risk assessment that considers both sets of issues pertaining to the adult with the mental health problems and the children they care for, this can provide a useful starting point from which to move forward. CPA reviews or section 117 discharge planning meetings should provide an opportunity to share and update information between child and adult care workers about any risks arising from the adult's mental health problems. Where a Local Authority children and families team is involved with a child or young person whose parent is receiving a mental health service the child care workers

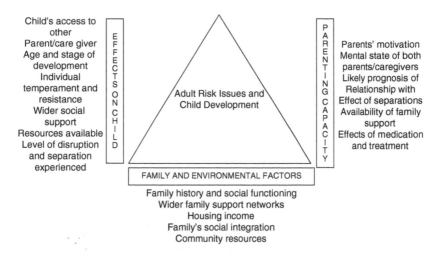

Figure 8.2 Biopsychosocial issues for assessment in child development

should at least know who the parents' Care Coordinator is and be able to feed information into the risk assessment process through this relationship.

Where child care and adult mental health practitioners are in the process of conducting an assessment the following framework has proved useful in training sessions as it is based on the assessment framework already familiar to child care workers (DH, 2000a) and embodies the biopsychosocial issues outlined.

At a team level an interdisciplinary approach is hampered by the separate legal frameworks that exist for children and adults. Where children or adults have very specialist needs that are being met through a contracted out service or out of area placement this can also render a collaborative approach difficult. Whilst a better understanding of the different perspectives of adult and children and families services may help in respect of approaches to integrated approaches to assessment and interventions across teams this is also sadly lacking. This is compounded by qualifying training programmes that require workers to specialize in their area of chosen practice early on. Whilst workers may have good grounding in either adult mental health or child care issues by the time they qualify, their exposure to a knowledge base of the 'other' area is likely to be lacking.

Falkov (1998) suggests that improved collaboration at a team level could be enhanced through communication between the different teams as soon as possible following a referral and that confidentiality should not be used as a cover for the absence of good practice. One of the difficulties in fostering a collaborative approach across teams is that often specialism specific jargon acts as a barrier to communication and teams are unaware of referral criteria. This is a particularly salient issue since the disbanding of generic Community

Table 8.3 Parenting checklist to support interdisciplinary working

1. Depression	Comments
• How secure are the attachments to the child? Is there evidence of insecure attachments? Is there another parent/caregiver who can offer secure attachments?	
• Is the parent over-sensitive to the child's negative behaviour?	
• How do symptoms of depression relate to the individual's own poor parenting experience?	
• Does depression pervade all aspects of family life? Explore daily routines, social networks, hobbies and interests.	
• How compliant is the individual with antidepressant medication? Explore over and under compliance.	
• Does the parent express suicidal thoughts or carry out self-harming behaviours?	
• What steps does the parent take to protect the child from the parent's self-harming?	
2. Anxiety Disorders	
• How pre-occupied is the parent with anxiety symptoms or phobias?	
• Do the anxiety disorders affect the child's adjustment? Explore preoccupation with physical symptoms and avoidance routines.	
• How do the anxiety problems affect attachment behaviour?	
• Where the parent experiences obsessive thoughts do these involve the child directly? e.g. ideas about contamination.	
• Does the parent involve the child in ritualistic behaviours? e.g. washing, self-harming, eating rituals.	
3. Psychosis	
• How is the psychosis characterized by positive or negative symptoms or both?	
• How severe are the positive symptoms? Remember the more severe the symptoms and lack of contact with reality the more significant the risk to child's safety.	
• Is the child included in the content of the delusions?	
• Is the parent able to spot signs of psychotic episodes and take protective action?	
• If there are lots of negative symptoms is this affecting attachment and motivation?	
• Does the child experience feelings of abandonment and neglect?	
• Does the parent experience command or persecutory delusions? Is the child a focus of these?	
• Is there a history of suicidal or aggressive behaviour?	
• Is there a history of morbid jealousy? Is the child a focus?	
• Is there a history of substance or alcohol abuse?	
4. Puerperal Psychosis	
• Is the newborn baby included in the delusions?	
• Is there any rough handling or physical aggression to the child?	
• Is there supervision available from other relatives?	

Mental Health Teams into more specialist services. In respect of accessing mental health services this increasing functionalization has the potential to hinder shared access to assessment and care planning for children and families teams even further.

Training workers together from the different range of agencies involved is one way of promoting a more collaborative approach across teams. In Birmingham, this was developed through the Area Child Protection Committee in collaboration with mental health colleagues in higher education. A collaborative training programme was designed that adopted a shared learning approach and was run over a day and half.

On the morning of the first day child care workers and adult mental health workers received different sessions to cover the knowledge base each group reported to be lacking. Thus the adult mental health workers covered the child protection framework including consideration of significant harm and the assessment framework. At the same time the child care workers received an introduction to the signs and symptoms of adult mental ill health, the CPA as the care planning framework and the referral criteria being used by local mental health teams. This helped to demystify much of the language teams used and increased team members' confidence in sharing information. During the afternoon of Day One all workers joined together to map out their respective referral routes and explore potential junctures for collaboration.

A half-day follow-up session was provided approximately two weeks later where the emphasis was on developing the framework for a collaborative approach to risk assessment based on the model described in Chapter 5. Workers considered a parenting checklist (see Table 8.3) together with the assessment framework above (see Figure 8.2) in respect of three case studies. Their task was to identify how a more integrated approach to working with the three families could be adopted.

Feedback from several cohorts of workers undertaking the programme has been unquestionably positive. Some workers negotiated further shadowing placements in the agency setting with which they were least familiar to further enhance their knowledge of either child care or adult mental health. Some teams have since invited colleagues from their locality mental health or child care team to team meetings to discuss complex cases or share more information generally about referrals routes.

Such inter-agency training as Falkov refers to it is one of seven key principles he describes that needs attending to promote a more integrated approach at the organizational level. Other principles relate to:

- Coherent coordinated and integrated service structures;
- Procedures to ensure needs of parents and children are jointly considered;

- Inter and intra-agency communication;
- Long-term support strategies and a variety of services in place;
- Flexible and accessible community resources;
- Support for the family as a whole.

With the continuing change afoot in both mental health care, as PCTs transfer to Foundation Trusts, and in the child care arena as education becomes a lead agency in the management of services, it is likely that promoting the above principles will continue to pose difficulties at least for the foreseeable future. One way that the government has attempted to tackle this and promote more effective interdisciplinary working at a strategic level is through the setting up of the Children and Young Peoples' Emotional Wellbeing and Mental Health National Support Team (DH, 2010). The Team has visited services to find out what works in respect of a whole system approach to children's emotional health from prevention through to specialist services. The majority of the key elements of best practice that the Team has highlighted echo the messages contained in this chapter and relate to:

- Joint commissioning of a mix of provision;
- Strong partnerships;
- Staff capabilities to support practical and evidence-based approaches of what works;
- Access to mental health services through schools and primary care;
- Joint pathway development for children with special needs;
- Well-integrated CAMHS;
- Early years intervention through multiprofessional children's centres.

Young Carers

Young carers are defined by the Carers (Recognition and Services) Act 1995 as 'children and young people (under 18) who provide or intend to provide a substantial amount of care on a regular basis' to other family members. In a family where a parent has a mental health problem a young carer may be providing care to that adult and/or to siblings and/or taking on the general running of the household when their parent is unable to do so. The role of being a young carer may be especially burdensome in a single parent household where the young person may feel isolated an unsupported in their role.

According to Falkov (1998) it is the consequences of caring for the adult with mental health problems that in turn can impact on the young person's mental health. Consequences can include: impaired educational opportunities, bullying and teasing, isolation from peers and lack of time for usual childhood activities. In addition, feelings of being stigmatized, poorly understood and lack of recognition for their contribution can contribute to a young person's impaired self-esteem inextricably linked to emotion disorders such as depression and anxiety. It is therefore not surprising that Meltzer et al. (2000) found that children with parents who screened positive on the GHQ12 (12-item General Health Questionnaire) were three times more likely to have a mental disorder than those whose parents had sub threshold scores.

The above experiences can be particulary difficult for the young person to cope with if they feel that the mental health professionals involved are working solely with the adult. A recovery model of mental health encourages an approach that nurtures existing family, community and social support networks thus placing an onus on adult mental health workers to be aware of and at least acknowledge the young person's needs as part of their assessment and intervention with the adult. The assessment frameworks included in this chapter are provided as examples that may help adult mental health workers to be more cognisant of the child care dimension.

A more formalized multiprofessional approach may be promoted with recourse to the relevant legislative frameworks. A young carer has a right to an assessment from the Local Authority social services departments either under the Children Act 1989 or the Carers (Services and Recognition) Act 1995, which is outlined in the adult mental health National Service Framework as inextricably linked with the CPA process.

In 2004 the carers (Equal Opportunities Act) requires Local Authorities to inform young carers of their rights to such an assessment. In addition, Local Authorities should ensure they are working in partnership with other bodies or agencies (for example, education) to provide a seamless service for young people and those they care for.

Where mental health workers are providing a service to the adult they should be continually informing the young person of their rights in order to promote a more integrated approach to meeting the needs of the family as a whole. This may involve assisting the young person to make contact with the local social services department or taking this forward on their behalf. Where mental health workers have particular skills in providing family interventions these can be especially useful particularly if delivered in partnership with a child care worker who may also be involved with the family. The focus of family work could be to assist with communicating and providing information about the parent's mental health problems or about exploring practical strategies to help the young person cope. The workers' skill will lie in achieving a balance between providing sufficient and useful information which does not undermine the young person in their role but that also guards against them taking excessive responsibilities to the detriment of their own wellbeing.

Very often a multiprofessional approach that involves the adult mental health and children and families workers will not occur for a variety of reasons. Firstly there may be a reluctance to assess young carers under either of

the Acts (Dearden and Becker, 1998) or the Local Authority may not adver-
tise a young carer's right to an assessment because of raising expectations
where services are lacking (DH, 1999). The different philosophies of adult
mental health workers and child care workers can act as a hindrance. This
can be especially evident if the adult mental health worker feels the young
person needs support but the child care agencies will only provide this where
the young person is considered to be suffering significant harm and is in need
of protection. Where it is deemed that the impact of the caring role does
not meet this threshold of need this can result in the young person being
denied a service. Very often young people themselves are reluctant to seek
help because of the fear that care proceedings may be implemented.

According to Underdown (2002) many young carers surveyed give strong
messages about the importance of partnership working both between agencies and children's and adults' services. Where they are able to articulate their
needs these centre on:

- Receiving information about their parents illness;
- Recognition of their role in the family;
- Practical and domestic help;
- A person who they can contact in a crisis;
- Someone to talk to – not necessarily formal counselling.
  (Falkov, 1998, p. 121).

Many of these needs can be met by well-coordinated inter-agency working
between the statutory and voluntary sector. A potential starting point is the
emphasis on a preventative approach so that the young person can receive
appropriate leisure activities, maintain contacts with friends and spend some
time away from home in chosen activities knowing that the services are providing support to their parent.

Whilst genuine attempts have been made to involve adult carers and users
of mental health services in developing a more interdisciplinary response
to care delivery the involvement of young carers and young people using
CAMHS has featured less prominently. A number of studies point to the
ethical, professional and practical issues in considering how to genuinely
engage young people in this process (Walker, 2001; Kent and Read, 1998;
Nixon and Northrup, 1997). However, work conducted by the Mental Health
Foundation, through its youth crisis project, has provided valuable information about how young people want to be involved, and their key concerns
arising from their direct use of mental health services (Vasiliou-Theodore and
Penketh, 2008 and Garcia et al., 2007). By integrating young people's experience into service planning this affords an opportunity to move one step closer
to interdisciplinary working in children's and young people mental health.

Summary

Children and young people's mental health is everybody's business, primarily because healthy emotional development in childhood is a precursor for resilience and mental health in later years. Where children need help and support to deal with mental health problems this is most effective where it is well-coordinated by a range of agencies, is easily accessed and tailored to the level of the young person's needs.

Interdisciplinary working that listens to young people and includes their views alongside those of the professionals is particularly important across the interface of child and adult mental health. This can include when a young person reaches the age of 18 and moves into adult services or where young people come into contact with adult mental health services either because their parent has a mental health problem and/ or they may be involved as caregiver.

Effective integrated working is also important where a parent's mental health impacts significantly on their ability to care and protect their children. Policy guidance provides a framework for an interdisciplinary response drawing together National Service Frameworks together with child protection procedures and guidance. The overall emphasis is upon partnerships to create a whole system way of working across health, social services, education and agencies in the independent sector. Interdisciplinarity is therefore key to this very ethos.

9

Interdisciplinary Working with Older Adults with Mental Health Needs

---

Key Issues:

Integrated working in respect of older adults with mental health problems spans several domains of practice:

- Older adults with cognitive impairments, most commonly, dementias;
- Older adults who experience emotional distress and or mental illness as secondary to physical health issues;
- Diagnosed mental health problems that may have begun earlier in a person's life and are present in late adulthood, the most common of these being depression.

In respect of the above the literature reveals several interconnected themes that are important to state at the outset of this chapter.

- Firstly, the language used in the literature reflects a concern with integrated services primarily at an inter-agency level rather than interprofessional or interdisciplinary working between teams and professions. This is because for older people their physical and mental health needs are so often inextricably linked, thereby requiring a response from a number of agencies and care sectors.
- A second and related issue is the realization that the nature of older peoples' mental health needs are complex, reflecting the heterogeneity of the service user group that therefore requires a whole system response spanning mental health promotion through to acute care, crisis prevention and intervention.

Historical Developments in Integrated Working

According to the DH (2005), the achievement and maintenance of good mental health are prerequisites for a fulfilling later life. Everybody's Business, launched on 14th November 2005 clearly stated that older peoples' mental health spans a range of services from mainstream to specialist. Care includes that provided to meet health and social, physical and mental health needs. The Health Education Authority (1997) defines mental health as 'the emotional and spiritual resilience which enables us to enjoy life and to survive pain, disappointment and sadness. It is a positive sense of well being and an underlying belief in our own and others' dignity and worth'. The World Psychiatric Association and World Health Organization's consensus statement on the organization of care for older people states that this care should be based upon the delivery of comprehensive, multidisciplinary and integrated services (World Health Organization and World Psychiatric Organization, 1997).

Towards the end of the 1990s a proliferation of research into the needs of older adults with mental health problems highlighted their plight of being overlooked. Koffman et al. (1996) identified the scarcity of services for this client group in the UK compared with Norway, Holland and France resulting in people being trapped in hospital with no way out. Also in 1996, the Alzheimer's Disease Society (as it was then called) surveyed more than thirty draft continuing care policies to see how much consideration there had been of the needs of older people with dementia. It concluded that less than half of these policies mentioned dementia at all and only four defined the condition.

In 1997, the DH/Social Services Inspectorate (SSI) published the results of a survey into the inspection of services for older adults with dementia in the community spanning eight Local Authorities. At the individual level of practice, good working relations were revealed – typified by staff working flexibly; blurring the boundaries of their activities and taking a broader view of their role. Threats to more integrated care at team and organizational levels arose as a result of disagreements between health and social care about how costs should be apportioned and a need to define boundaries more clearly was highlighted. A second report by Barnes (1997, p. 9) attempted to provide a more detailed analysis of the current issues for service delivery for older adults with mental health problems and continued to highlight 'the need to cross organisational boundaries in health and social services'. Additional barriers to an integrated approach to care for this service user group emerged as follows:

- Management of services resting with different sectors;
- Fragmentation of provision due to budget constraints;
- Confusion arising from competing health Trusts;
- Difficulties shifting the hospital focus to community care;
- Lack of co-terminosity between health and Social Services Departments (SSDs);
- Time needed to develop joint strategies;
- Organizational turbulence experienced by health and SSDs.

These factors led Barnes to conclude that generally care for older people with mental health problems 'confronts different professional value systems as a balance is sought between protection and treatment, independence and risk. It requires typically a multi-agency and multiprofessional response. Even so older people with mental health problems are often nobody's priority' (p. 1) and 'Like books supported by bookends the care of an older mentally ill person alone can collapse if either side of the support is missing. To maintain this support a flexible response from both types of services was felt to be crucial' (p. 54).

In addition to these structural barriers, evidence suggested that integrated care delivery was being further compounded in relation to older adults with mental health problems because of attitudinal barriers. Hagebak and Hagebak (1980) identified these as stemming from the elderly themselves who were dissuaded from using mental health services and from engaging with workers who demonstrated a discriminatory response in their practice.

Key concept 9.1: Barriers to working with older adults with mental health problems

Adapted from Hagebak and Hagebak (1980)

Attitudinal barriers from workers	Attitudinal barriers from older people
1. An older person has a lifetime of learning behaviours which can only be overcome with great difficulty.	1. As in 6 below the older person accepts their declining memory which dissuades them from seeking help.
2. Coming face to face with the unpleasant realities of their own mortality and the effects of the ageing process results in fear or resentment of this forced personal awareness.	2. Because they have lost many of the most meaningful life roles such as work, parenthood, marital relationship the older person has no role except 'me'. This may lead to reduced feelings of self-worth and mirrors the "why bother" approach seen in the worker.
3. There is little point in working with people who have a short life expectancy and little potential to resume an active role in society.	3. Fierce independence and 'do it for yourself' attitudes leads to rejection of public services that are seen as equated with welfare.
4. There is a reversal of roles due to age differences and the worker responds to the older person as if to a parent.	4. Distrust and fear of mental health services and/or of being labelled mentally unwell.
5. Treating the older person as 'just like a child' failing to see that while dependency issues may be similar a lifetime of experience and accumulated knowledge makes the dynamic very different.	5. Behaving as expected in accordance with stereotypical views of the general public reinforcing the role of child or parent adopted by the worker. The older person behaves in a depressed way because they have been led to believe old age is depressing and a sense of 'hope' is lost.
6. A belief that all older people lose cognitive abilities as they grow older and forgetfulness becomes a natural part of ageing results in failure to treat organic problems.	

The situation by the end of the 1990s called for re-prioritizing the needs of this service user group. However, whilst the National Service Frameworks were intended to improve standards of care in the NHS; the delay between the publication of the NSF for Mental Health (DH, 1999a) and the NSF for Older People (NSF-OP) (DH, 2001a) encouraged a cessation of planning services for older people with mental health needs in comparison to those for working age adults that were pushed ahead and resourced (Royal College of Psychiatrists, 2006, p. 13).

The Audit Commission's Reports, Forget Me Not (2000) and Forget Me Not (2002) provided testimony that a number of areas still needed improvement. Similarly national inspection reports by the Social Services Inspectorate (2003) and the Commission for Health Improvement (2003) called for improvements in service commissioning, noted the continued lack of priority given to services for older people and the failure to meet the standard in the NSF-OP for access to integrated mental health services. This latter point was reiterated by Ian Philp in his introduction to Securing Better Mental Health for Older Adults in 2005 (DH, 2005b). Philp stated that; providing care to older people with mental health problems was still posing a challenge even though reviews of progress against the NSF standards had been undertaken in the previous year.

It is therefore only within the last five years that a flurry of policy documents and national initiatives have attempted to redress this imbalance, seeking at last to drive forward the agenda for improving mental health services for older people. Everybody's Business (DH, 2005a) set out four objectives which reflect the political agenda. These are to:

- Improve older people's quality of life;
- Meet complex needs in a coordinated way;
- Provide person-centred care;
- Promote age-equality.

As a result of these developments service models and components are being increasingly articulated alongside the need for a value base that recognizes the heterogeneity of the older adult population and seeks to be more inclusive. In this respect these developments reflect the key issues highlighted in other chapters of this book as being integral to a more interdisciplinary approach to mental health working. These will now be explored in more detail below.

Older Adults with Mental Health Problems

The number of older adults in global society is currently growing. According to Age Concern (Lee, 2007), the number of people over the age of 65 years in the United Kingdom is estimated to increase over the next 15 years by over one third from 9.6 million in 2006 to 12.7 million in 2021. There is widespread acceptance that depression and dementia are the most common mental health problems in later life (Lee, 2007; Royal College of Psychiatrists, 2006; DH, 2005a and 2005b) with the prevalence of the latter increasing exponentially with age. According to the Alzheimer's Society (2007) one person in 20 is affected over the age of 65 rising to one in five over the age of 80 years. Depression is even more common affecting around 15 per cent of older adults (Beekman et al., 1999). In order to highlight the ranging prevalence of mental health problems in later life the Royal College of Psychiatrists (2006) describes this in respect of a typical GP practice.

> A typical general practice with a list size of 10,000 will include approximately 1,500 people aged 65 and over. These are likely to include around 75 with dementia, 225 with depression (including 30 with severe depression), 30 with psychoses and 30 others with various less common though significant conditions. A service planning population of 250,000 will include 37,500 people aged 65 and over. Among these will be approximately 2,000 with dementia, 5,600 with depression (750 severe), 750 with psychoses and 750 with other conditions. These figures do not include groups such as younger people with dementia, older adults who have a learning disability in addition to mental distress and/or dementia and older adults within the prison system who have mental health problems (Royal College of Psychiatrists, 2006, p.10).

Within this diverse group of service users there are a range of ways in which individuals come into contact with mental health services (Tucker et al., 2007).

First, there are a significant proportion of older adults who have been living with long-term mental health conditions that have necessitated their involvement with adult mental health services up to the age of 65 and will need continuing care and support beyond this somewhat arbitrary divide. Whilst in the minority by comparison, there are adults aged 65 years and over who develop severe and enduring mental health problems for the first time and who may be better served by mental health services targeted at the 16–65 age group.

Second, there are people who may never have been in contact with mainstream adult mental health services but as a result of chronic or acute physical health care issues, bereavement and loss or the assumption of caring responsibilities in later life experience mental distress of a severity that requires specialist intervention, alongside physical care.

Third, there is the group of individuals who develop organic mental health problems such as dementia, some of whom may fall into a younger than 65 age group.

Finally, given that older people occupy two-thirds of NHS beds (Royal College of Psychiatrists, 2006; DH, 2001a) and a significant number will be care home residents (MacDonald et al., 2002; Margallo-Lana et al., 2001; Mann et al., 2000; Office for National Statistics, 1999), it is understandable that the need for older people to access mental health services from within these settings will be quite commonplace.

A Whole System Response to Older Adults with Mental Health Needs

Everybody's Business highlights that because of these different routes into services the task of providing care for this client group becomes increasingly a whole system issue. According to Jones and Bowles (2005, p. 642) a whole system can be defined as: 'the coordination of different, yet connected teams and services in order to provide high-quality flexible care and services in the most appropriate environment for the person'. Within a whole systems approach there appears to be consensus in the literature that this in turn includes: soft systems that relate to the collective activity of players in the system and are changeable, reflecting the unpredictable behaviour of human beings (Brenton, 2007; Checkland, 1972) and hard systems that are the distinct elements with their clearly defined purposes and outcomes. Standard 7 of the NSF-OP (DH, 2001a) sets out the overarching service model for older people with mental health problems, stating that this should include:

- Mental health promotion;
- Early detection and diagnosis;
- Assessment and treatment;
- Support for carers;
- Specialist old age psychiatry services.

This is reflected in the National Dementia Strategy (DH, 2009) which sets out the vision for transforming jointly commissioned services for people with dementia. The strategy hints at interdisciplinary working in respect of services working together to improve care, links between general hospital services and older peoples' mental health needs and visits to care homes by specialist mental health teams. In the compendium to the strategy (DH, 2011) examples of best practice are provided, several of which highlight the importance of interdisciplinary working in more detail. Taken together the National Dementia Strategy, Everybody's Business (DH, 2005a) and Raising the Standard (Royal College of Psychiatrists, 2006) have provided further detail on the components of care provision as shown in Figure 9.1. For each component models of service are further specified together with the key elements the service should be able to deliver. The Community Mental Health Teams for Older People (CMHT-OP) are one such component, recognized as the backbone to a modern specialist older person's service. Their remit is to provide services ranging from advice and support to other health and social care professionals, through to assessment (including a memory assessment

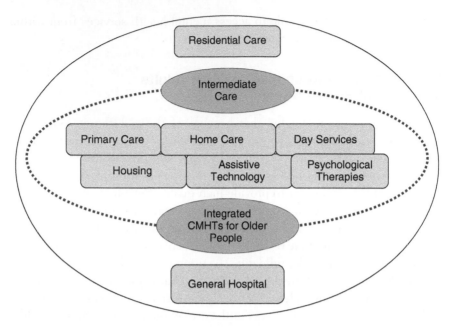

Figure 9.1 Hard elements of a whole system of care for older adults with mental health problems

service), care planning, in-reach support to general hospitals and psychological interventions. These in essence then feature as the 'hard' system elements of CMHT-OP.

In order that a CMHT-OP can function effectively there are several styles of teamworking proposed by the Royal College of Psychiatrists (2006) that are judged to be more or less effective according to the evidence base and reflect some of the differences previously identified in earlier chapters between uni/multiprofessional and multi/interdisciplinary working. In essence the team approach adopted reflects the soft system element.

Consultant Referral Teams operate according to a traditional uniprofessional model of care, only accepting referrals from a Consultant Psychiatrist who acts as the gatekeeper to limited and specialist resources. This model is based on the role of the Consultant being the professional responsible for larger numbers of service users and the director of other professionals, who thus have limited autonomy. This approach is likely to lead to continuing workload problems for the team and the Consultant Psychiatrist in particular.

GP Referral Teams will take referrals from any source with the agreement that this is appropriate from the service user's own GP who ultimately retains medical responsibility. Individuals may be allocated to different members of the CMHT-OP which in theory frees up the Consultant Psychiatrist in the team to concentrate on more complex cases. Team members have more autonomy which is more akin to a multiprofessional method of working.

Teams may be multidisciplinary, including a range of health and social care disciplines and may demonstrate as a result improved coordination, efficiency of assessments and less duplication of workload. Such teams may be combined with social care services with varying degrees of collaboration from very little through to joint management, a shared team base and ultimately full integration. Integrated care is defined by Kodner and Spreeuwenberg (2002, p. 3) as 'a discrete set of techniques and organisational models designed to create connectivity, alignment and collaboration within and between the cure and care sectors at the funding, administrative and/or provider levels'. According to Leutz (1999) there are three stages of integration that are outlined below. These would appear to reflect the stages of multidisciplinary working identified for adults of working age in Chapter 1.

Linkage enables individuals' mild or moderate care needs to be met by health and social care services that serve the whole population and don't have to rely on special relationships. Different professional groups establish links with others by noticing if, for example, an individual is not taking medication and contacting the appropriate medical personnel. Providers in different agencies know who is responsible for provision and follow the rule of eligibility and coverage rather than trying to renegotiate responsibility. The main task is provision of information and administrative connections. This reflects very much a multiprofessional or multi-agency response.

Coordination is where explicit structures are put into place to coordinate care across different systems and sectors. Although a more structured form of integration than linkage this still focuses on coordinating simultaneous or sequential care on a short or long-term basis. The main tasks are focused on coordinating service use, sharing information in a planned way, managing transitions for service users and assigning primary responsibility for care coordination. A critical difference between this and linkage is that when urgent or complex issues arise there are systems and personal relationships in place to identify changes and ensure coordination. This accords more closely with multi-agency and multidisciplinary working.

An example of this way of working was found by Tucker et al. (2009) in two-thirds of Consultant Old-Age Psychiatrists who identified formal protocols for the shared care of people being prescribed anti-dementia medication. However, fewer than four out of ten of these Psychiatrists reported similar arrangements with GPs for the care of older people with depression or moderate dementia and where protocols had been agreed these were rarely used.

Full integration is where resources from multiple systems are pooled to provide new programs of care and is likely to be most appropriate for a subset of the service user group who require specialist types of intervention and close collaboration between the professionals involved. This combines responsibilities as well as resources in an interactive way across care sectors and settings through joint commissioning and works from a shared record system. This reflects an increasingly inter-agency or interprofessional way of working.

Benefits of full integration of services for older adults are reported to include: faster and more appropriate responses to requests for care and reduced costs to care providers (Challis et al., 2004; Øvretveit, 1993). These in turn support a more flexible service response with access to a social worker specializing in this service user group. Depending upon how full integration is achieved drawbacks include different management styles and approaches between health and social services. Øvretveit highlighted that multidisciplinary comprehensive assessment can only be systematic if the integrated teams are led by a single team manager. Conflict over resources and multi-professional roles and responsibilities must be balanced with the knowledge that no single professional group has the skills or knowledge to offer comprehensive care or assessment (Webb and Hobdell, 1978).

Care Planning for Older Adults with Mental Health Needs

Within mainstream mental health services the CPA provides the glue which holds together specialist care from the respective teams and services (see Chapter 4). For older people the Single Assessment Process (SAP) was introduced by the NHS Plan in 2000 aiming to ensure a more person centred approach to assessing care needs and planning services across all sectors and agencies. The SAP identified four levels of assessment to match the complexity of service users' needs. These range from contact and overview for people with mild to moderate problems through to specialist and comprehensive care for individuals as their needs become increasingly complex. Towards this latter end of the spectrum it is expected that more than one professional will be involved and that relevant information across agencies and teams will be collected, stored and shared in summary form with the individual's consent. Where a service user has complex needs that are being met by a range of services the coordination of these inputs should by managed by one professional.

In essence the SAP and CPA therefore have certain features in common which are identified by Everybody's Business (DH, 2005a, p. 15). These include:

- Placing the service user and their families at the centre of the assessment process;
- Improving standards of assessment and care planning using a common approach across agencies and care settings;

- Providing a framework for multidisciplinary and multi-agency working;
- Providing assessments that are responsive to the level of need;
- Enabling carers to access an assessment in their own right.

The key issue for services working with older adults with mental health problems is how to dovetail the two approaches to care coordination as the CPA has only two levels of assessment (standard and enhanced) compared to the SAP's four. In some services the CPA is being maintained as a separate specialist assessment and care planning framework that is 'bolted on' when the older person has mental health needs in addition to other health and social care requirements. In other areas organizations are trying to incorporate key elements of the CPA into a specialist mental health focused assessment that is conducted as part of the SAP.

Challis et al. (2004) reported that where the SAP was working effectively a comprehensive assessment was targeted at highly vulnerable older people and undertaken jointly by specialist social workers and clinicians. In these circumstances the benefits of interdisciplinary working were reaped in respect of a reduction in functional decline, improvement in carer wellbeing and reductions in care home admissions and health care costs.

A key area where it is important for the two care planning frameworks to dovetail is in respect of risk assessment, planning and management. As identified in Chapters 4 and 5 the CPA provides the mechanism for coordinating an interdisciplinary approach to risk assessment, planning and management for working age adults with mental health needs. Older adults are a particularly vulnerable group and may pose a risk to themselves or be at risk of ill treatment or exploitation by others in their social networks or indeed professionals within the health and social care system. Irrespective then of how the two frameworks are brought together there needs to be a mechanism in place for collating and sharing information about risks and safety factors from the range of different disciplines involved including the service user and their caregivers. A resulting plan for managing the risk factors identified also needs to dovetail with any safeguarding measures, be shared with service providers and the individuals who are delivering care on a regular basis. One way to achieve this is that when an overview assessment is undertaken as part of the SAP that highlights mental health needs and concerns about risk this is passed to the specialist mental health services to which the service user is referred. The mental health team can then implement the CPA including the risk assessment, planning and management element and feed this information back via the Care Coordinator to the most relevant colleagues who are responsible to implementing the SAP.

The tensions between the two frameworks are likely to arise when the older person has complex needs requiring a response from a range of services and when it is unclear whether mental health or physical needs are the priority. According to Chevannes (2002) this can result in professionals being driven by their specific agency procedures and operating outside the integrated, multidisciplinary assessment process. This can cause tensions between care providers and lead to confusion about which framework should offer the route into a specialist assessment. Perhaps then it is not surprising that Challis et al. (2004) found that a systematic approach to comprehensive assessment for older people with complex needs was largely absent across the whole of the UK and multiprofessional teams operating in a truly integrated way was not the norm.

PRACTICE FOCUS 9.1

The Complexities of Interdisciplinary Working with Older People

Frank is a 69-year-old retired carpenter, living alone, who was referred by the local CMHT for specialist mental health assessment by the liaison psychiatry service following an attempt at suicide using a cut-throat razor. He was already known to social work services, aligned with, but not fully integrated with the CMHT. His GP had made the referral to gain help for Frank in securing re-housing and other practical and emotional support in view of his depressed mood and social isolation.

An assessment under the Care Programme Approach established that Frank had become increasingly depressed following the death of his wife five years ago. His depressed state of mind was associated with increasing social isolation, increasing use of alcohol, and chronic indigestion which he felt was the 'last straw' that triggered his suicide attempt resulting in an admission to a general hospital. Given his stated intention to 'finish things off' a mental health assessment was instigated and on discharge a joint application was made by the Approved Mental Health Professional (a social worker), and the admitting psychiatrist, for detention under Section 2 of the Mental Health Act (1983, as amended in 2007). During the subsequent two weeks in a psychiatric hospital Frank's mood improved – attributable to low-dose antidepressants, a better diet without alcohol, and antacid treatment for his stomach condition (diagnosed provisionally as oesophageal reflux).

A multidisciplinary discharge meeting, attended by the practice nurse on behalf of Frank's GP, established a care plan with Frank's input which included prompt discharge from the psychiatric hospital; continuation of antidepressant medication, with a view to withdrawal once his social circumstances had improved; attendance at the local (Age Concern) active pensioners' group, and rehousing in a more supported setting. This element of the care plan was to be coordinated by the social worker, who assumed responsibility for care coordination; and more active investigation and treatment of Frank's gastric symptoms.

This plan, though complex and involving sequential care initially, worked out well in most respects. Frank's GP's efforts to secure a reliable diagnosis of the cause of his stomach pains successfully identified a small gastric ulcer as the cause, which was effectively treated with diet and appropriate medication. Although rehousing proved problematic due to cost and eligibility issues, Frank's Care Coordinator made progress in monitoring his depression more closely, advised periodically by the Community Psychiatric Nurse (CPN). Together they observed an improvement in his mood,

Practice Focus 9.1 – *continued*

attributable to better physical health, and the social contact offered by the regular visits to the Pensioners Group. In the light of this Frank was discharged from specialist mental health services four months after his suicide attempt, with overall clinical responsibility reverting to his GP.

Where older people with complex mental health needs are considered to be at risk and living in care homes, The Guidance on Developing and Implementing Multi-agency Policy and Procedures to Protect Vulnerable Adults from Abuse (DH, 2000b) should be used as a tool for ensuring protection becomes an interdisciplinary issue. Barriers identified to not using the No Secrets Policy and Procedures, include a view that people with functional mental health problems such as schizophrenia and manic depression are not as vulnerable as the other groups such as older people with dementia that the policy was designed to cover. Also attitudes to people with severe and enduring mental health problems as dangerous and contaminated may be used to justify such discrimination in the way procedures may or may not be implemented (Ingram, 2004). Diagnoses such as schizophrenia can feed into a debate about the reliability of reporting that can also apply to older people experiencing cognitive impairment where there is an issue over mental capacity. In addition, practitioners may view adult protection procedures as over-bureaucratic and a lack of integration with existing practice such as the CPA renders their use even more cumbersome (Ingram, 2004). By denying older people with mental health needs access to these policies their isolation and vulnerability is perpetuated and the likelihood of an interdisciplinary approach more problematic.

According to Everybody's Business, to arrive at a truly person-centred approach to care coordination for older adults with mental health problems there are significant cultural, organizational and systemic barriers to be overcome. The way forward for achieving this is seen to rest with 'strong and sustained' leadership that promotes collaborative working with others to cross the organizational and professional boundaries in order to achieve a common goal. This approach is identified as important for interdisciplinary working generally in Chapter 12 but perhaps becomes especially important where leaders have to get to grips with integrated working at an inter-agency level and when the whole system of care provision is demonstrably complex. In such situations leaders and managers of services for older people with mental health problems need to become increasingly skilled at promoting a biopsychosocial approach, negotiating interface issues, developing joint strategies and pooled resources. They must also be able to champion the needs of older people with mental health problems as a service user group who have suffered from being nobody's priority for a significant period of the modernization agenda in mental health.

Involving Older Adults in Care Decisions

The involvement of service users and their carers in the decisions that affect care delivery is highlighted as a key theme for service development in the National Service Framework for Older People, Everybody's Business and the Dementia Strategy although there is scarce detail about how this might feature in the models of service advocated. For this reason it seems that progress towards a truly interdisciplinary approach in services for this group with mental health problems is at an earlier stage than in mainstream mental health services for working age adults. This is probably attributable in part to the increased complexity of care delivery across a number of different interfaces and the specific issues impacting upon service user and carer involvement that have been discussed so far.

In order to move towards more fully integrated services for older people with mental health problems that transcends agency and sector boundaries local partners are asked to prepare a joint strategy for the promotion of older people's mental health (DH, 2005a, p. 12). This should dovetail with the needs of carers with mental health problems and the local suicide prevention strategy and should cover: information provision, physical health needs, public attitudes, staying active, social networks and standards of living. This chimes with a biopsychosocial model for the delivery of integrated care to older adults which recognizes the importance of interventions in their widest sense providing simultaneously for medical, psychological and social needs (McWhinney, 1997).

The Importance of a Biopsychosocial Approach

Indeed the NICE/SCIE guidelines (2006) for improving care provision to people with dementia advocates a coordinated and integrated approach between health and social care that includes pharmacological treatments, cognitive stimulation and social interventions. The latter is deemed especially important by the Alzheimer's Society (2007) that recommends low-level support to enable people to remain in their own homes and retain their independence and dignity which consists of help with practical tasks such as cleaning, shopping, DIY and gardening.

Another reason why the biopsychosocial model may be helpful in understanding and responding to older adults' mental distress is because of the double discrimination they experience (Cabinet Office, 2006; DH, 2001a). According to Age Concern and the Mental Health foundation (Lee, 2006) age is the most common type of prejudice encountered by people who are aged 55 and over which has a negative effect on their mental health. If ageism is compounded by the stigma attached to having a diagnosable mental health problem this can multiply the difficulties for the service user and their families concerned.

For people with dementia this can mean an assumption that they are unable to give their views or contribute to the decision making process

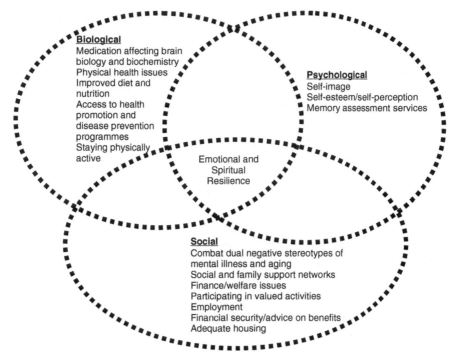

Biological
Medication affecting brain biology and biochemistry
Physical health issues
Improved diet and nutrition
Access to health promotion and disease prevention programmes
Staying physically active

Psychological
Self-image
Self-esteem/self-perception
Memory assessment services

Emotional and Spiritual Resilience

Social
Combat dual negative stereotypes of mental illness and aging
Social and family support networks
Finance/welfare issues
Participating in valued activities
Employment
Financial security/advice on benefits
Adequate housing

Figure 9.2 Biopsychosocial model of mental distress in older people

that affects their care. Adopting such a stance perpetuates disabling procedures which denies service users opportunities and also restricts their right to self-determination (CSIP, 2007). By including a social perspective in an interdisciplinary approach this enables the professional to see the person with dementia as not just someone who has an illness, but rather as an individual who is living with cognitive impairment together with a range of social restrictions that can encompass economic, cultural and environmental barriers to full participation as an active citizen in society. It is from this standpoint that services can then seek to involve service user and care groups in a more meaningful dialogue about how to tackle such barriers reflecting an interdisciplinary approach at a more strategic level.

The Mental Capacity Act and Interdisciplinarity

The Mental Capacity Act (MCA) (2005) supports such a participatory approach for people with organic mental health problems at a more individual level because it is predicated upon an assumption that a person has capacity and should not be treated as unable to make a decision unless all practicable steps to help them to do so have been taken without success.

Where it is agreed that the older person is unable to make a decision for themselves either because; they are unable to understand the information relevant to the decision, to retain that information, use it as part of the decision making process, or communicate their decision to others; anyone acting on their behalf must take certain steps in order to determine what is in their best interests. In accordance with the legislation this involves encouraging the person to participate as fully as possible in the decision making process and paying due consideration to their past and present wishes and feelings. In addition, it is a requirement of the MCA (2005) that the views of anyone named by the person as someone to be consulted should be taken on board together with the views of anyone engaged in caring for the person or interested in his welfare. The legislation thus provides support for an interdisciplinary approach to decision making for older adults with mental health problems who have particularly complex needs.

Where a change of residence or serious medical treatment is proposed for an older person who lacks capacity and where they have no family or friends with whom it is appropriate to consult, the legislation requires that an Independent Mental Capacity Advocate (IMCA) must be appointed. The IMCA should take the necessary steps to support the older person they have been instructed to represent so that they may participate as fully as possible in any relevant decision. The IMCA should also contribute to the interdisciplinary decision making process by:

- Obtaining and evaluating relevant information in relation to the older adult's care;
- Finding out what the person's wishes and feelings would be likely to be;
- Ascertaining the beliefs and values that would be likely to influence the person if they had capacity;
- Exploring what alternative courses of action are available;
- Obtaining a further medical opinion where treatment is proposed and the advocate thinks that one should be provided.

The importance of the ICMA is reflected by the training that has been available to individuals wishing to act in this role.

Summary

Care for older adults with mental health problems is complex, reflecting the need for inter-agency services that cross sector boundaries and settings and respond to the heterogeneity of the service user group. Integrated care that is founded on a biopsychosocial model and supported by a robust integrated care planning framework and interdisciplinary leadership offers the best chance of improving care in the future.

10

Interdisciplinary Working with Individuals with Complex Care Needs

> **Key Issues:**
> - People with complex needs include people with mental health and substance misuse issues and offenders with mental health problems in the criminal justice system.
> - Interdisciplinary working with these service user groups is supported but also undermined by government policy and legislation.
> - Initiatives to coordinate improved interdisciplinary and inter-agency working include 'mainstreaming' and the 'equivalence principle'.
> - The Care Programme Approach and the Offender Mental Health Care Pathway provide mechanisms for delivering more holistic, interdisciplinary care that addresses the interrelatedness of service users' difficulties.

Perhaps the greatest test of whether interdisciplinary working is being implemented effectively is how it is experienced by people who have complex care needs who often need access to more than one service at any one time. This chapter seeks to understand the experience of these individuals in more detail and explore the social policy context for interdisciplinary working in order to offer some models and suggestions for guiding good practice.

Understanding the Experience of People with Complex Care Needs?

Individuals who have complex care needs are likely to have vulnerabilities spanning the biopsychosocial domains of health and wellbeing. These in turn contribute to the onset of, or exacerbate, existing mental health problems. For example, individuals may have poor physical health which contributes to depression or experience physical symptoms from substance misuse. Psychologically they are more likely to have low self-esteem, developmental or learning disabilities and/or poor emotional literacy. Socio-economic factors too such as poverty, a lack of employment and isolation are likely to be more evident.

A combination of these factors can render service users at risk of further stigma and discrimination from wider groups in society that compounds their vulnerability. One way of understanding how these individuals come to the attention of mental health services is to understand how their experiences of stigma and discrimination can contribute to their presentations of mental distress.

Individuals may experience direct discrimination – for example, being made redundant for reasons relating to their age, gender or mental health diagnosis. Alternatively indirect discrimination is more subtle and operates through the application of rules or requirements that place particular groups at a disadvantage. An example of this would be the 'not in my back yard' syndrome whereby local community groups recognize the need for a new psychiatric hospital but covertly resist moves to build it near to where they live.

The media also contributes to the unequal treatment of certain groups in society through the process of stereotyping whereby misinformation is used to justify treating these groups differently. For example, the link between mental ill health, offending behaviour and substance misuse is a common connection that has been fuelled in the press by some particularly high profile cases such as the alleged attack by Richard Cazaly on Abigail Whitchalls in 2005.

When individuals internalize these experiences of differential treatment, stigma and stereotyping, their thoughts and beliefs can be acted out in rule breaking behaviour that seems out of control. This is when sanctions such as compulsory hospitalization and incarceration may be used as a means of containment. This is represented diagrammatically in Figure 10.1.

Understandably individuals struggle with the internal tensions and emotions that accompany the process of being stereotyped or labelled. This in turn is likely to place them in an invidious position of needing to make a choice, often subconsciously about whether or not to comply with the overriding messages from the dominant group and change their behaviour accordingly.

If individuals choose the 'conformist' option, compliance with negative images and labels such as 'psycho', 'pervert' and 'druggy' can create psychological dissonance and distress as the individual struggles with a course of action or lifestyle that does not fit with their 'internal' sense of self and which they are not wholly in agreement with. This can lead to further stress, lowered self-esteem and lifestyle choices that compound a sense of failure. Ultimately symptoms of this distress can be diagnosed as paranoia, depression and anxiety and lead to the individual being formally labelled as 'MAD'. If, on the other hand, individuals choose not to adhere to the stereotyped messages regarding their place in society and follow a more non-conformist path their behaviour will be seen as rebellious and rule breaking to the point

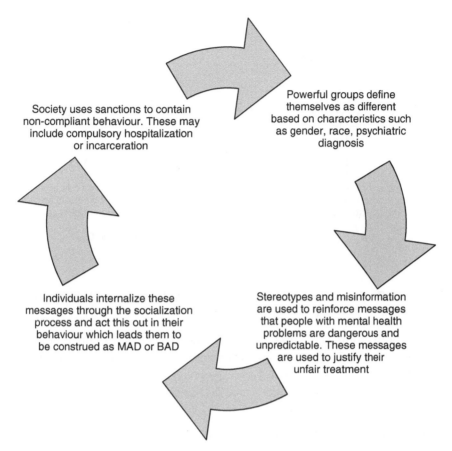

Figure 10.1   The cyclical process to explain the internalization of discrimination and its impact on behaviour

where legal and penal sanctions may have to be imposed and the individual is labelled as 'BAD'.

Glasby et al. (2003) identify this as the MAD versus BAD debate and point out that in practice, because of the complex needs of these individuals such distinctions are difficult to determine. Irrespective of the route into either the mental health or the criminal justice system there is a higher incidence of transitions for individuals between the two systems. This is one of the reasons why a more interdisciplinary response is required in order that their interrelated care needs can be dealt with more effectively (see Figure 10.2).

As the main groups associated with the MAD versus BAD debate are people with mental health and substance misuse needs or people with mental health problems in the criminal justice system this chapter will focus on interdisciplinary working in respect of these two groups. Over the past

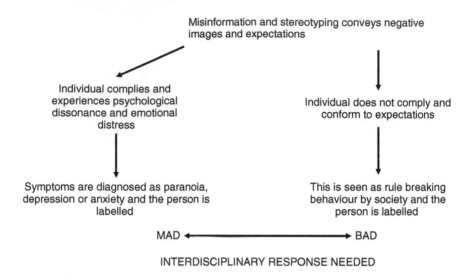

Figure 10.2 The pathways to the label of MAD or BAD for people with complex care needs

decade both groups have attracted increasing attention in Britain as organizations have attempted to rise to the challenge of modernizing care services to provide what is acknowledged within the policy framework as an interdisciplinary approach to contemporary care delivery.

The Prevalence of Complex Needs

One of the difficulties that arise when talking about prevalence rates for people with complex care needs is the variable language used in research studies and in practice. For example, in relation to people with mental health and substance misuse issues two terms are commonly used to refer to their presentation; co-morbidity or dual diagnosis. The latter is a vague term that according to Bean (2001) merely indicates the presence of two interdependent disorders at any one time. Another difficulty with the term 'dual diagnosis' is that it is also used to refer to people with mental health issues and learning disabilities.

Despite the lack of linguistic clarity, over a decade ago, Krausz (1996) articulated that the coincidence of severe mental illness and addiction was becoming a recurrent challenge for psychiatric services, highlighting the structural weaknesses in interdisciplinary interventions between mental health and addictions services.

As a reflection of this growing area of concern a systematic review of the relevant literature in the field of dual diagnosis was undertaken in Britain by the Royal College of Psychiatrists in 2001. The review provided in-depth

Table 10.1 Prevalence rates of dual diagnosis

Authors	Country	Population Investigated	Lifetime rate of substance use	Current rate of substance use
Drake and Wallach (1989)	USA (Community mental health)	Chronic mental illness		32%
Barbee (1989)	USA	Emergency mental health service all patients		47%
Regier et al. (1990)	USA	Households those diagnosed with schizophrenia		47%
Duke (1994)	UK	Schizophrenia and alcohol	22%	
Menezes (1996)	UK	Psychosis	32%	37%
Fowler (1998)	Australia	Schizophrenia	27%	60%
Cantwell (1999)	UK (Early Intervention)	Psychosis		37%
Wright (2000)	UK (Community mental health)	Psychosis	33%	13%

information on the prevalence rates of specific mental health conditions and their relationship with the substances used by individuals (Crawford, 2001).

Depending on the sample of the population studied and the research methodology employed, studies in both the United States and in Britain suggested that between 30 per cent and 50 per cent of people with mental health problems also had substance use issues (see Table 10.1). This range reflected the heterogeneous nature of the population identified by Watkins (1997, p. 313) who pointed out that 'both mental illness and substance use disorders will vary over a spectrum from mild to severe and will overlap with normal behaviour' over an individual's life course.

Generally speaking service users with mental health and substance misuse needs tend to do poorly on a number of outcomes. Thorley (1997) identifies co-morbidity as a constant predictor of poor prognosis often associated with poor compliance with medication, higher rates of violence, homelessness and suicidal behaviour. Additional multiple problems include criminal behaviour (Bean and Wilkinson, 1988; Keene, 1997; Hammersley et al., 1990; Swanson et al., 1990) and self-neglect relating to a deterioration in general physical health (Quinton et al., 1995). A number of mental health inquiry reports have also emphasized the increased risk posed to members of the public from people with dual diagnosis (Ward and Applin, 1998 and Reith, 1998, p. 122–125).

A similar picture of heterogeneity is seen for individuals who use forensic mental health services or those with mental health problems in the criminal justice system. Official figures identify that around 90 per cent of the 140,000 prison population have a diagnosable mental health issues or substance use problems or both. This proportion rises to 95 per cent for young people under the age of 21 (DH, 2001c).

In 1997, a survey conducted by the Office for National Statistics (reported in Lester and Glasby, 2005) suggested that nine out of every 10 prisoners had at least one of five types of mental disorder (neurosis, psychosis, personality disorder, drug dependency or alcohol abuse) and between 12–15 per cent of sentenced prisoners had four of the five.

In a study of 157 prison suicides between 1999 and 2000, 72 per cent were people with at least one psychiatric diagnosis, 62 per cent had a history of drug misuse and 32 per cent of alcohol misuse (Shaw et al., 2003). According to the authors at least 90 per cent of the sample could have been considered 'a risk' at reception to prison because of a history of previous mental health care, a lifetime of mental disorder, current symptoms or treatment or a history of drug misuse, alcohol misuse or self-harm. Such figures support McCann (1999) who explains that mentally disordered offenders exhibit a range of diagnoses and span the spectrum of criminal offences.

Within the forensic mental health, and prison population there is increasing acknowledgement that women with complex needs are a particularly vulnerable group. Women who use substances are more likely than men to be diagnosed with depression or a personality disorder (Grella, 1997). Other studies have highlighted the link between women's mental health issues and a past history of sexual or physical abuse (Fiorentine et al., 1999; Jarvis and Copeland, 1997).

Women with post-traumatic stress disorder who also use substances have been found to have a more severe clinical profile including more criminal behaviour and a higher number of suicide attempts than women who do not use substances (Najavits et al., 1999). The Corston Report (Corston, 2007) specifically focused on the needs of women in the criminal justice system highlighting that women had an increased incidence of suicide, and self-harming behaviours. In addition, their offending behaviour, mental ill health and drug misuse were more likely to be compounded by child care and relationship issues such as domestic violence.

All of the above research emphasizes that people with complex mental health needs are increasingly vulnerable in a society that perpetuates social inequalities resulting in a lack of opportunities for employment, decent housing and benefits. Where the social and professional response to such individuals is to deny these interrelated complexities when they present to services this has the potential to be more disabling to the individual than the impairments themselves (Williams and Keating, 2000).

If services are to be responsive to this diverse group of service users they will therefore need to be delivered with an increasingly interdisciplinary, and inter-agency focus. As a starting point, Keene (2001) has shown that service mapping can highlight service user groups that overlap between agencies; providing information that can be combined to produce an inter-agency needs assessment profile. This can be used to inform service planning, develop inter-agency assessment procedures and influence subsequent joint policies. Such an approach Keene argues is centred on multidisciplinary assessment and continuing care associated with a shift in emphasis from treatment to maintenance and rehabilitation. This allows for the combining of approaches such as assertive outreach for individuals who are likely to be difficult to engage, with assistance with social problems, drug/alcohol misuse and crime related behaviour. For those service users who need maintenance care this can be provided while psychosocial interventions such as cognitive behavioural therapy and motivational interviewing can be targeted at others who want to change their behaviour.

The Health and Social Care Policy Context for People with Complex Needs

Over ten years ago, Rorstad and Checinski (1996) viewed the introduction of the contract culture of the NHS and CCA (1990) as an opportunity to highlight the gap in services for individuals with complex needs for two reasons.

Firstly, the legislation meant that services would be more open to scrutiny and care managers would follow up, more proactively people being required to leave residential care because of substance misuse or offending issues. This, in turn, would highlight if service users had any related mental health needs that could then be considered by the health authority extra-contractual referral panel when considering future funding for a treatment package.

Secondly, the growing emphasis on the need to provide more adequate care for Mentally Disordered Offenders (MDOs) would indirectly raise the profile of people with mental health difficulties and substance misuse needs within the criminal justice system.

Since the introduction of the NHS and CCA the health and social care policy agenda in Britain has provided a supportive backdrop for interdisciplinary working for people with complex care needs but also accounts for why this has been difficult to achieve in practice.

Common themes that have emerged are:

- The increasing focus on community-based services (Richards and Horder, 1999; Groves and Farrell, 1996);

- The recognition that chemical dependency, mental disorders and offending are intertwined and can be understood from a biopsychosocial perspective;
- The high rates of relapse and recidivism within this service user group, together with the related issue of risk and finally;
- A notion that 'recovery' and rehabilitation for these groups should be increasingly defined in social rather then medical terms (Durcan, 2006; Carling, 1996; Polak, 1993; Harrison et al., 1985).

Over the last ten years mental health and substance use agencies have been encouraged by government policy to focus on community-based services, although these appeared a decade earlier in the drug and alcohol field and in forensic services than in mainstream mental health (DH, 1998d). The difference in timescales for service developments have contributed to a fragmented system which has made it difficult for subsequent joint working to take place. The modernization of mental health services has been governed by the National Service Framework and the NHS Plan whilst the National Treatment Agency for Substance Misuse has dealt with drug and alcohol services (National Treatment Agency, 2006).

Responsibilities for service implementation have thus been held by different bodies at different times. For example, in the early part of this decade the Drug Action Teams (DATs) were responsible for commissioning drug and alcohol services while the Local Implementation Teams (LITs) were responsible for commissioning in mental health. This division of responsibility at a strategic level hampered progress towards more integrated services. It is only during the last five years that the commissioning of all health care, including mental health and substance misuse services in prison settings, has been transferred to the Primary Care Trusts. This significant policy development should facilitate a more coordinated approach, particularly for those with the most complex care needs.

The main thrust of forensic services in the community has been to divert people with mental health problems away from the criminal justice system and this has required collaboration between the police, courts, prisons and mental health services. Initiatives have included the appointment of Arrest Referral Workers, a role that draws skills and approaches from drugs work and social work. This means that at the point of arrest individuals can receive an assessment of substance misuse, mental health and offending behaviour and be referred on to the most appropriate service to provide help with their priority needs. The Offender Mental Health Care Pathway (DH, 2005c) highlights the role for a Criminal Justice Liaison team made up of Approved Social Workers, psychiatric nurses, psychiatrists, psychologists and learning disability specialists to facilitate the early detection of offenders with mental health problems and divert them out of criminal justice and into the NHS system for care and treatment.

In tandem with these diversion schemes Judge et al. (2004) and Mohan et al. (2004) identify new mental health services being developed in the community which differ in the extent to which they demonstrate interdisciplinary working. Services range from parallel models of care with forensic specialists responding to referrals from the CMHT while at the other end of the spectrum forensic specialists have been integrated into the teams. Similar practices have developed in relation to community-based services for people with dual diagnosis within the last five years.

However, in terms of legislation the Mental Health Act (2007) continues to reflect the historic separation of services. In section 1(3) the Act makes it explicitly clear that dependence on alcohol or drugs is not considered to be a disorder or disability of mind. This clause continues to perpetuate the division of services between statutory mental health care and drugs work and continues to dissuade agencies from collaborative working with particularly high risk groups of people who have combined needs in relation to their mental health and substance misuse problems.

In the light of the policy thrust towards improving interdisciplinary working the legislation seems rather out of step particularly with the key approaches being advocated. These are 'mainstreaming' for people with coexisting problems of mental health and substance misuse and 'equivalence' of service for those with mental health needs in the criminal justice system. These policy developments advocate interdisciplinary working in respect of organizational collaboration, teamworking and relationships and individual practice.

The Mainstreaming Approach

According to government guidance, mainstreaming hinges upon a number of systems and structures being in place as shown in Figure 10.3.

Whilst mainstreaming may seem to policy makers as a positive way forward, placing the responsibility clearly with one agency risks denying the contribution from non-statutory drug and alcohol services, based largely in the independent sector. This is evidenced by a number of research projects conducted over a six-year period by Keene (2001). During this time a range of 168 service users and 72 different professionals were interviewed and revealed significantly different perspectives between the two groups regarding the contribution of services.

Keene found that service users with mental health and substance use needs had developed their own lifestyles, routines, structures and communities to cope with their complex problems and difficult circumstances. In these communities they were accepted for who and what they were. Many reported that the therapeutic programmes offered by the professionals were likely to 'soften

Mainstreaming Hinges On	
Local services developing definitions of dual diagnosis to reflect local needs and targets groups	Staff in Crisis Resolution, Early Intervention, CMHTs and inpatient services must be suitably trained
Definitions agreed between agencies	Services and need for client group should be mapped
Specialist teams of dual diagnosis workers should provide support to mainstream mental health teams	Local project teams working to the LITs should prepare a focused definition together with care pathways and clinical governance guidelines
All staff in Assertive Community Treatment services must be trained to work with dual diagnosis	All people with dual diagnosis should be subject to CPA and risk assessment

Figure 10.3 Requirements for effective mainstreaming as set out in the Department of Health: Dual Diagnosis Good Practice Guide (DH, 2002). Reproduced under the Open Government license (v.1.0)

them up' to a point where they lost their survival strategies and became less connected to their social networks. Service users wanted the ongoing maintenance, support and friendship they valued from the non-statutory workers but the expertise, contacts and resources of the statutory services when necessary.

The 'Equivalence' Principle

As evidenced by the shift in commissioning of health care services in prisons to the PCTs the principle of 'equivalence' has been underpinning prison reform over the past decade (NHS Executive and HM Prison Service, 1999). It simply seeks to ensure that the health care services available to offenders are equivalent to those provided to the general population. Consequently it is acknowledged that in respect of meeting mental health needs many of the interventions required will be at the primary care level with the support of more specialized mental health provision for individuals whose presentations are more complex. As a result of the equivalence movement virtually every prison in Britain now has access to a prison in-reach team providing specialist prison focused mental health care (Durcan, 2006).

In recognition that prison mental health reform also hinges upon social care interventions, Changing the Outlook (DH and HM Prison Service, 2001) sought to emphasize the social work contribution to these in-reach teams. However, the success of health and social care integration at the team level has been patchy. In some prisons, teams are modelled along the lines of CMHTs and are multiprofessional in composition while in others they consist predominantly of mental health nurses. The degree of integration of the team within the prison also varies from teams that are dedicated to one establishment and based within it to others that have an external base and provide sessional input to a number of prisons.

Suicide prevention in prisons is encouraged through the Assessment, Care and Custody in Teamwork (ACCT) Approach which is a multiprofessional case management system that aims to identify individuals who are at risk of suicide and self-harm and offer individualized care and support in advance, during and after a mental health crisis. The approach hinges upon effective communication and referral between operational and health care staff in prisons and identifying and training a multiprofessional team who will respond quickly to prisoners when they are judged to be at risk.

Unfortunately there is little evidence available on the impact of these new ways of working including whether the nature of team composition and multiprofessional working makes a difference. For these reasons it is questionable whether these teams can be considered to be offering an equivalent service to that provided by specialist mental health teams who are adopting an increasingly interdisciplinary approach in the community.

Both the guidance on mainstreaming and Changing the Outlook highlight the Care Programme Approach as the mechanism for coordinating care for people with complex needs across services and agencies. In relation to people with dual diagnosis it is expected that care coordination will be led by staff in mental health services. In relation to prisoners with mental health problems Care Coordinators in community mental health services should be in contact with the in-reach service as part of the prison's reception process to ensure transfer of relevant information into the prison health care system. The in-reach service should then take responsibility for contacting the Care Coordinator prior to an individual's release in order to ensure a multidisciplinary pre-discharge team meeting is arranged to agree transfer of care responsibilities. This way of working is set out clearly in the Offender Mental Health Care Pathway.

While care coordination for people with dual diagnosis is likely to remain local and ongoing, the biggest hurdle to care continuity for those in the criminal justice system is the geographical distance between the prison and the community mental health services that are often in different regions. This can lead to problems with engagement and poor information exchange at key points of transition between agencies. A common problem is the engagement and commitment to CPA by staff that aren't trained as mental health professionals. Workers in substance misuse and alcohol agencies and front line prison officers and health care staff understandably have different priorities and don't necessarily see the CPA as part of their core business. A recent example of this is the introduction of the Offender Management System that is geared at reducing offending and is more coercive in its application than the CPA. This has the potential to undermine care planning and the involvement of service users in the process thereby diluting further opportunities for improved interdisciplinary working.

Inter-agency working therefore emerges as a prerequisite if mainstreaming and equivalence approaches are to be successfully implemented. Such an approach will need to be able to combine the expertise of working with people with complex care needs from both the statutory and independent sectors in order to create a more integrated service system. In addition, there will be a need for improved collaboration between those with responsibility for commissioning services such as the Primary Care Trusts and the service providers, such as Her Majesty's Prisons as custodians.

Developing Interdisciplinary Working

One of the challenges of moving towards an increasingly interdisciplinary way of working is that of involving service users who by the very nature of their complex needs and experiences of using services have encountered practice that has sought to exclude their involvement rather than encourage it. Invariably service users receive one service for one problem and for some problems no service at all. Illustrated from a service user perspective this approach is experienced as particularly unhelpful as shown in Key concept 10.1 below.

Key concept 10.1: Service users' experiences of services for people with complex needs

'I was pushed around like a tennis ball. The alcohol people said I had a mental illness and the mental illness group said I had a drink problem. Neither of them did very much for me' (Rorstad and Checinski, 1996, p. 9);

'All these different departments, all these different agencies, are all separate, they don't seem to act as one although they communicate with each other, they only communicate on a part time basis' (Keene, 2001, p. 75);

'There didn't seem to be anybody available then who was interested enough to help or perhaps it's too difficult a story' (Keene, 2001).

The starting point for interdisciplinary working from a service user's perspective therefore is the process of assessment and identification of the interrelatedness of their needs highlighted by the service users in Keene's research above. Service users need professionals to understand that they have a range of complicated problems that often seem unresolvable.

Moreover their ability to cope with these problems and make changes to their lifestyles varies and at times cannot be tackled.

Interdisciplinary working with these individuals needs to draw upon the biopsychosocial model outlined in Chapter 3 as a way of including service users' perspectives about the interrelatedness of factors contributing to their presentation.

Firstly then it is important to ensure these factors are included and documented as part of an ongoing assessment. This is difficult if assessment documentation is reductionist and of a tick box format.

Research has shown that for some individuals with mental health problems their physiological vulnerability is such that using even small amounts of drugs and alcohol can precipitate a psychotic crisis. These individuals will need a different response to those who have developed long-term mental health needs as a result of prolonged substance or alcohol misuse.

There is also evidence reviewed previously in this chapter that how service users think, feel and perceive their situation and their ability to do something about it may be affected by their previous life experience together with cognitive capacities such as memory and self-efficacy. This may require a response based on motivational interviewing techniques (Miller and Rollnick ,1991) and/ or the transtheoretical model of change (Prochaska and DiClemente, 1992) to assist service users to focus on aspects of their behaviour and lifestyles that they want to change.

In addition, it is highly likely that social factors will need to be addressed by virtue of their presentation as service users in the criminal justice system and those with dual diagnosis will be socially excluded and have experience of, or risk unemployment, homelessness, limited numeracy and literacy skills and debt problems. A significant number of the prison population are also likely to have been in Local Authority care as children (Social Exclusion Unit, 2002).

One example of an assessment tool that attempts to reflect the complexity of service users' needs is the Forensic Assessment Format (Carey, 2006) that is adapted from the Material-Discursive-Intrapsychic model, (Ussher, 2000). The framework aims to provide a more collaborative focus to the content and process of assessment where the professionals work with the service user to discover the level of needs, and how best to meet them. This allows the assessment process to be experienced as a more collaborative encounter. The tool is currently being validated in a study in the North East of England.

Two different professionals from the Forensic Community Mental Health Team undertake complimentary assessments using the FAF. They may be from a medical, nursing, psychology or social work background depending on the disciplinary perspectives that are considered by the team to be the most relevant to the service user's situation. The assessment will cover what has happened in service users' lives, how they fit into and communicate with the world around them and how this impacts upon their coping strategies and self-esteem. The assessment provides information about needs, risk and safety factors and is described in more detail in Key concept 10.2 below.

Key concept 10.2: The material intrapsychic discursive model applied to people with complex forensic mental health needs (Carey, 2006)

Material aspects are subdivided into three sections, health, social and institutional factors. Questions guide a discussion about medical history; body image, including appetite, weight and eating disorders; sleep pattern; and any use of illicit substances or alcohol. Social factors considered include gender and relationships, economic factors, environment, abuse, bereavement; and employment. Institutional factors cover the impact of prison, psychiatric hospital and care homes/social services on the service user and how they believe this has influenced their life course.

Questions relating to **discursive aspects** assess communication skills; stigma; role conflicts, including expectations and aspirations; developmental problems, taking account of life stories and the quest for, or lack of, autonomy.

Intrapsychic factors will include the impact of stressors, such as neglect, guilt and separation, and the defence mechanisms used to cope with them. The internalized expectations of the service user, such as gender role and idealized fantasy will be explored, as well as self-esteem/self-worth. Current roles and relationships will be discussed such as whether a service user is a parent, sibling, son or daughter and how this sits with their role as a prisoner or service user. The intrapsychic elements also include psychological defence mechanisms, and coping strategies, to understand in more detail how the service user perceives themselves and their internalized self-concept.

In future, it is expected that holistic assessments such as the Forensic Assessment Format will strengthen the evidence base for a combination of simultaneous interventions that span counselling, drug/alcohol misuse, and physical health promotion.

In respect of the latter, Paterson et al. (2007) report that simple interventions to increase the levels of physical activity can improve offender's mental health and their abilities to cope with the emotional and psychological issues they experience in the criminal justice system. In Britain currently there are a growing number of projects to increase offenders' access to healthy lifestyle advice and physical exercise promoted through government initiatives such as Walking the Way to Prison Health and (DH, 2002) and Choosing Health (DH, 2004).

One example of a programme aimed at bringing together physical exercise and offender management is an Exercise on Referral Programme at Her

Majesty's Prison Everthorpe. This is presented as a practice focus example below to illustrate how an interdisciplinary way of working can be used to promote mental health.

PRACTICE FOCUS 10.1

Her Majesty's Prison Everthorpe Exercise on Referral Programme (Paterson et al., 2007)

The Exercise Referral Programme at HMP Everthorpe links physical exercise with offender management and has required a restructuring of the social environment in the gaol that has included a complete re-education of all staff around the importance of physical activity and its contribution towards improving mental health. The aim of the project is to support offenders trying to change their health and activity habits.

With the offenders' consent, the gym staff, the Health Care department and mental health teams contribute to the Exercise Referral programme by sharing information in a much more joined-up and holistic way. All parties work together in an interdisciplinary approach to discuss issues, risks and possible interventions for individual service users. Physical education staff have undertaken mental and public health awareness training in order to inform the work they do with individuals.

The gym team and Offender Management Unit at HMP Everthorpe take the view that referral for physical activity is not just about fitness but also about developing confidence, social skills and gaining social capital. More importantly, it can prepare and equip individuals for the more intense psychological interventions that are offered where attitude and commitment play such a large part in determining success or failure.

Any offenders can be referred into the scheme. Through being encouraged and working together with staff, the door can be opened to helping individuals to address their mental health and offending behaviour. Responses from individuals also suggests that such interdisciplinarity is beginning to break down preconceived ideas about the Prison environment and its staff. By taking part in the programme the offender often feels, possibly for the first in their life, they have achieved something positive.

The staff at HMP Everthorpe work hard to ensure all departments communicate progress whilst involving the offender as much as possible. The exercise referral system is only in its infancy but the benefits are potentially huge. Prisons run on relationships and the key to success is developing these not just on a one-to-one level between a staff member and the offender but also at a team level with departments which did not traditionally communicate.

The main ingredient that the Forensic Assessment Format and the Exercise on Referral Programme have in common is the ability to provide some hope for individuals with complex needs that they can improve their situation. By working collaboratively as a team and involving the service users in the approach this starts to offer an alternative way of working to what has happened in the past when individuals may have felt abandoned and isolated by the mental health and social care system.

The importance of hope as integral to the process of recovery and rehabilitation is well-documented and needs to be linked with a range of outcomes spanning reductions in substance misuse and offending through to improved mood and self-esteem to enable individuals acquire more effective coping strategies and improved social and interpersonal skills.

Summary

People with substance misuse issues, offending and mental health problems are by definition individuals with complex care needs who require an increasingly interdisciplinary and inter-agency response. This needs to enable to them tackle their difficulties often simultaneously, supported by interdisciplinary assessments and interventions that promote a sense of hope for improvement. The policy agenda has made some provision for the greater integration of services to people who present with complex needs but may continue to be hindered by factors such as structural oppression, institutional discrimination and media stereotyping. Wherever possible gaps in services need to be identified and addressed strategically. Teamworking can be encouraged by improved communication and information sharing in a way that sees the individual's needs as complex and interrelated rather than as separate and in competition.

11

Interdisciplinary Education and Training

Key Issues:

- Interdisciplinary learning and education is about the interactiveness of the learning encounter between professionals and non-professionally affiliated staff, service users and carers. It involves learning with, from and about each other with the explicit aim to improve collaboration and the quality of care.
- The need for interprofessional education has been supported by a raft of policy developments since the mid 1990s.
- Interprofessional education becomes interdisciplinary when service users, carers and non-professionally affiliated groups in the workforce interact with professionals to learn with, from and about each other to improve collaboration and the quality of care delivered.
- Interdisciplinary learning needs to be planned, designed and delivered with the explicit aim of enhancing collaborative practice.

No book on interdisciplinary working would be complete without a chapter dedicated to interprofessional learning and education. This is because training mental health practitioners to learn to work more effectively together is often identified as the panacea for solving many of the problems associated with poor practice in mental health. High profile inquiries outlined in Chapter 5 have consistently identified that interdisciplinary or inter-agency communication is a systematic failing alongside risk assessments that aren't shared (Reith, 1998, pp. 85, 100, 112, 118). By providing more opportunities to learn to work collaboratively it is postulated that some of these shortfalls in practice can be overcome.

This message is clearly articulated in government policy since 1997 and is synonymous with the modernization of the health and social care workforce agenda. Interprofessional education (IPE) as it has become commonly referred to in the academic and professional literature, has increasingly developed in mental health through a number of related initiatives. The National Service Framework (DH, 1999a) and the NHS Plan (DH, 2000) set out the need for a skilled workforce, able to work collaboratively, in order to ensure the delivery of effective mental health services.

Seven years later in 2007 the Creating an Interprofessional Workforce (CIPW) programme was launched relating to the health and social care workforce generally. This followed on from a number of Common Learning Pilot Site Projects that reached their completion in 2004 (Coster et al., 2007). The programme originated within the Department of Health and aimed to 'mainstream' the development of IPE across the Strategic Health Authorities in England. 'Mainstreaming' refers to the steps being taken, promoted by government, to integrate IPE 'in organisational, financial, regulatory and theoretical terms – into professional education with which its relationship had previously become tenuous and marginal' (Barr and Ross, 2006, p. 97).

This chapter will begin by outlining how some of the policy initiatives that have deliberately set out to foster IPE generally have been implemented in mental health. It will then consider what is meant by IPE, and its importance in mental health training. Finally the chapter will consider how IPE can be applied as part of a workforce development strategy to promote increased interdisciplinary working in contemporary mental health services.

Background to the Development of IPE

According to Barr (2002, p. 8) the IPE movement in the UK began as far back as the 1960s, occurring as a set of discrete initiatives to 'improve working relations between health, social care and sometimes other professions'. Taken together these developments aimed to: improve practice and the delivery of care whilst enhancing the status of the professions, allowing them to gain collective strength and secure a place in higher education provision.

With the change of government in 1997 the policy agenda was set to embrace these rather ad hoc developments within a more coherent approach. The NHS Plan called for a new core curriculum, supported by joint training that would equip the NHS workforce with the knowledge and skills needed to meet the increasingly diverse needs of service users. In addition, a common Foundation Programme was earmarked as a mechanism to allow students and staff to switch careers in health and social care more easily.

These ideas were further supported by the NHS Workforce Strategy (DH, 2000c) that called for genuinely multiprofessional training to promote:

- Teamwork;
- Partnership and collaboration between professions, agencies and with service users;
- Skill mix and flexible working;

- Opportunities to switch training pathways to expedite career progression;
- The introduction of new types of workers into the health service workforce.

Since the strategy was first launched these priorities have been realized in different ways in mental health with contributions coming from a number of directions.

Firstly, in the late 1990s a number of shared or joint learning programmes began to develop with a focus on psychosocial interventions for people with severe and enduring mental health problems (Brooker et al., 2003; Milne et al., 2000; Carpenter et al., 1999; 2000). One of these was a three-year Masters Programme in Community Mental Health at Birmingham University (known as the RECOVER Programme). This was funded by what was then the West Midlands NHS Executive. This programme will be used as a good example of IPE throughout this chapter as it was systematically evaluated over a five-year period and was explicitly interdisciplinary in its design, delivery and evaluation.

Such programmes were usually required to be delivered in partnership between the funders, representatives from the different professions, agencies and service user organizations in order to support the interprofessional learning model. This approach has continued with the commissioning and delivery of subsequent mental health training programmes for other groups of workers that have been introduced into the mental health workforce (Bailey, 2007).

One way that interdisciplinary education has been supported nationally between the providers of mental health training in the higher education sector in England together with the professional bodies and employers is through the Mental Health in Higher Education Project. Interdisciplinary education has also been supported through joint events between the Higher Education Academy subject centres. The funding of two interdisciplinary Centres for Excellence and Teaching in Mental Health in 2005, (one at Birmingham and one at Middlesex University) was a deliberate attempt by the Higher Education Academy to support national learning developments that fostered IPE in mental health learning, teaching and practice.

Attempts to develop an increasingly shared skill mix among mental health professionals was supported initially through The Capable Practitioner framework of 2001 (Sainsbury Centre for Mental Health, 2001). This set out a list of capabilities that were linked to the NSF standards and covered the knowledge, skills and values deemed necessary for contemporary mental health practice across all professions. This framework evolved into the more succinct Ten Essential Shared Capabilities (DH, 2004) that is now recognized as the blueprint for the underpinning curriculum of all mental health training initiatives. A series of learning materials to support the implementation of these capabilities has also been designed and made available through the Centre for Academic Workforce Innovation at the University of Lincoln.

Teamwork has been explicitly fostered since 2004 through the New Ways of Working initiative, with the Creating Capable Teams Approach being launched at the NWW Conference in April 2007. Packs to support the development programme are available through the National Mental Health Development Unit's internet site (www.nmhdu.org.uk). There is an associated programme of training and development for workshop facilitators in order that they can enable the implementation of the approach locally. In addition, many mental health training programmes delivered in the higher education sector, such as the one for Graduate Primary Care Workers at the University of Birmingham have a module or parts of their curriculum dedicated to teamworking.

In general, higher education institutions have differed in the extent to which they offer interprofessional training at the qualifying level for health and social care workers. This reflects a debate about whether IPE should be reserved until after initial qualification when workers are actually engaged in collaborative mental health practice that affords a direct opportunity to transfer their learning. Post qualification IPE in mental health may also overcome some of the logistical issues of bringing professions together when they are at different stages of their basic training. Professionally accredited degree programmes tend to have very specific systems and structures geared to the requirements of the particular professional body responsible, which often militates against joint accreditation and delivery. Despite these issues, in some places, such as Teesside University, students wishing to pursue a career in mental health nursing or social work do have the option of a common foundation curriculum during their degree which then leads into specialist pathways later on in their training.

The new types of worker roles in mental health services have gathered momentum over the last five years with a significant increase in the numbers of non-professionally affiliated staff such as Support Time and Recovery Workers and Gateway Workers in Primary Care Mental Health. An overview of the development of these roles is provided by Dickinson et al. (2008). An evaluation (jointly undertaken by Newcastle and Durham Universities) has sought to establish how these, together with the new ways of working for other professionals, are being implemented nationally and the implications for the education and training of the workforce.

All of the above developments serve to reinforce the fact that in the field of mental health working and learning IPE is set to hold centre stage for the foreseeable future.

What is IPE?

Chapter 2 of this book suggests that interdisciplinary working in mental health is not about everyone being able to do the same job but about a collaborative, inclusive approach that hinges on both distinct and shared contributions from the respective disciplinary groups. McGrath (1991) encapsulates the essence of what we are trying to achieve as follows:

> Interprofessional working is not about fudging the boundaries between the professions and trying to create a generic care worker. It is instead about developing professionals who are confident in their own core skills and expertise, who are fully aware and confident in the skills and expertise of fellow health and care professionals, and who conduct their own practice in a non-hierarchical and collegiate way with other members of the working team, so as to continuously improve the health of their communities and to meet the real care needs of individual patients and clients. (McGrath, 1991 quoted in CAIPE, 2007)

Similarly, Finch (2000, p. 1138) identifies the purposes of interprofessional working as:

- To 'know about' the roles of other professional groups;
- To be able to 'work with' the roles of other professionals, in the context of a team where each member has a clearly defined role;
- To be able to 'substitute for' roles traditionally played by other professionals, when circumstances suggest that this would be more effective;
- To provide flexibility in career routes (moving across).

If we accept that this is what we are seeking to achieve, then it is only right that interprofessional education should be part of an overall workforce development strategy to equip mental health workers with the skills, knowledge and attitudes so that they are confident in their own contribution and can collaborate for the benefit of service users and services with others.

Carpenter and Dickinson (2008, p. 9) suggest that: 'Despite – or perhaps because of – the current interest in IPE, there are a number of prefixes (multi/inter/uni/trans), adjectives (professional/disciplinary) and nouns (education/training/learning/studies) which are married together in any number of ways to refer to a range of phenomenon which fit broadly within this area'. They go on to provide the following helpful definitions in an attempt to clarify the concept:

Key concept 11.1:   Helpful definitions of IPE as summarized by Carpenter and Dickinson (2008, p. 10)

- *Uniprofessional education* – Occasions when professionals or students from one profession learn together.
- *Multiprofessional education* – Occasions when two or more professions learn side by side in parallel.
- *Interprofessional education* – Occasions when two or more professions learn with, from and about each other to improve collaboration and the quality of care (Centre for Advancement of Interprofessional Education (CAIPE) 1997).
- *Transprofessional education* – Occasions in real practice where professional boundaries have been crossed or merged.
- *Shared learning* – Similar to multiprofessional learning, where students or professionals learn alongside each other, but they do not necessarily interact.
- *Common learning* – A term preferred by the Department of Health (DH) which suggests that health and social care students should, in part, follow a common curriculum.

Apart from the latter two of these terms (that relate more to how IPE is delivered) there is an explicit focus on the term 'professional'. As suggested in Chapter 2 this detracts from the involvement of the growing numbers of non-professionally affiliated staff within the mental health workforce and implies the exclusion of service user and carers.

CAIPE (2007) refers to this issue on page 8 and goes on to emphasize that in terms of the Creating an Interprofessional Workforce (CIPW) programme participants recognized that IPE embraced the wider workforce including administrators, care assistants, patients, service users and carers. They suggest that the term professionalism is 'used to describe the principles and values held and demonstrated by an individual, regardless of whether they are a member of a registered profession'. Both Tew et al. (2004) and Carpenter and Dickinson (2008) state the importance of involving service users in mental health training. This stems from the valuable knowledge and expertise they bring to the learning encounter as a result of their direct experience of mental distress and the responses they have received from professionals as a result.

The crux of the issue here is the *interactiveness* of the learning encounter; the learning with, from and about each other to improve collaboration and the quality of care. Where service users collectively and individually are able to contribute their distinct disciplinary expertise alongside that of trained mental health workers, from a position of equal status and importance this is where interdisciplinary learning and working occurs. It is this shift in the power dynamic that demarks interdisciplinary education from that which is referred to as interprofessional.

From the typology provided by Carpenter and Dickinson there are parallels between the range of terms defined here and those that are discussed in Chapter 1 to refer to mental health professionals working together. Interprofessional differs from multiprofessional education by virtue of the level of interactedness of the approach. Multiprofessional programmes do not usually involve service users as participants, often adopting a shared learning methodology so that different professionals can learn the same knowledge and skills. These programmes usually fail to consider how such knowledge and skills are shaped by each other's different professional backgrounds, and the ways different practitioners implement them in their job role. In the absence of these considerations it becomes difficult to see how such learning opportunities can impact upon collaborative practice at the individual, interpersonal and organizational dimensions in mental health as outlined in Chapter 2.

CAIPE (1996) suggests that IPE is a subset of multiprofessional education typified by its purpose to enhance collaboration and the joint training methods that it uses to do so. It is thus the *process* of learning collaboratively that is of equal importance to, and changes the essence of, the content of what is learned. Where service users are involved as active participants in this process, either as educators and/or participants, interdisciplinary education is fostered.

This was particularly the approach on the interdisciplinary Programme in Community Mental Health at Birmingham University which is presented below as a practice example.

PRACTICE FOCUS 11.1

Birmingham University's RECOVER Programme: An Example of Interdisciplinary Education

The RECOVER programme at Birmingham University set out explicitly to increase the skill mix amongst mental health practitioners and allow more flexible ways of working in new mental health services as they emerged in line with the National Service Framework requirements. The programme's aims were to promote interprofessional working and service user involvement in care planning and delivery in addition to giving practitioners the skills and knowledge to use evidence-based psychosocial interventions with individuals and families (Carpenter et al., 2003). The course was designed collaboratively by professionals and service users. Modules were included on teamworking, and working in partnership with service users alongside more 'skills-based' modules on medication management and cognitive therapy for psychosis.

In year 1 a Foundation Module was provided. One of the key topics covered on this module was working in accordance with the Care Programme Approach. All the participants (professionals and service users) who joined the course had learned about the Care Programme Approach (CPA) either as a case worker responsible for its

Practice Focus 11.1 – *continued*

implementation or as a recipient. What they had not experienced was an opportunity to consider how the team as a whole was working with the CPA and whether this was similar to or different from the way other teams worked. Also, they had not considered how service users were being more directly involved in the CPA in different part of the West Midlands region and how they experienced the care planning process overall.

In the advent of the increasing functionalization of Community Mental Health Teams (CMHTs) it was particularly important for staff and service users to learn together about the challenges and opportunities for implementing CPA more effectively.

CPA input on the Foundation Module was therefore taught in such a way as to focus on these key issues with a view to increasing service users' involvement in their care plans and promote shared risk taking with their Care Coordinators. Service users provided taught inputs alongside professionals and training exercises required collaborative discussion and formulation of care plans. The principles of interdisciplinary education on this occasion, thus accorded with those identified for IPE proposed by Barr in 2002 and included:

- Putting service users at the centre of the care planning process and exploring a shared risk taking approach;
- Promoting collaboration between practitioners and service users and between different professions;
- Reconciling competing objectives for care plan implementation between service users and professionals; and,
- Complementing common learning that all had experienced about CPA with comparative learning about each other's approach to implementation and respective roles and responsibilities.

In addition to the principles that need to underpin interdisciplinary learning Barr (1996) identifies eleven dimensions of IPE that can be used to understand how the educational experience is being provided. These are reproduced by Carpenter and Dickinson (2008, pp. 15–16) as follows:

Key concept 11.2: Barr's 1996 dimensions of IPE as cited in Carpenter and Dickinson (2008)

- *Implicit or explicit* – IPE might go unrecognized in everyday work or may occur through serendipitous multiprofessional learning. This learning is implicit and may be consolidated and verified when it is made explicit. Explicit IPE is often through courses, workshops, and conferences.
- *Discrete or integrated* – IPE might consist of freestanding modules designed to improve quality of care through better collaboration or could be integrated into other MPE or uniprofessional education as an specific area of learning.
- *All or part of a programme* – IPE might be the entirety of a programme or just an aspect of it. It is unlikely to ever be the whole of a pre-qualification course, although it could be all of a post-qualification programme.

Key concept 11.2 – *continued*

- *General or particular* – The IPE may concentrate on a particular user group, method or setting, or be more broadly based.
- *Positive or negative* – IPE might have a positive impact on relationships and collaborative work, but there is the potential for a negative impact to be produced also and educators should be wary of this.
- *Individual or collective* – IPE might focus on individual learning and assessment or collective learning through small groups of students collaborating.
- *Work/employment-based or college-based* – IPE can occur in the workplace informally or formally (or the two combined). College-based IPE does usually tend to include practice or work-based placements.
- *Shorter or longer* – IPE can be brief (in a meeting or over a lunch break), or could be extended (and last anything from weeks to years).
- *Sooner or later* – IPE can be introduced at many different stages in qualifying/post-qualifying learning and subsequently at any stage throughout lifelong learning.
- *Common or comparative* – IPE can be concerned with learning needs across all the professions included or about respective roles, responsibilities, powers, duties, and perspectives to inform collaboration in practice.
- *Interactive or didactic* – IPE tends to usually use small groups and interactive methods where different professionals can interact whereas didactic lecturing approaches tend to be used much less.

This time Carpenter (2006, p. 147) illustrates these dimensions in practice with reference to the Interdisciplinary Programme in Community Mental Health at Birmingham University.

PRACTICE FOCUS 11.2

Dimensions of IPE as Illustrated by the RECOVER Programme in Community Mental Health at Birmingham University

The Birmingham programme 'was *explicit* in its focus on learning to promote collaboration. It was *integrated* in that interprofessional education was a distinct emphasis reflected in the design, content and learning methods. Explicit teaching about interprofessional collaboration however comprised only *part* of the programme which also emphasized learning about psychosocial interventions and service user participation. It was of course *particular* in its concern for people with severe mental health problems. The learning methods and assessments were generally *individual* rather than collective. Although all students were working in mental health services, the teaching programme was *college-based*, but with work-based assignments. It was a *long* course, lasting one day a week for two academic years and at a *later* stage of education; students had been qualified practitioners for at least two years. The curriculum contained both *common* elements, such as learning about psychosocial interventions and *comparative* study of respective roles and responsibilities and perspectives to inform interprofessional practice, especially in the modules on teamworking, inter-agency collaboration and assessment. These modules, especially, used *interactive* learning methods extensively, but others, for example a module on psychiatric symptoms and pharmacology, were essentially *didactic*'.

From the above discussion it is evident that IPE in mental health can be considered in relation to a number of different parameters, including purpose, principles, content and structure. Where service user involvement is integrated from the outset so that it becomes fundamental to the overall learning and development experience, this sees a shift towards interdisciplinary education (IDE).

Theoretical Underpinnings of IPE

Support for the integral part that service users must play in interdisciplinary education in mental health comes from Clark's (2006) analysis of the theoretical underpinnings of IPE.

Firstly, he considers that the social aspects of learning follow the real world context in which knowledge is acquired, that is created in the social exchange among team members. Where team members are interacting on a daily basis with service users it follows that in order to develop a knowledge base about how to manage mental distress collaboratively the service user's perspective is equally as important as that of other team members.

Clark goes on to assert that 'clinical judgement is based more on the relationships between people than between "people and things"'. In mental heath clinical judgement is based on the relationship service users form with professionals and can explain why a service user who is deemed to engage and possess 'insight' into their condition receives Assertive Community Treatment while another who does not is admitted to hospital under the Mental Health Act. Clarke argues that this process of 'clinical learning' is facilitated by IPE experiences.

Thirdly, Clarke draws attention to the social construction of knowledge that he refers to as 'the basic cognitive structures of a discipline'. Where disciplines can work and learn together a shared sense of the reality of mental distress is co-constructed between workers and service users. This means that not only will interdisciplinary learning potentially impact on how professionals work with individuals who have mental health problems it will also enable service users to develop a revised social construct of their experiences of professionals and using services. Through an iterative learning process service users and workers from other disciplines can co-create a revised social construct of their experiences of collaboration.

Finally, as stated in Chapter 1, a level of conflict and resistance comes with the territory of progressing to a more interdisciplinary way of working in mental health. Clarke acknowledges this and draws from the work of the learning theorist Kolb (1984) to suggest that 'out of the conflict comes the development of insight, understanding and skill'. Different disciplines in mental health will also bring to the interdisciplinary learning encounter different learning styles and ways of interacting with others. Some of these will relate to their professional training experience, others to personal factors.

All learners need the range of experiences Kolb described as concrete experience, abstract conceptualization, active experimentation and reflective observation in order to learn successfully, make decisions and solve problems. Thus Clarke concludes IPE is a continuous process grounded in experience not in outcomes. It is therefore important for successful interdisciplinary education to include the experiences of all those involved in the mental health care process.

Planning, Delivering and Evaluating IDE

In order to develop interdisciplinary education it is important to consider a number of issues such as:

- The shared learning needs of the participants and how these are influenced by their different backgrounds and experiences;
- Whether the learning methods themselves foster increased collaboration;
- How the training is delivered and whether this models or undermines interdisciplinarity;
- Whether interdisciplinary learning brings about actual changes in practice.

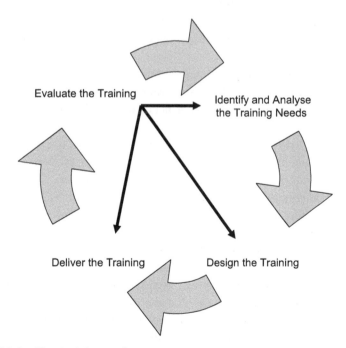

Figure 11.1 The training cycle

One way of approaching the planning, delivery and evaluation of interdisciplinary learning opportunities is to apply what is commonly recognized in the training and education literature as the training cycle. This focuses on each of the stages in turn in order to develop training and development solutions. Using this model it becomes possible to consider systematically what is known from the growing evidence base for interprofessional education at each stage.

Identify and Analyse the Training Needs

Whilst having a recognized framework of knowledge, skills and attitudes for all mental health workers such as the Ten Essential Shared Capabilities this cannot be relied upon as the only source of information on the shared training needs of the mental health workforce.

As Carpenter and Hewstone (1996) point out merely bringing groups of workers together will not necessarily effect a change in practice, rather, workers need to be brought together for a common purpose with equal status, backed by institutional support (Hewstone and Brown, 1986).

The purpose of identifying and analysing interdisciplinary training needs is therefore to establish what the common learning agenda is, both in terms of content (for example: changes to the mental health legislation) and process (how to communicate together more effectively when conducting Mental Health Act assessments). Information is also needed about the training backgrounds and the experience that different groups bring to the learning encounter so that these can be drawn upon in a positive way rather than act as a potential source of conflict.

For these reasons it important to undertake some sort of information gathering exercise prior to the start of designing an IDE programme to identify in more detail the training needs that need to be addressed by the learning encounter.

Bailey (2002) provides an example of this in relation to training on dual diagnosis for specialist drugs workers and Approved Social Workers (ASWs). Information about the training needs for the drugs workers was drawn from a systematic survey that asked individuals to rate their confidence and competence in dealing with specific areas of practice, including working with individuals with co-morbid problems. In relation to the ASWs, information was collected more anecdotally from Mental Health Act assessments and feedback from Community Mental Health Teams. This suggested that a vast proportion of time and resources was being increasingly consumed by service users with both substance use and mental health problems, with little effective interaction to address their needs occurring between mental health teams and the specialist drugs teams locally.

The training needs of the two groups, whilst therefore similar in some respects, were also different. Both groups needed to know how to work together to provide a better response to these individuals with complex needs; in particular, how to manage risk and tailor interventions to address both mental health and substance misuse issues. In order to collaborate more effectively ASWs needed to know how to access drugs services and what effect illicit substances could have on a person's mental health. Drugs workers needed to know more about the signs and symptoms of mental distress, the CPA and the mental health legislation together with how mental health services were organized. Once these similarities and differences were identified it became possible to design a training programme that would respond to both sets of needs effectively.

Designing Interdisciplinary Training

As part of the design phase questions need to be asked about whether all the participants need to receive the same content or whether, as in the case described above, some separate and some shared learning sessions are required. Thus staying with the dual diagnosis training programme as an illustration of interdisciplinary learning, once the training needs of the ASWs and drugs workers were established they were used to inform the design of the training programme. In respect of the five day programme that was commissioned shared learning sessions were included on risk assessment and the interaction of mental health medication and illicit substances and alcohol. There were also shared learning sessions with case related exercises on joint approaches to assessment and intervention. During the first two days of the training course ASWs received input as a separate group, which included topics such as drug policies and the types of inventions used by the drugs teams. At the same time parallel sessions were provided to the drugs workers covering the CPA and mental health legislation.

Table 11.1 Relationship between the types of learning necessary for interprofessional education and corresponding examples of training methodologies (Barr et al., 1999)

Type of learning	Examples of methods of delivery
Received Learning (RL)	Lectures and other didactic teaching
Exchange-based Learning (EBL)	Case discussion
Observation-based Learning (OBL)	Joint home visits
Action-based Learning (ABL)	Problem-based learning
Simulation-based Learning (SBL)	Games, exercises, role plays and experiential groups
Practice-based Learning (PBL)	Placements and work-based assignments

The design of the inputs across the whole five day programme was directly informed by strategies that Barr et al. (1999) have demonstrated as effective for promoting IPE within an overall adult learning approach. These are shown in Table 11.1.

At the beginning of the course all participants took part in a general introductory session that involved some action-based learning to agree the common learning agenda. After the parallel sessions the two groups came back together again in an exchange-based learning session to share information about their respective agencies and how to access services. Case studies, role plays and group exercises were included in the shared learning sessions alongside didactic inputs to maximize the opportunities for interprofessional learning to take place.

Delivering the Training

Rather than simply lecturing in the didactic sense, interprofessional educators need to adopt a flexible approach that also includes elements of facilitation. According to Barr (1996, p. 244) the role of the facilitator is essential in IPE as they need to be 'attuned to the dynamics of interprofessional learning, skilled in optimising learning opportunities, valuing the distinct experience and expertise which each of the participating profession brings'.

It is also important for those leading the IPE sessions to model effective interdisciplinary working and learning together. This was achieved on the Interdisciplinary Programme in Community Mental Health at Birmingham University by sessions being led jointly between professionals from different disciplinary backgrounds where the duality of perspectives was used as a strength in the way that information was presented and critically reflected upon.

Some sessions were jointly delivered by a professional and one or more service users. This was particularly important for communicating a message that service users have an important role to play in interdisciplinary learning and that this can reinforce collaboration in a positive way. However Tew and colleagues (2004) point out that the direct delivery of training can be a daunting prospect for service users and carers and it is unlikely that effective learning will take place if they are left to deal with critical messages and feedback from professional participants on their own. For this reason, serious thought must be given about how best to support service users before, during and after the training session. When training collaboratively it is helpful to establish a set of ground rules beforehand about how it is intended to deliver the session jointly including who takes responsibility for leading specific exercises and eliciting learner feedback. It is also helpful to agree in advance how a professional might step in part way through without undermining the service user or carer's contribution if they find the experience too stressful or anxiety provoking.

Table 11.2 Kirkpatrick-Barr evaluation framework of outcomes

Level of evaluation	outcomes
1. Reaction	Learners' views on the learning experience and its interprofessional nature
2a. Modification of attitude/ perceptions	Changes in reciprocal attitudes or perceptions between participant groups. Changes in perception or attitude towards the value and/or use of team approaches to caring for a specific client group
2b. Acquisition of knowledge/ skills	Including knowledge and skills linked to interprofessional collaboration
3. Behavioural change	Identifies individuals' transfer of interprofessional learning to their practice setting and changed professional practice
4a. Change in organizational practice	Wider changes in the organization and delivery of care
4b. Benefits to patients/clients	Improvements in health or wellbeing of patients/clients

Source: Barr (2000).

Evaluating the Training

Evaluating the interdisciplinary learning experience becomes increasingly important in order to demonstrate its effectiveness. One of the frameworks that has been widely used in the IPE literature is the Kirkpatrick-Barr framework of outcomes which seeks to establish the impact of IPE across a number of levels as shown in Table 11.2.

However, a systematic review of mental health training (Bailey et al., 2003) reveals that very few evaluations go beyond the collection of data at level 3 and where information is gathered about the acquisition of knowledge and skills this tends to be very subjective from self reports of the participants. Evaluators therefore need to ensure that opportunities to test knowledge and skills such as before and after case vignettes or objective knowledge-based questionnaires are included as tools alongside more qualitative data collection.

The crux of whether interdisciplinary learning and working is effective is the impact it has on service users and their families. This was documented in relation to the Interdisciplinary Programme in Community Mental Health by Barnes et al. (2000) and showed that the programme, that was by design focused on service user involvement, resulted in improved care outcomes for those who were using services.

Tew et al. (2004) highlight the need for service users and carers to work alongside the commissioners and providers of mental health education to establish from the outset the criteria that will be used to evaluate programme outcomes as these maybe quite different to the criteria that professional participants would use to judge their experience.

One of the limitations of the Kirkpatrick-Barr framework is the lack of consideration given to the context in which the interdisciplinary learning encounter takes places. Bailey (2007) has highlighted the importance of this in relation to shared learning for graduate primary care workers. Where interdisciplinary learning is thwarted from the outset by the competing agendas of commissioners, managers and supervisors this will, in turn, influence the training experience and the transfer of interdisciplinary learning back into practice. It is therefore important to include as part of the evaluation process an examination of the context in which the learning programme is delivered as this may help to explain the success or limitations of subsequent interdisciplinary practice.

Summary

This chapter has set out to explore how IPE has developed in line with contemporary mental health care and what is recognized as IPE in mental health education today. It is suggested that interdisciplinary education or IDE is a more inclusive approach, aiming explicitly to promote more interactive ways of working between professionals and service users. In training and education this involves service users alongside professionals in setting the training agenda, designing and delivering the training programme and evaluating its impact. The training cycle can be used as a simple framework for considering relevant issues that need to be tackled systematically in respect of promoting more effective interdisciplinary learning and education.

12

Managing Interdisciplinary Working and Practice in Mental Health

---

Key Issues:

In order to manage interdisciplinary working and practice, managers of mental health services need to be able to:

- Manage themselves, manage and lead others and the service.
- Achieve a balance between leading and developing people and ensuring that the tasks of the team are completed.
- Interface effectively between their team, the organization to which they belong and other teams/networks that interlink to provide a service including collaboration with service users.
- Ensuring processes are in place for professional development and supervision that takes account of individual disciplinary contributions and collective roles and responsibilities.

It is undisputable that the world of mental health and social care is changing. Over the past 20 years this change has been continuous, resulting in an increasingly complex landscape of reconfigured services, new ways of working and a more diverse mental health workforce. As a result, mental health staff are likely to be working as members of a team as well as forming part of a wider network. Managers of teams and services are therefore facing a challenge which involves two sets of complementary activities; managing complexity of service delivery on the one hand and managing people from different disciplines and backgrounds on the other.

The ultimate aim of change in mental health services has been to re-orientate the culture of care delivery; moving further away from the traditional model of medical treatment of diagnosable disease towards mental health promotion and prevention of ill health. Responsibility for mental wellbeing is seen as being shared between mental health professionals, carers and service users, supported through a collaborative care planning process that promotes and sustains involvement and inclusion.

Whilst on the one hand such significant change can present a welcome challenge with energizing opportunities, if not managed and led effectively it can also result in stress, conflict, sickness absence, staff burn out and demoralization. According to Borrill et al. (1996) and (2000) poor health in the workplace means that both the quality and quantity of care for those who use services can be reduced.

It is also often the case that mental health workers, who find themselves in positions with leadership and management responsibilities, do so more by default than design. Promotion within the professional hierarchy is likely to reflect effective clinical practice with service users rather than managerial and leadership training and expertise. Whilst skills learned in one-to-one practice are often transferable to management and leadership roles, workers also need new skills and knowledge to develop their confidence and competence in changing themselves and others in response to the organizational development agenda.

This chapter seeks to provide some models and frameworks to assist individuals understand the tensions of interdisciplinary leadership and management in more detail. It will also present qualitative data gained from a study involving managers of mental health services and service users that set out to identify what were the areas of greatest training need and how these might be overcome.

The Context of Interdisciplinary Leadership and Management

The White Paper Working for Patients (DH, 1989), alongside the development of Primary Care Groups and Trusts signalled the move to a primary care led NHS and a 'reframing of the relationship between the NHS and the public in terms of competition, choice and consumerism' (Rowe and Shepherd, 2002, p. 276). This change was reinforced by the National Service Framework (DH, 1999a) and the NHS Plan (DH, 2000) that set out the agenda for the overall redesign of the mental health service including how it would be more responsive to the needs of those who use it. The New NHS: Modern Dependable (DH, 1997) placed a formal duty on NHS, Local Authorities and not-for-profit organizations to work in partnership. This, in turn, was supported by the 1999 Health Act that allowed the NHS and Local Authorities to pool budgets, delegate commissioning of services to one agency on behalf of partner organizations and integrate health and social care staff. As a consequence of these changes leaders and managers find themselves in charge of services that increasingly reflect a mixed economy of care spanning the statutory, private and independent or voluntary sectors; with an increasing contribution from service users and their families through informal support networks.

Subsequently Commissioning a Patient Led NHS (DH, 2005d) and the White Paper Our Health Our Care Our Say (DH, 2006) reinforce further change in the types of environments where health care is delivered. According to McNichol (2007) over the next ten years the provision of health care by social enterprisers is set to increase significantly. Such flexibility is a deliberate intention of government policy to promote improved health care outcomes for individuals and communities. Leaders and managers of mental health services must therefore be prepared to work in partnership with agencies and individuals to deliver a whole system of integrated care provision. This in itself is a complex task for a number of reasons.

First, according to Wildridge et al. (2004) there is confusion about the definition and terminology of partnership working with many other labels such as collaboration, coordination, cooperation, joint working, inter-agency working and networking being used interchangeably (p. 4). Second, to be effective partnership or collaborative working needs to occur at different levels spanning strategic decision making through to direct work with service users (DH, 1998e; Glendinning, 2003). Finally a number of barriers to partnership working have been identified. These include work overload and increased bureaucracy (Peck et al., 2002), a perceived imbalance of power between partners that destabilizes collaboration (Balloch and Taylor, 2001) and culture clashes based on stereotypical views of collaborators and their contributions (Wilson and Charlton, 1997). For all of these reasons the process of managing change in interdisciplinary working must be done well; hinging increasingly upon effective human interaction alongside the successful management of resources and service redesign.

Managing and Leading Interdisciplinary Change

In order to assist mental health managers in rising to these challenges successfully it was decided to introduce a pathway of leadership and management training and development for them as part of the interdisciplinary RECOVER Programme at the University of Birmingham. When the programme had been originally introduced in 1997 it was in direct response to the National Service Framework in mental health and set out to equip practitioners with knowledge and skills in psychosocial interventions, interdisciplinary teamworking and strategies for involving service users as more integral partners in care planning and delivery. From the outset a number of practitioners who embarked on the programme were quickly promoted into managerial positions with responsibility for reconfiguring hospital and community services in line with the new functional mental health teams proposed by the Policy Implementation Guide (DH, 2001). As a result of these developments it became apparent to the University as an education provider that managers needed a complementary but different focus to their training. Whilst practitioners needed to be able to deliver psychosocial interventions to service users and their families, managers needed the skills and strategies to support the delivery of these evidence-based interventions at an organizational level.

As a starting point it was decided to conduct a series of focus groups with managers to explore from their perspective what they identified as their key training and development needs. In order to ensure that these complemented the aspects of managerial competence judged to be important by service users it was decided to include people who were using services in the groups alongside the managers. Invitations to participate were sent to managers and service users via members of the programme's Management Board, thus ensuring the involvement of all professions, (nursing, social work, occupation therapy (OT), psychology and psychiatry) and a range of mental health Trusts across the West Midlands region. Service user groups who contributed to the programme in a number of ways were also approached and asked to nominate participants. As a result six managers and four service users volunteered to take part in the focus groups, the first of which followed a predominantly unstructured format in order to give managers and service users an opportunity to discuss the issues before identifying specific training solutions. The second focus group was structured around the issues that emerged from the initial discussion and asked participants to consider how best to design and deliver the training and development inputs.

The focus group discussions were tape recorded by agreement with all participants and the recordings were transcribed into a typed record for content analysis. Detailed notes were taken during the group discussions so that the meaning attached to pertinent issues raised could be recorded in context. Responses quoted from the group discussions are coded below as responses from managers (FGM) and those from service users (FGSU).

The responses were then thematically analysed using an interpretive phenomenological approach (Smith and Osborn, 2003) to identify the common and different issues identified (D'Cruz and Jones, 2004). Main categories emerged from direct quotes which were then coded, and grouped according to a number of sub themes (Patton, 1990) as shown in Figure 12.1.

In the first focus group (FG) a number of topic areas were highlighted as important including change management, leadership, financial and project management, performance management and managing multidisciplinary teams. With more discussion in the second workshop it was possible to reach broad agreement that training needs fell into two main categories; effective managers needed to be able to manage people and manage the service. This fits with the general literature on leadership styles that advocates a balance between task centred and person centred methods of leading that focus

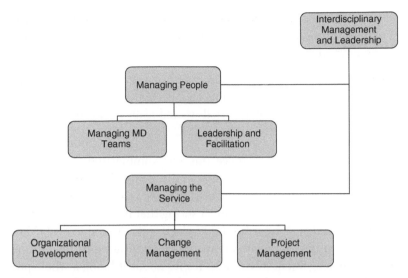

Figure 12.1 Categories and themes emerging from the focus group discussions with managers and service users

simultaneously on meeting targets and managing performance whilst valuing individuals and team's contributions. The leader's ability to foster a sense of trust between colleagues that supports a collaborative approach to getting the job done is important for person centred leadership (Hamer and McNichol, 2006; Boak and Jones, 2002).

In respect of managing people the key concern was how to manage staff from a range of backgrounds to work collaboratively with service users.

> 'Well it's multi disciplinary teams isn't it? You've got managers of different disciplines and backgrounds managing others of different disciplines and backgrounds'. (FGM1)
>
> This latter issue was of particular concern: 'Looking at management of other disciplines I think it is really important to somehow to be clear about management and their professional management and how that might differ'. (FGSU1)
>
> 'It's really trying to define, which is really difficult, what is a management role and what is a professional role within that'. (FGM3)

Supervision of staff was seen as key to the above and a discussion ensued about supervision of staff in their day to day working practice and work-load management as compared with professional supervision. Participants debated whether these should be separate functions or in some instances whether staff should have two supervisors and be managed by a three way meeting. This emerged as a complex issue with no readily identifiable solution.

However, the consensus in both groups was that leadership and facilitation skills were interlinked and were important in order for managers to encourage collaboration.

'I think leadership skills are very important because I think those form the basis of everything else you can build on'. (FGM3)
'Leadership skills and facilitation skills should really go together because on their own they don't stand do they?' (FGSU2).

In relation to managing the service this was summarized by one manager with agreement from other participants in the group: 'Well on the whole it's performance management isn't it? About your service it's also managing the performance of individuals within in, ensuring that its targets are met, objectives are done, quality standards [are] in place and adhered to'. (FGM4)

Organizational development was seen as a starting point for putting the performance management in context: 'Yes it's about it being a whole process isn't it and not just that particular individual and their team. That must be the bigger picture really' (FGM6).

Change management was identified as important by all six of the managers in the groups and was supported by the service users as an area that needed to be addressed. It was agreed that this should include: implementing and evaluating change, knowing when you've achieved it and how to take people with you on the change journey including service users and their carers.

Within a context of continual change in mental health services managers reported they were frequently being asked to do things with very little notice: 'It's the thing about being able to write up a project or a report, because you are suddenly asked to do something like that and it's quite difficult trying to find out actually how to lay it all out and nobody seems to tell you'. (FGM3)

This developed into an in-depth discussion of project management that needed to cover budgetary resources, financial management and funding streams, business planning, action planning, clinical governance issues and reaching targets. This was seen to be connected more with the hard aspects of management although depended upon the soft skills of managing people.

In the light of the above, the remainder of this chapter is devoted to exploring some of the strategies and theories that can inform leading and managing interdisciplinary change in mental health.

Given the extensive nature of the issues raised it will not be possible to go into all aspects in detail, rather some further reading material will be identified at the end of the chapter focusing on particular aspects.

Management and Leadership as Interrelated Activities

The first point to make is that the themes identified above in Figure 12.1 are all interrelated and this was clearly apparent in mental health services from the discussions in the two focus groups. This reflects Onyett's (2003) analysis of the management of mental health teams in which he distinguishes between the need for a combination of transactional leadership or management and transformational leadership. The former is concerned with the organization and planning of the use of resources, dealing with problems as they arise and monitoring activities aimed at meeting targets. The latter involves 'challenging the status quo and is about creating new visions and scenarios to stimulate the creative and emotional drive in individuals to innovate and deliver excellence' (Onyett, 2003, p. 162). Maintaining the relationship between the overall vision for the service and the means by which this can be achieved thus becomes a fundamental issue for managers and leaders in interdisciplinary mental health settings.

One way to conceptualize this relationship is to use the framework outlined in Figure 12.2. This illustrates the links between management and leadership.

One of the first steps in a successful strategy for leading and managing change is the need for a shared vision so that staff can understand the overall goal that may relate to new options for services. In interdisciplinary working this needs to be agreed across services and should involve all stakeholder groups including those who use services and their families. This is important because, as Onyett (2003, p. 168) points out, 'leadership may reside with more than one person and vary with the domain of activity that is being led'. A related mission statement articulates how the vision will be delivered and often relates to standards of care. It is important in interdisciplinary working that the mission reflects the collective achievements of the different disciplines.

As outlined previously a number of tensions are likely to beset interdisciplinary working in mental health including power relations between the different professions and role conflict. In order to counterbalance these, the process of arriving at a shared vision and mission are important as a starting point for building mutual trust between collaborators. In addition, once these

Figure 12.2 Managing and leading interdisciplinary mental health services

are signed up to it is likely to be easier to reach agreement about the different ways in which collaborators can pursue their individual ways of achieving set objectives whilst collectively the service is moving in one direction. According to Onyett (2003, p. 168) 'the aims of the service should be broken down into a statement of the overarching purpose of the service, and the more specific objectives which the service intends to meet'. In the diagram above these are referred to as goals.

Underpinning the framework is the need for a value base that respects and recognizes the contributions of the different collaborators and considers these to be equally valid even though some partners or their contributions will be smaller than others. It's about the resources and knowledge partners bring to the collaborative exchange thus value statements need to be developed through a process that promotes ownership by all stakeholders. According to Hosking and Morley (1991) the extent to which shared values can be achieved will depend on the level of group cohesion within teams and services. Onyett (2003) asserts that the team provides a vehicle for an ideology or value base to be translated into practice. If the values do not translate into achievable outcomes then the team risks disillusionment or loss of faith.

The translation of a vision and mission into a service strategy needs to reflect joint ownership of decision making, collective accountability for the direction of travel and shared resources such as pooled budgets. At a team level strategic agreement will need to be reached in relation to referral routes and sources, eligibility criteria and how workloads will be allocated and managed. Things like corporate governance arrangements (Wildridge et al., 2004) may be just as important as agreeing the respective agencies, teams or individual's contributions. Ultimately the service strategy needs to foster joint commitment that is reflected in the goals set and will be visible through the behaviours of collaborators.

Goals need to be clearly agreed including those that need to be met through collaboration between partners and those that partners can meet independently but still contribute to the overall mission and vision. Behaviours that promote interdisciplinarity are likely to demonstrate the skill of working across professional, organizational or other boundaries. According to Wildridge et al. (2004) individuals who have these skills are sometimes described as 'boundary spanners' or 'reticulists' and are often working at the front line. Onyett (2003) highlights that team managers have the dual task of facing outwards when representing the team and its members to higher management and inwards when acting to communicate management expectations for the service or communicating strategic goals. This part of the role is seen as living on the boundary and according to Roberts (1999) requires an effective manager to be 'in touch' with both the internal state of the team and the outward demands placed upon it. This is where developing allies both within the team and elsewhere in the organization can play an increasingly important role in assisting the manager to feel less isolated and more supported in discharging the complex requirements of their role.

A clear communication strategy often best written down; is an intrinsic link to all the elements in the process. Collaborators need to understand the outcomes to be achieved, the resources, tools, support systems and structures to help them achieve them. Effective mechanisms for providing information to and receiving it from different stakeholder groups, teams and/or individuals is important to ensure their continued involvement in translating the vision and mission into the day to day goals, behaviour and results.

Having established the interrelatedness of leadership and management activities in interdisciplinary working the issue then arises about how to demonstrate this skill mix in practice.

As a starting point it is worth pointing out that key to the above is the ability to manage oneself, the ability to manage others and the ability to manage the interactions between the service and those who use it. Hamer (2006, pp. 17–18) describes this as the three dimensional approach to leadership and management as all three elements, together with the context in which they occur, are interdependent. Any significant change in one will impact upon the others and is depicted as follows:

Each of these three elements will now be discussed in some detail.

Managing Oneself in Interdisciplinary Working

Whilst the bulk of professional training is geared towards the uniprofessional contribution practitioners make to mental health and social care services this is likely to become increasingly diluted for staff in management positions. This is because of the role managers play in promoting collaboration within and between teams and services. It is worth acknowledging that in order to

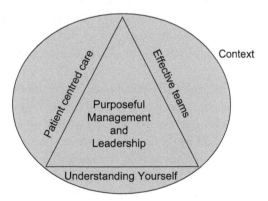

Figure 12.3 Hamer's 3-dimensional approach to leadership and management (2006)

be effective managers and leaders need to retain a sense of their original disciplinary identity either as nurse, social worker, psychologist etc whilst also developing a sense of direction in terms of where they wish to take the service. According to Engel and Gursky (2003, p. 49) managing collaboration involves balancing professional independence with professional interdependence in order to 'recognise the value of each member's skills and to magnify these skills many times through the skills of other professionals'.

Effective managers also need to understand and be able to work with the organization's systems and structures in which they are trying to manage. These may vary on a continuum. Some organizations will be characterized by a very top down, vertically aligned, and multilayered hierarchy which presents little opportunities for senior and middle managers to have direct experience of what is happening in day to day practice. Other organizations may adopt a 'flattened' management structure and encourage a more 'bottom up approach' that hinges directly on the diversity of collective decision making and sharing of expertise. This can be very challenging for professionals who have traditionally worked in a team where a vertical chain of command was in operation.

In attempting to strike a balance between these two extremes the manager of interdisciplinary services needs to develop a sense of belonging both within the team as the leader/manager but also within the organization as a whole. Onyett (2003) claims that teams need a manager who can cope with being used both by the team members in the way the manager represents the team to the organization but also how they in turn represent the organization to the team. Engel and Gursky (2003, p. 51) call for managers to be 'impartial arbiters of bidirectional information and honest brokers of the organisation's mission'. In order to do this, managers need to retain their own skills and be subject to scrutiny and performance appraisal by more senior managers and the workers for whom they are responsible. The downside of managers who can't achieve this balancing act effectively is that the staff and team may cling together and externalize senior managers as the enemy in the organization which subsequently leads to the internalization of negativity and personalized conflicts.

It is clear from the leadership and management literature that as well as retaining a pivotal position in relation to power dynamics within organizations effective managers also need to be able to switch between getting the job done and supporting and enabling their workers. This is often referred to in the literature as the 'task' and 'people' domains of leadership. Tasks such as time management, workload prioritization and allocation together with ensuring minimum standards and safety requirements are met fall within the task domain. Developing good practice guidance about how work should be allocated within the team to which everyone signs up, will involve canvassing the opinion of staff about the different options available and how this fits with the underpinning values of collaborative practice. This kind of management activity falls more clearly into the supporting people domain. In summary, managers of interdisciplinary teams would do well to remember that in order for individuals to function in their role successfully they need a sense of:

- The direction of travel for the team and the service;
- Personal and professional belonging and a sense of identity; and,
- To feel cared for with praise and recognition for the job they do and the contribution they make to the team.

These needs will be fostered in teams where members have the opportunity to take some autonomous responsibility for their practice and be able to pursue stimulating new experiences in the course of their work.

Managers need to ensure they seek these fundamental needs for themselves through their peers and allies in the service as well as putting them in place for members of their team.

Managing Others

An individual's overall success as a manager therefore depends to a significant extent on the successful relationships they are able to build with people at all levels within their organization and other agencies with whom they work in partnership. Studies of staff working in community mental health settings have highlighted the importance of working in a team and relationships with colleagues as among the strongest sources of reward (Onyett et al., 1995; Carson et al., 1995; Knapp et al., 1992). Building in time for contact between team members in order to foster interdisciplinary working therefore becomes important. Onyett (2003) highlights the need for this to include: individual peer consultation, mentoring and supervision.

One of the obvious contact points for colleagues is in the form of team meetings or care planning and review meetings. According to Hewstone and Brown (1986) the contact effect is promoted when:

- Participants are brought together for a common purpose and with equal status (as articulated in the values underpinning the collaborative practice of the team or service);
- Interdisciplinary teamwork is promoted and supported at the higher levels of the organization;
- Contact opportunities are created that are pleasing or rewarding;
- Colleagues engage in functionally important activities (such as a collaborative approach to risk, assessment, planning and management) with common goals that are rated of higher importance than individual goals.

Managing the way in which clinical team meetings work is therefore an opportunity for managers to promote interdisciplinary contact that embodies these positive outcomes and fosters collaboration. Morgan (1996) highlights the need to engender a 'culture of support' in the team alongside more formal decision making about day to day working practice such as workload management. Colleagues need to be attuned to the psychological impact of working with people with mental health issues because as Scheid (1996) points out, their role requires commitment at an emotional level, to be caring, as well as acting in a caring way. This is echoed by Ramon and Williams (2005, p. 15) who advocate replacing a distanced 'hands off' approach in mental health with a more 'hands on' way of working that demonstrates emotional closeness to the service user and an interest in their everyday concerns.

Inevitably, interdisciplinary working is not without conflict arising as a result of role rivalry, power dynamics, professional stereotyping and competition between disciplines (Onyett, 2003; Onyett et al., 1995). While addressing these issues can pose a challenge for managers it is important that they are addressed rather than allowed to develop as a sub-culture that can undermine collaboration. According to West and Farr (1989) successful organizations manage rather than suppress conflict and that everyone in the team should take some responsibility for conflict management. Onyett (2003) identifies the need for well-defined responsibilities within teams together with clear lines of accountability as a means of making conflict resolution easier. Watts and Bennett (1983) highlight that disagreements over clinical work can result in positive outcomes. These include guarding against 'Groupthink' that can arise when teams become over-cohesive and strong social pressures are brought to bear on anyone challenging collective assumptions. The crux of interdisciplinary working is to value the expression of difference within the team as a means of ensuring that the intellectual contributions from the different professions become intrinsically less valuable in order to ensure that the service users' experiences and understanding of their mental health issues are also taken into account.

Effective communication for the purpose of interdisciplinary decision making is key to the management of others. Colleagues and service users need to come together with a clear understanding of what needs to be accomplished together with information about the resources and capabilities they have to achieve the desired outcome. Onyett (2003, p. 195) identities the preconditions for such effective communication in mental health teams as follows: a recognized need to communicate, a shared social reality about what they are doing and a shared language with which to describe this reality, together with support to take the perspective of others into account including both their emotional and cognitive position. He acknowledges that these preconditions are often a characteristic of maturing teams that have stable membership.

With this is mind, managers of interdisciplinary mental health teams and services can benefit from an understanding of team processes as outlined by Tuckman (1965). Tuckman's team development model is based on the premise that small groups or teams go through various stages before they are able to work together effectively. These are shown in Figure 12.4. The model can be used to understand the emotional climate of a new team as it develops and to help managers understand the dynamics in existing teams. For example, if the team is engaging in significant levels of argumentative behaviour managers may want to consider whether this is part of the storming stage of team development or is arising as a result of another issue such as workload pressure that needs to be managed effectively.

In the forming stage team members tend to be anxious and uncertain. They look to the manager for direction as they attempt to understand the nature of the work within the overall aim and objectives for the service. In this stage teams members are likely to be polite to each other and more aware of their own uniprofessional backgrounds. Interpersonal relationships tend to be superficial.

The storming stage is characterized by conflict, questioning of the aims and objectives and in some instances the manager's role in helping the team to achieve these. In interdisciplinary teams this stage will be characterized by professional stereotyping and jockeying for position between the disciplines. There is often resistance to the demands of the task and the manager has to demonstrate an effective balance between managing the task and containing the conflict, a balance between giving direction while supporting and coaching. This is not a good stage for decision making in teams.

Stage 3: NORMING	**Stage 2: STORMING**
Success occurs Appreciation and trust built Team is creative Individual motivation increased	Express differences React to leadership Trying new ideas Splinter groups form Competition is high
Stage 4: PERFORMING	**Stage 1: FORMING**
Team very motivated Individuals defer to team needs High openness and support Superior team performance	Making contact and bonding Norms of the team not established Trust not yet developed Politeness and dependency

Figure 12.4 Tuckman's team development model

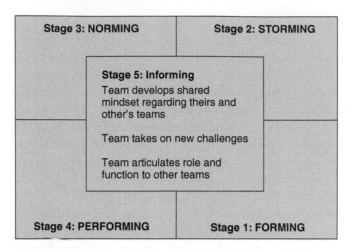

Figure 12.5 Tuckman's Team Development Model as developed by Kur (1996). This is the author's diagrammatical representation based on Tuckman's (1965) model

When teams enter the norming stage this is manifest by increased group cohesion and clarity about the direction of travel. This stage presents an opportunity for managers to foster an increased appreciation of the combining of different disciplinary perspectives. Team members are more likely to engage in the decision making process in the forming phase as they search for mutual support amongst their colleagues and a sense of team identity is fostered.

Performing teams have resolved their interpersonal conflicts and are able to achieve a heightened level of interaction and collaboration to get on with the task at hand. Roles become more flexible and interchangeable as the team become more focused on finding solutions. Their energy for the work increases and their anxiety about individual contributions is diminished. In this stage the manager can take on more of a delegation role to enhance the effective level of interaction that is occurring.

In 1996, Kur added a fifth stage to Tuckman's original model referred to as the 'informing' stage. Informing occurs where teams are able to articulate and demonstrate to other teams their collective contribution to the wider goals of service delivery. This is especially important in mental health services where specialist teams coexist and need to interact effectively in order to promote continuity of care for service users and their families. This requires a level of coexistence and interaction between managers of teams and with other agencies to facilitate their team's overall contribution to the overall service strategy.

Where teams are brought together for a specific, time-limited task they may disband once the task is complete. Tuckman refers to this stage as adjourning and the manager's role is to recognize how the collective contributions have resulted in the achievement of the objectives and facilitate successful closure.

Managing the Service

Managing the delivery of increasingly interdisciplinary care in mental health is a complex task and hinges upon managers being able to manage the expertise of their workforce effectively. Learning lessons, as teams and services move through the process of change, can be just as important for managers as whether change is implemented successfully or is experienced as beset with difficulties. According to Hayes (2002, p. 39) 'the collective nature of learning is especially important in complex and turbulent environments because in such circumstances senior managers may not be the best-placed individuals to identify opportunities and threats'.

Interdisciplinary learning and change can be fostered by the opportunities for training and education that are made available to individuals and teams (see Chapter 11) and needs to 'harness the intellectual treasure' (Engel and Gursky, 2003) that is intrinsic to a truly interdisciplinary approach. While clinical team meetings serve a function in terms of promoting contact between team members as outlined above they can also be instrumental in ensuring the delivery of the service accords with an overall aim of promoting interdisciplinarity. Morgan (1996), cited in Onyett, (2003) suggests that team meetings can be managed to promote:

- Hope: by inculcating a view of service users as whole people with futures and valuable roles to play;
- Affirmation: by recognizing the work being undertaken;
- Information: by sharing and clarifying details;
- Ideas: by generating new options;
- Fun: by ensuring colleagues in the team are enjoying their work.

It is interesting to note that the values of hope, affirmation and information are akin to a recovery model for service users with mental health problems. This implies that if the manager can adopt such a 'strengths-based' model of leadership this could more easily be transferred to a recovery approach to service delivery. By involving mental health service users in the team approach (see Bracken and Cohen, 1999) this can help the team to stay reflexive in the way that it discharges its care and retains the focus on improving the outcomes that are most important to service users.

Performance management is one way of ensuring that the aims of the service are realized through the objectives set for individual team members. Managers of interdisciplinary mental health services need to be able to make transparent how the overall vision and mission for the service can be achieved through the disciplinary contributions of individuals. Collectively these contributions can realize team aims and objectives thus embodying the multiplicative effect of working together outlined in Chapter 2. Supervision and staff appraisal are two routes that can support the performance management process as outlined in Figure 12.6.

The overall purpose of the appraisal process is for the manager to review the job role of the individual within the wider context of the goals and targets set by the organization. An appraisal discussion with a team member is likely to focus upon their key responsibilities, accomplishments, current workload, factors affecting performance together with opportunities for professional development and progression.

Supervision in contrast to appraisal is a more formal process of professional support and learning that enables practitioners to develop their knowledge and competence and assume responsibility for their own practice. It also enhances consumer protection and the safety of care in complex situations (DH, 2003). The link between supervision and managing the service to the service user is shown in Figure 12.7.

Supervision and service delivery are therefore linked as part of a dynamic process that involves the supervisor, the worker (or in some cases a trainee) and the person who is using the service. If one element in the relationship is affected this will have a knock on effect in the other areas.

For example, the supervisor's role is more easily discharged if: there are clear procedures and realistic administrative demands, the supervisor has the opportunity to be involved in developing the organization's policy, appraisal schemes are in place and their link or separateness from the supervision process is clearly delineated. In interdisciplinary working supervisors also need to have the opportunity to network with other agencies and maintain some direct contact with service users. They will be less effective in their role if there is information about the team or the individual worker that is bypassing supervision, they are uncertain about their authority to supervise or how they can match their supervisory style with the learning needs of the individual. Where there is less communication about practice upwards to senior management and supervisors lack their own supervision arrangements, these factors can also contribute to the ineffectivess of supervisors.

The needs of the service user are more likely to be met by the service where the agency publicizes clear information about mental health provision and there are opportunities to work in partnership that embodies anti-discriminatory practice. Where service users have access to complaints procedures, advocacy services and supportive community groups and networks they are more likely to be able to keep the service informed about their changing needs. Where agencies are too busy to listen, provision is service led; evaluated by quantity not quality, or where there is an acute lack of resources, service users'

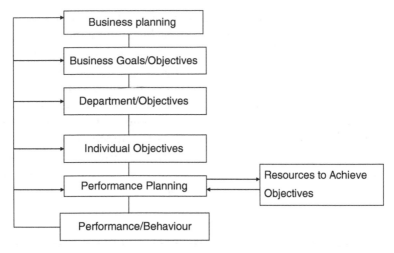

Figure 12.6 Performance management and business planning

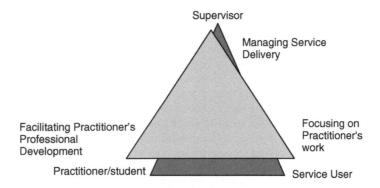

Figure 12.7 Supervision and service delivery

needs are likely to feature less prominently in the way the service is delivered and evaluated

The worker is more likely to actively contribute to the supervision process if they have a good understanding of their professional needs and how these link with the competences and occupational standards they are required to demonstrate in practice. Workers who are enthusiastic about their role and learning opportunities, and have a balance between autonomy and dependency with opportunities for self-reflection are likely to be more effective in the care they provide. They are less likely to be supported in supervision where the emphasis is skewed towards the needs of the supervisor or service user or where there is uncertainty about their identity and role.

In respect of managers supervising staff from different disciplinary backgrounds it may therefore be important, as highlighted by the managers and service users who contributed to the focus group discussion reported at the start of this chapter, to separate out the managerial function of supervision from that of ongoing professional development that hinges upon the distinct disciplinary contribution that the individual brings to collaborative practice. Provided that the respective lines of accountability and responsibility are clarified and those involved in providing the supervisory and management functions do not require workers to behave in ways that create conflict between the two processes supervision can be an effective tool for promoting interdisciplinary mental health care delivery.

PRACTICE FOCUS 12.1

Managing Interdisciplinary Working

Initially a CMHT, East D Team has specialized further to work with individuals with psychosis. The team is comprised of social workers, Community Psychiatric Nurses (CPNs), OTs, a consultant psychiatrist and consultant psychologists. Team members also include support workers and link workers who work under the guidance and direction of professionally qualified staff. The team has a team manager who is a CPN by background and several administrative staff.

The team manager is responsible for the overall day to day running of the team and the allocation of clinical work. This is done weekly through 'allocation meetings' which all team members attend. The team manager oversees an interdisciplinary way of working in that all CPNs, social workers and OTs are first and foremost Care Coordinators and service users are often unaware of their disciplinary contribution. As a result caseload size is managed across disciplines and averages at 35.

All Care Coordinators provide a combination of psychological therapies and learn basic skills in Cognitive Behavioural Therapy and Dialectical Behaviour Therapy. Where more specialist therapeutic skills and/or assessment is needed, service users are referred to the consultant psychologists and staff members from other disciplines who have advanced skills and expertise in therapeutic interventions.

One senior Approved Mental Health Professional (AMHP) who is a social worker by background, has been promoted to the role of 'expert practitioner' and provides supervision to some of the social workers in the team. This is in addition to caseload management and performance appraisal which is undertaken by the team manager. Where such professional support is provided in addition to workload management this system seems to work well. However, in a 'sister' team in the same locality both the team manager and 'expert practitioner' roles are held by CPNs. In this team social workers express significant concern about the lack of disciplinary specific supervision particularly in relation to their statutory social work duties.

Feedback from interviews with team members as part of a current study reveals increasing support for interdisciplinary working within the team but with the proviso that interdisciplinary management can be augmented by opportunities for professional supervision where this is necessary to ensure practice that is responsive to service users' needs.

Summary

This chapter has summarized the interrelatedness of leadership and management and the need for managers of interdisciplinary mental health services to be able to integrate the vision and mission of the service with an overall operational policy or strategy and the individual goals of staff in order to realize objectives and outcomes. Communication is key to the overall process and managers need to balance managing the task element of service delivery whilst ensuring that teams and individuals are supported throughout the process of change.

Concluding Comments

This book has attempted to explore the evolution of interdisciplinary working in mental health and has defined this as an extension of multiprofessional working; to include meaningful interactions between disciplines including service users and carers to achieve enhanced care delivery.

Whilst over the last 100 years systems and structures in mental health services have evolved to a point where they can support interdisciplinary practice the latter is thwarted by the lack of an agreed language to describe collaboration and the patchy implementation of disciplines interacting effectively. For interdisciplinarity to underpin properly coordinated care delivery, that involves service users and carers as key stakeholders in the process, support is required at all levels from one-to-one working through to integration within teams and effective organizational structures that transcend traditional health and social care boundaries. Whilst the policy agenda in mental health has re-oriented to support this way of working, by virtue of its complexity interdisciplinary working is costly. Costs occur in respect of time and human resources as well as the costs incurred by role confusion and role rivalry that arise between professionals. For interdisciplinary working to be successful it needs to be predicated on a shared value system that promotes a recovery oriented focus in mental health treatment and interventions. The new legislative framework has gone some way to support this but in some respects could be criticized for further blurring the roles of mental health professionals in its attempt to define mental illness and treatments more widely.

With the advent of increasing numbers of non-professionally affiliated staff and the New Ways of Working initiative the care planning and delivery process inherently includes a more diverse range of contributions. The essence of interdisciplinary working is the way in which these are coordinated to deliver a more seamless service to service users and their families. Paradoxically, the diversification of the workforce coupled with the increasing specialization of mental health teams has in some respects detracted from interdisciplinary working rather than improved it.

Inter-agency working is reserved for integrated approaches that straddle agency boundaries and promote partnership working at structural and strategic levels. This is becoming increasingly important in the light of current economic constraints although pooled budgets to support inter-agency partnerships have not been readily forthcoming.

Interdisciplinary working is key to effective risk assessment planning and management given the need to collect information specific to individuals' circumstances alongside more general information about how different types of mental health problems present and should be effectively managed. In a climate of increasing litigation and public concern about risk, a more inclusive approach to information gathering can help to guard against the influence of biased thinking in the risk assessment and decision making process. By involving service users and carers in interdisciplinary working this should support a greater emphasis on risk taking strategies that are shared between providers and recipients of services. Values which recognize the valid and positive experience of service users living with mental health problems in relation to the recovery model of mental health will also support interdisciplinary working arrangements for more effective risk management practice as a collaborative endeavour.

Research has shown that involvement in care delivery and the process of decision making about services at local and national levels can be intrinsically valuable for individuals who use services, resulting in enhanced self-esteem and a broadening of their experience and skills. In the light of this it is therefore disappointing that the New Ways of Working agenda has not sought more actively to support service user contributions to the workforce as was originally envisaged in the role of Support, Time and Recovery Workers.

Interdisciplinary working is especially important for groups who have always tended to fall through the network of mental health care provision such as children and young people, older adults and individuals with complex needs such as substance misuse and interrelated mental health issues. Interdisciplinary working that is attuned to care continuity across the interface of services is therefore especially important and requires joined-up policies to support collaborative practice. Increasingly for these groups the overall emphasis needs to be upon partnerships to create a whole system way of working across health, social services, education and agencies in the independent sector.

Interdisciplinary working will not be sustained unless supported by effective training and development. This needs to be available at all levels to support individual practitioners, teams and joint working between organizations. Managers of services are key to this and understandably find the task of managing and leading an increasingly diverse mental health workforce daunting and beset with challenges. It is important that the training agenda reflects the body of interprofessional education research that reinforces a clear message: interdisciplinary working is not about all mental health workers being able to do the same things. Interdisciplinary working is fostered when workers have some shared skills and others that are unique to their profession. This diversity is needed because of the wide ranging presentation of mental distress and the individuality of service users. What is crucial is how interprofessional opportunities encourage workers to learn and collaborate together in ways that enhance their unique and shared expertise for the benefit of the service users and their families. Managers and leaders who can harness this synergy in the workplace will be skilled in interpersonal communication, managing change and creative in the way they deliver professional supervision versus workload management.

Finally, interdisciplinary working is synonymous with the modernization of mental health services. It is underpinned by a modern day value system that promotes flexibility in relation to issues of professionalism, power and occupational culture. In a political climate of increasing social inclusivity it is the way forward underpinned by approaches that seek to enhance recovery from mental distress, promote citizenship and harness the collective expertise of an ever diversifying mental health workforce.

References

Adorian, D., Silverberg, D. S., Tomer, D. and Wamosher, Z. (1990) 'Group Discussions with the Health Care Team: A Method of Improving Care of Hypertension in General Practice', *Journal of Human Hypertension*, 4(3), pp. 265–268.

Aitken J. B. and Curtis, R. (2004) 'Integrated Health Care: Improving Client Care while Providing Opportunities for Mental Health Counselors', *Journal of Mental Health Counselling*, 26(4), pp. 321–331.

Allott, P. and Holmes, P. (1993) 'Involving Service Users', in Dean, C. and Freeman, H. (eds), *Community Mental Health Care: International Perspectives on Making It Happen*, London: Gaskell & The Centre for Mental Health Services Development.

Alzheimer's Society (2007) *Dementia UK: A Report into the Prevalence and Cost of Dementia, The Full Report*, London: Alzheimer's Society.

Anderson, E., Shepherd, M. and Salisbury, C. (2006) '"Taking off the Suit": Engaging the Community in Primary Health Care Decision Making', *Health Expectations*, 9(1), pp. 70–80.

Anthony, E. J. and Cohler, B. J. (eds) (1987) *The Invulnerable Child*, New York: Guilford Press.

Anthony, W. A. (1993) 'Recovery from Mental Illness: The Guiding Vision of the Mental Health Service System in the 1990s', *Psychosocial Rehabilitation Journal*, 16(4), pp. 11–23.

Armstrong, E. (1992) 'Facilitators in Primary Care', *International Review of Psychiatry*, 4(3–4), pp. 339–341.

Armstrong, E. (2000) 'Mental Health Problems in Primary Care', in Bailey, D. (ed.), *At the Core of Mental Health: Key Issues for Practitioners, Managers and Mental Health Trainers*, Brighton: Pavilion, pp. 129–153.

Askheim, O. P. (2003) 'Empowerment as Guidance for Professional Social Work: An Act of Balancing on a Slack Rope', *European Journal of Social Work*, 6(3), pp. 229–240.

Atkin, D., Lunt, N., Parker, G. and Hurst, M. (1993) *Nurses Count: A National Census of Practice Nurses*, York: Social Policy Research Unit, University of York.

Audit Commission (1994) *Finding a Place: A Review of Mental Health Services for Adults*, London: HMSO.

Audit Commission (1999) *Children in Mind: Child and Adolescent Mental Health Services*, London: Audit Commission.

Audit Commission (2000) *Forget Me Not: Mental Health Services for Older People*, London: Audit Commission.

Audit Commission (2002) *Forget Me Not 2002: Developing Mental Health Services for Older People in England*, London: Audit Commission.

Bacon, P. (1997) 'Assessing Risk: Are We Being Over Cautious?', *British Journal of Psychiatry*, 170 (Supplement 32), pp. 30–31.

Badger, F. and Nolan, P. (1999) 'General Practitioners' Perceptions of Community Psychiatric Nurses in Primary Care', *Journal of Psychiatric and Mental Health Nursing*, 6(6), pp. 453–459.

Bailey, D., (1997) 'What is the Way Forward for a User-led Approach to the Delivery of Mental Health Services in Primary Care?', *Journal of Mental Health*, 6(1), pp. 101–106.

Bailey D. (2002) 'Training Together: An Exploration of a Shared Learning Approach to Dual Diagnosis Training for Specialist Drugs Workers and ASWs', *Social Work Education*, 21(5), pp. 565–581.

Bailey, D. (2002a) 'Training Together Part Two: An Exploration of the Evaluation of a Shared Learning Programme on Dual Diagnosis for Specialist Drugs Workers and ASWs', *Social Work Education*, 21(6), pp. 685–699.

Bailey, D. (2005) 'Using an Action Research Approach to Involving Service Users in the Assessment of Professional Competence', *European Journal of Social Work*, 8(2), pp. 165–179.

Bailey, D., (2007) 'Training Graduate Primary Care Mental Health Workers for Collaborative Practice: Part 1', *The Journal of Mental Health Training, Education and Practice*, 2(3), pp. 12–22.

Bailey, D., Carpenter, J., Dickinson, C. and Rogers, H. (2003) *A Systematic Review of Post Qualifying Mental Health Training*. Prepared for the Department of Health, University of Birmingham, Institute of Applied Social Studies.

Bailey, D., Casey, B., Paxton, R. and Linde, K. (2012) 'Understanding the Whole Mental Health System: Identifying a Conceptual Framework', *Journal of Interprofessional Care*, (forthcoming).

Balloch, S. and Taylor, M. (eds) (2001) *Partnership Working: Policy and Practice*, Bristol: Policy Press.

Bambling, M., Kavanagh, D., Lewis, G., King, R., King, D., Sturk, H., Turpin, M., Gallois C. and Bartlett, H. (2007) 'Challenges Faced by General Practitioners and Allied Mental Health Services in Providing Mental Health Services in Rural Queensland', *Australian Journal of Rural Health*, 15(2), pp. 126–130.

Barham, P. and Hayward, R. (1991) *From Mental Patient to the Person*, London: Tavistock/Routledge.

Barlow, J. and Underdown, A. (2008) 'Attachment and Infant Development', in Jackson, C., Hill, K. and Lavis, P. (eds), *Child and Adolescent Mental Health Today: A Handbook*, Brighton: Pavilion Publishing/Mental Health Foundation, pp.47–54.

Barnes, D. (1997) *Older People with Mental Health Problems Living Alone: Anybody's Priority?* London: Department of Health.

Barnes, D., Carpenter, J. and Bailey, D. (2000) 'Partnerships with Service Users in Interprofessional Education for Community Mental Health: A Case Study', *Journal of Interprofessional Care*, 14(2), pp. 189–200.

Barnes, M. and Bowl, R. (2001) *Taking Over the Asylum: Empowerment and Mental Health*, Basingstoke: Palgrave.

Barr, H. (1994) 'NVQs and Their Implications for Interprofessional Collaboartion', in Lethard, A. (ed.), *Going Interprofessional: Working Together for Health and Welfare*, London: Routledge.

Barr, H. (1996) 'Ends and Means in Interprofessional Education: Towards a Typology', *Education for Health*, 9, pp. 341–352.

Barr, H. (2000) 'Working Together to Learn Together: Learning Together to Work Together', *Journal of Interprofessional Care*, 14, pp. 177–179.

Barr, H. (2002) *Interprofessional Education Today, Yesterday and Tomorrow: A Review*. Commissioned by the Learning and Teaching Support Network Centre for Health Sciences and Practice from the UK Centre for the Advancement of Interprofessional Education. London: LTSN for Health Sciences & Practice.

Barr, H. (2003) 'Unpacking Interprofessional Education', in Lethard, A. (ed.), *Interprofessional Collaboration: From Policy to Practice*, Hove: Brunner/Routledge, pp. 265–279.

Barr, H., Freeth, D., Hammick, M., Koppel, I. and Revves, S. (1999) Evaluating Interprofessional Education: A United Kingdom Review for Health and Social Care, London, British Association for the Advancement of Interprofessional Learning/Centre for Advancement of Interprofessional Education.

Barr, H., Freeth, D., Hammick, M., Koppel, I. and Reeves, S. (2000) *Evaluations of Interprofessional Education: A UK Review for Health and Social Care*, London: British Educational Research Association and the United Kingdom Centre for the Advancement of Interprofessional Evaluation.

Barr, H., Koppel, I., Reeves, S., Hammick, M. and Freeth, D. (2005) *Effective Interprofessional Education: Argument, Assumption and Evidence*, Oxford; Malden, MA: Blackwell.

Barr, H. and Ross, F. (2006) 'Mainstreaming Interprofessional Education in the United Kingdom: A Position Paper', *Journal of Interprofessional Care*, 20(2), pp. 96–104.

Bean, P. (2001) *Mental Disorder and Community Safety*, Basingstoke: Palgrave.

Bean, P. and Wilkinson, C. (1988) 'Drug Taking, Crime and the Illicit Supply System', *British Journal of Addiction*, 83, pp. 533–539.

Beecham, J., Knapp, M. R. J. and Scheider, J. (1996) 'Policy and Finance for Community Care: The New Mixed Economy', in Watkins, M., Hervey, N., Carson, J. and Ritter, S. (eds), *Collaborative Community Mental Health Care*, London: Arnold, pp. 44–77.

Beeforth, M. (1993) 'Users are People', in Williamson, V. (ed.), *Users First: The Real Challenge for Community Care*, Brighton: University of Brighton.

Beekman, A. T. F., Copeland, J. R. M. and Prince, M. J. (1999) 'Review of Community Prevalence of Depression in Later Life', *British Journal of Psychiatry*, 174, pp. 307–311.

Birchwood, M., Mason, R., MacMillan, F. and Healy, J. (1993) 'Depression, Demoralization and Control Over Psychotic Illness: A Comparison of Depressed and Non-depressed Patients with a Chronic Psychosis', *Psychological Medicine*, 23, pp. 387–395.

Blom-Cooper, L. (1996) *The Case of Jason Mitchell: Report of the Independent Panel of Inquiry*, London: Duckworth.

Blount, A. (2003) 'Intergrated Primary Care: Organising the Evidence', *Families, Systems and Health*, 21, pp. 121–134.

Boak, G. and Jones, H. (2002) *Leading Innovation and Change in the Health Service*, Chichester: Kingsham Press.

Bond, A. J. and Lader, M. H. (1996) *Understanding Drug Treatment in Mental Health Care*, Chichester: John Wiley and Sons.

Bond, J., Cartlidge, A. M., Gregson, B. A., Philips, P. R., Bolam, F. and Gill, K. M. (1985) *A Study of Interprofessional Collaboration in Primary Health Care Organizations*, Report No. 27, vol. 2, Newcastle upon Tyne Health Care Research Unit: University of Newcastle upon Tyne.

Boote, J., Telford, R. and Cooper, C. (2002) 'Consumer Involvement in Health Research. A Review and Research Agenda', *Health Policy*, 61(2), pp. 213–236.

Borrill, C. S., Carletta, J., Carter, A. J., Dawson, J. F., Garrod, S., Rees, A., Richards, A., Shapiro, D. and West, M. A. (2000) *The Effectiveness of Healthcare Teams in the National Health Service*, Birmingham: Aston University.

Borrill, C. S., Wall, T. D., West, M. A., Hardy, G. E., Shapiro, D. A. and Carter, A. J. et al (1996) *Mental Health of the Workforce in NHS Trusts: Phase 1 Final Report*, Sheffield and Leeds: Institute of Work Psychology, University of Sheffield and Department of Pyschology, University of Leeds.

Bownds, D. (1999) *The Biology of Mind*, Bethesda: Fitzgerald Science Press.

Bracken, P. and Cohen, B. (1999) 'Home Treatment in Bradford', *Psychiatric Bulletin*, 23, pp. 349–352.

Bracken, P. and Thomas, P. (2004) 'Postpsychiatry is not another model!' *Openmind*, Jan/Feb, 125, pp. 6–7.

Bradshaw, J. (ed.) (2001) *Poverty: The Outcomes for Children*, London: Family Policy Studies Centre.

Brearley, P. C. (1982) *Risk in Social Work*, London: Routledge and Keegan Paul.

Brenton, K. (2007) 'Using Soft Systems Methodology to Examine Communication Difficulties', *Mental Health Practice*, 10(5), pp. 12–16.

Bronstein, L. (2003) 'A Model for Interdisciplinary Collaboration', *Social Work*, 48(3), pp. 297–306.

Brooker, C., Saul, C., Robinson, J., King, J. and Dudley, M. (2003) 'Is Training in Psychosocial Interventions Worthwhile? Report of a Psychosocial Intervention Trainee Follow-up Study', *International Journal of Nursing Studies*, 40(7), pp. 731–747.

Burns, T., Millar, E., Garland, C., Kendrick, T., Chisholm, B. and Ross, F. (1998) 'Randomized Controlled Trial of Teaching Practice Nurses to Carry Out Structured Assessments of Patients Receiving Antipsychotic Injections', *British Journal of General Practice*, 48(437), pp. 1845–1848.

Byng, R., Single, H. and Bury, C. (1999) *Developing Primary Care for Patients with Long-term Mental Illness. Your Guide to Improving Services*, London: Kings Fund.

Cabinet Office (2006) *Reaching Out: An Action Plan on Social Exclusion*, London: Cabinet Office/Social Exclusion Task Force.

CAIPE (1996) (Centre for Advancement of Interprofessional Education) *Principles of Interprofessional Education*, London: CAIPE.

CAIPE (2007) *Creating an Interprofessional Workforce: An Education and Training Framework for Health and Social Care in England*, London: Department of Health.

Campbell, H., Hotchkiss, R., Bradshaw, N. and Porteous, M. (1998) 'Integrated Care Pathways', *British Medical Journal*, 316(7125), pp. 133–137.

Campbell, P. (2002) 'Doing it for Ourselves', *Mental Health Today*, October, pp. 28–30.

Canvin, K. Bartlett, A. and Pinfold, V. (2002) 'A "Bittersweet Pill to Swallow": Learning From Mental Health Service Users' Responses to Compulsory Community Care in England', *Health and Social Care in the Community*, 10(5), pp. 361–369.

Care Services Improvement Partnership (2005) *Our Choices in Mental Health*, London: Care Services Improvement Partnership.

Carey, J. (2006) 'A Safe Society: Effective Assessment, Prevention and Treatment in Forensic Mental Health', Paper presented at International Association of Forensic Mental Health Services Conference, 14–16 June 2006, Amsterdam, The Netherlands.

Carling, P. (1996) *Return to the Community: Building Support Systems for People with Psychiatric Disabilities*, New York: Guilford Press.

Carpenter, J., Barnes, D. and Dickinson, C. (1999) *Birmingham University Programme in Community Mental Health. Progress Report 1 from the External Evaluation Team*, Centre for Applied Social Studies, Durham: University of Durham.

Carpenter, J., Barnes, D. and Dickinson, C. (2000) *Birmingham University Programme in Community Mental Health. Progress Report 2 from the External Evaluation Team*, Centre for Applied Social Studies, Durham: University of Durham.

Carpenter, J., Barnes, D. and Dickinson, C. (2003) *Making a Modern Mental Health Careforce: Evaluation of the Birmingham University Interprofessional Training Programme in Community Mental Health 1998–2002*, Durham: University of Durham, Centre for Applied Social Studies.

Carpenter, J., Barnes, D. and Dickinson, C. (2006) 'Outcomes of Interprofessional Education for Community Mental Health Services in England: A Longitudinal Evaluation of a Post-graduate Programme', *Journal of Interprofessional Care*, 20, pp. 145–161.

Carpenter, J. and Dickinson, H. (2008) *Interprofessional Education and Training*, Bristol: Policy Press in association with Community Care (Better partnership working series, book 3).

Carpenter, J. and Hewstone, M. (1996) 'Shared Learning for Doctors and Social Workers: Evaluation of a Programme', *British Journal of Social Work*, 26(2), pp. 239–257.

Carpenter, J. and Sbaraini, S. (1996) 'Involving Service Users and Carers', *CPA Journal of Mental Health*, 5(5), pp. 483–488.

Carson, D. and Bain, A. (2008) *Professional Risk and Working with People: Decision Making in Health, Social Care and Criminal Justice*, London; Philadelphia: Jessica Kingsley Publishers.

Carson, J., Fagin, L. and Ritter, S. (eds) (1995) *Stress and Coping in Mental Health Nursing*, London: Chapman and Hall.

Challis, D., Clarkson, P., Williamson, J., Hughes J., Venables, D., Burns, A. and Weinberg, A. (2004) 'The Value of Specialist Clinical Assessment of Older People Prior to Entry to Care Homes', *Age and Aging*, 33(1), pp. 25–34.

Chambers, R., Boath, E. and Wakley, G. (2001) *Mental Healthcare Matters in Primary Care*, Abingdon: Radcliffe Medical Press.

Checkland, P. B. (1972) 'Towards a Systems Based Methodology for Real World Problem Solving', *Journal of Systems Engineering*, 3(2), pp. 87–116.

Chevannes, M. (2002) 'Social Construction of the Managerialism of Needs Assessment by Health and Social Care Professionals', *Health and Social Care in the Community*, 10(3), pp. 168–178.

Cigno, K. and Bourn, D. (eds) (1998) *Cognitive-behavioural Social Work in Practice*, Aldershot: Ashgate.

Clark, J., Johnson, D. and Whittingham, P. (1995) *Developing the Care Programme Approach: Building on Strengths*, Bristol: NHS Training Division.

Clark, P. (2006) 'What Would a Theory of Interprofessional Education Look Like? Some Suggestions for Developing a Theoretical Framework for Teamwork Training', *Journal of Interprofessional Care*, 20(6), pp. 577–589.

Cleaver, H., Unell, I. and Aldgate, J. (1999) *Children's Needs, Parenting Capacity: The Impact of Parental Mental Illness, Problem Alcohol and Drug Use and Domestic Violence on Children's Development*, London: The Stationary Office.

Close, A. W. and Corney, R. (eds) (1982) *Social Work and Primary Health Care*, London: Academic Press.

Colombo, A., Bendelow, B., Fulford, B. and Williams, S. (2002) 'Evaluating the Influence of Implicit Models of Mental Disorder on Processes of Shared Decision Making Within Community Based Multidisciplinary Teams', *Social Science and Medicine*, 56, pp. 1557–570.

Combs, B. and Slovic, P. (1979) 'Causes of Death: Biased Newspaper Coverage and Biased Judgements', *Journalism Quarterly*, 56, pp. 837–843.

Commission for Health Improvement (2003) *What CHI Has Found in Mental Health Trusts: Sector Report*, London: Commission for Health Improvement.

Corston, J. (2007) *The Corston Report: A Report by Baroness Jean Corston of a Review of Women with Particular Vulnerabilities in the Criminal Justice System: The Need for a Distinct, Radically Different, Visibly Led, Strategic, Proportionate, Holistic, Woman-centred, Integrated Approach*, London: Home Office.

Coster, S., D'avray, L., Dawson, P., Dickinson, C., Gill, E., Gordon, F., Humphris, D., MacLoed-Clark, J., Marshall, M., Pearson, P., Steven, A. and Barr, H. (ed.) (2007) *Piloting Interprofessional Education: Four English Case Studies*, London: Higher Education Academy, Health Sciences and Practice (Higher Education Academy Health Occasional Papers, 8).

Craven, M. A. and Bland, R. (2006) 'Better Practices in Collaborative Mental Health Care: An Analysis of the Evidence Base', *Canadian Journal of Psychiatry*, 51(6 Suppl. 1), pp. 7S–72S.

Crawford, M. J., Rutter, D., Manley, C., Weaver, T., Bhui, K., Fulop, N. and Tyrer, P. (2002) 'Systematic Review of Involving Patients in the Planning and Development of Health Care', *BMJ*, 325, 30th November, pp. 1263–1265.

Crawford, V. (2001) *Co-existing Problems of Mental Disorder and Substance Misuse (Dual Diagnosis): A Review of Relevant Literature. Final Report to the Department of Health*, London: Royal College of Psychiatrists' Research and Training Unit.

CSIP (2007) *Strengthening the Involvement of People with Dementia: A Resource for Implementation*, London: Care Services Improvement Partnership, National Older People's Mental Health Programme.

Davis, A. (1996) 'Risk Work and Mental Health', in Kemshall, H. and Pritchard, J. (eds), *Good Practice in Risk Assessment and Risk Management 1*, London: Jessica Kingsley Publishers, pp. 109–120.

D'Cruz, H. and Jones, M. (2004) *Social Work Research: Ethical and Political Contexts*, London: Sage.

Dearden, C. and Becker, S. (1998) *Young Carers in the United Kingdom: A Profile*, London: Carers National Association.

Deegan, P. E. (1988) 'Recovery: The Lived Experience of Rehabilitation', *Psychosocial Rehabilitation Journal*, 11(4), pp. 11–19.

Deegan, P. (1996) 'Recovery as a Journey of the Heart', *Psychiatric Rehabilitation Journal*, 19(3), pp. 91–97.

Department for Education and Skills (2003) *Every Child Matters*, London: The Stationary Office (Cm. 5860).

DfES (2004) *Every Child Matters: Change for Children*, Nottingham: Department for Education and Skills Publications.

DH (1989a) *Caring for People: Community Care in the Next Decade and Beyond*, London: HMSO (Cm. 849).

DH (1989b) *Working for Patients*, London: HMSO (Cm. 555).

DH (1990) Caring for People. The Care Programme Approach for People with a Mental Illness referred to the specialist mental health services. Joint Health/Social Services Circular C(90)23/LASSL(90)11. London: Department of Health.

DH (1994) *Guidance on the Discharge of Mentally Disordered People and their Continuing Care in the Community*, London: Department of Health/NHS Executive (HSG (94) 27).

DH (1994a) *Mental Illness: Key Area Handbook*, 2nd edn, London: HMSO.

DH (1995) *Building Bridges: A Guide for Arrangements for Inter-agency Working for the Care and Protection of Severely Mentally Ill People*, London: Department of Health.

DH (1997) The New NHS: Modern Dependable, London: The Stationary Office (Cm. 3807).

DH (1998a) *Modernising Mental Health Services: Safe, Sound and Supportive*, London: Department of Health.

DH (1998b) *Modernising Social Services: Promoting Independence, Improving Protection, Raising Standards*, London: Department of Health.

DH (1998c) *The New NHS: Modern and Dependable – Developing Primary Care Groups*, Leeds: Department of Health (HSC 1998/139: LAC (98) 21).

DH (1998d) *Tackling Drugs to Build A Better Britain: The Government's 10-year Strategy for Tackling Drug Misuse*, London: The Stationary Office (Cm. 3945).

DH (1998e) *Partnership in Action: New Opportunities for Joint Working Between Health and Social Services: A Discussion Document*, London: Department of Health.

DH (1999) *Effective Care Coordination in Mental Health Services: Modernising the Care Programme Approach – A Policy Booklet*, London: Department of Health.

DH (1999a) *National Service Framework for Mental Health: Modern Standards and Service Models*, London: Department of Health.

DH (1999b) *Still Building Bridges: The Report of a National Inspection of Arrangements for the Integration of the Care Programme Approach with Care Management*, London: Department of Health.

DH (1999c) *Working Together to Safeguard Children: A Guide to Interagency Working to Safeguard and Promote the Welfare of Children*, London: Stationary Office.

DH (1999d) *Caring About Carers: A National Strategy for Carers*, London: Department of Health.

DH (2000) *The NHS Plan: A Plan for Investment, A Plan for Reform*, London: The Stationary Office (Cm. 4818-I).

DH (2000a) *Framework for the Assessment of Children in Need and their Families*, London: The Stationary Office.

DH (2000b) *No Secrets: Guidance on Developing and Implementing Multi-agency Policy and Procedures to Protect Vulnerable Adults from Abuse*, London: Department of Health.

DH (2000c) *A Health Service of All the Talents: Developing the NHS Workforce*, London: Department of Health.

DH (2001) *The Mental Health Policy Implementation Guide*, London: The Stationary Office.

DH (2001a) *National Service Framework for Older People*, London: Department of Health (HSC 2001/007: LAC (2001) 12).

DH (2001b) *Workforce Action Team Special Report on Primary Care Mental Health*, London: Department of Health.

DH (2001c) *Changing the Outlook: A Strategy for Developing Mental Health in Prisons*, Department of Health / HM Prison Service / The National Assembly for Wales.

DH (2002) *Mental Health Policy Implementation Guide: Dual Diagnosis Good Practice Guide*, London: Department of Health.

DH (2002a) *The Mental Health Policy Implementation Guide*, London: Department of Health.

DH (2003) *The Victoria Climbiè Inquiry: Report of an Inquiry by Lord Laming*, London: The Stationary Office (Cm. 5730).

DH (2003a) *Fast-forwarding Primary Care Mental Health: Graduate Primary Care Mental Health Workers – Best Practice Guidelines*, London: Department of Health.

DH (2004) *The Ten Essential Shared Capabilities: A Framework for the Whole of the Mental Health Workforce*, London: Department of Health.

DH (2004a) *National Service Framework for Children, Young People and Maternity Services*, London: Department of Health and Department for Education and Skills.

DH (2004b) The Carers (Equal Opportunities) Act, London, DH.

DH (2005) *New Ways of Working for Psychiatrists: Engaging Effective Person-centred Services Through New Ways of Working in Multidisciplinary and Multi-agency Contexts*, London: Department of Health.

DH (2005a) *Everybody's Business: Integrated Mental Health Services for Older Adults: A Service Development Guide*, London: Department of Health.

DH (2005b) *Securing Better Mental Health for Older Adults*, London: Department of Health.

DH (2005c) *Offender Mental Health Care Pathway*, Department of Health & National Institute for Mental Health in England, London: Department of Health.

DH (2005d) *Commissioning a Patient Led NHS*, London: Department of Health.

DH (2006) *Our Health, Our Care, Our Say: A New Direction for Community Services*, London: The Stationary Office (Cm. 6737).

DH (2007) *Independence, Choice and Risk: A Guide to Best Practice in Supported Decision Making*, London: Department of Health.

DH (2007) *New Ways of Working for Everyone*, London: Department of Health.

DH (2008) *Refocusing the Care Programme Approach: Policy and Positive Practice Guidance*, London: Department of Health.

DH (2008a) *High Quality Care for All: NHS Next Stage Review Final Report*, London: Department of Health (Cm. 7432).

DH (2009) *Living Well with Dementia: A National Dementia Strategy*, London: Department of Health.

DH (2010) *Equity and Excellence: Liberating the NHS*, London: Department of Health (Cm. 7881).

DH (2010a) *Children and Young People's Emotional Wellbeing and Mental Health National Support Team: The Learning – 'What Good Looks Like'*, London: Department of Health.

DH (2011) *Living Well with Dementia: A National Dementia Strategy – Good Practice Compendium*, London: Department of Health.

DH and HM Prison Service (2001) *Changing the Outlook: A Strategy for Developing and Modernising Mental Health Services in Prisons*, London: Department of Health.

DHSS (1980) *Organisational and Management Problems of Mental Illness Hospitals: Report of a Working Group / Chairman: T.E. Nodder*, London: Department of Health and Social Security.

DHSS (1981) *Care in the Community: A Consultative Document on Moving Resources for Care in England*, London: Department of Health and Social Security.

DHSS (1988) *Community Care: Agenda for Action*, London: HMSO.

Dickinson, C., Lombardo, C., Pearson, P., Barnes, D. and Bailey, D. (2008) 'Mapping New Roles in Mental Health Services; The Development of Four New Mental Health Roles from 2004–2006', *Journal of Mental Health Training, Education and Practice*, 3(1), pp. 4–11.

Docherty, J. P. (1997) 'Barriers to the Diagnosis of Depression in Primary Care', *Journal of Clinical Psychiatry*, 58 (suppl. 1), pp. 5–10.

Downey, R. (2002) 'No One to Turn To', *Community Care*, 1–7th August 2002, pp. 30–34.

Duggan, C. (1997) 'Assessing Risk in the Mentally Disordered: Introduction', *British Journal of Psychiatry*, 170 (Supplement 32), pp. 1–3.

Duncan, J. (2003) 'Healthcare Professionals to Child and Adolescent Mental Health Clinicians: Developing a Generic Profession', *The Mental Health Review*, 8(2), pp. 26–29.

Durcan, G. (2006) 'Equivalent to What? Mental Health Care in Britain's Prisons', *The Journal of Mental Health Training, Education and Practice*, 1(4), pp. 36–48.

Dym, B. and Berman, S. (1986) 'The Primary Health Care Team: Family Physician and Family Therapist in Joint Practice', *Family Systems Medicine*, 4, pp. 9–21.

Engel, C. and Gursky, E. (2003) 'Management and Interprofessional Collaboration', in Lethard, A. (ed.), *Interprofessional Collaboration: From Policy to Practice*, Hove: Brunner-Routledge, pp. 44–55.

Engel, G. L. (1977) 'The Need for a New Medical Model: A Challenge for Biomedicine', *Science*, 8, pp. 129–136.

Engel, G. L. (1980) 'The Clinical Application of the Biopsychosocial Model', *American Journal of Psychiatry*, 137, pp. 535–544.

England, E. and Lester, H. (2005) 'Integrated Mental Health Services in England: A Policy Paradox', *International Journal of Integrated Care*, 5(3) [online]. Available at: http://www.ncbi.nlm.nih.gov/pmc/articles/PMC1475728/pdf/ijic2005-200524. pdf (Accessed 9 June 2011).

Falkov, A. (1996) *A Study of Working Together Part 8 Reports: Fatal Child Abuse and Parental Psychiatric Disorder*, London, Department of Health.

Falkov, A. (ed.)(1998) *Crossing Bridges: Training Resources for Working with Mentally Ill Parents and their Children. Reader – for Managers*, London: Department of Health.

Farrell, M., Schmitt, M. and Heinemann, G. (2001) 'Informal Roles and the States of Interdisciplinary Team Development', *Journal of Interprofessional Care*, 15(4), pp. 281–95.

Felton, A. and Stickley, T. (2004) 'Pedagogy, Power and Service User Involvement', *Journal of Psychiatric and Mental Health Nursing*, 11(1), pp. 89–98.

Finch, J. (2000) 'Interprofessional Education and Teamworking: A View from the Education Providers', *British Medical Journal*, 321, pp. 1138–1140.

Fiorentine, R., Pilati, M. L. and Hillhouse, M. P. (1999) 'Drug Treatment Outcomes: Investigating the Long-term Effects of Sexual and Physical Abuse Histories', *Journal of Psychoactive Drugs*, 31(4), pp. 363–372.

Fleury, M-J, Bamvita, J-M. and Tremblay, J. (2009) 'Variables Associated with General Practitioners Taking on Serious Mental Disorder Patients', *BMC Family Practice*, 10(41), 1471–2296.

Fortune, T. (2000) 'Occupational Therapists: Is Our Therapy Truly Occupational or Are We Merely Filling Gaps?', *British Journal of Occupational Therapy*, 63, pp. 225–230.

Foster, A. (1998) 'Thinking About Risk', in Foster, A. and Roberts, V. Z. (eds), *Managing Mental Health in the Community: Chaos and Containment*, London; New York: Routledge, pp. 85–96.

Freeman, G., Weaver, T., Low, J. and de Jonge, E. (2002) *Promoting Continuity of Care for People with Severe Mental Illness Whose Needs Span Primary, Secondary and Social Care: A Report for NCCSDP*, London: NCCSDP.

Fulford, K. W. M., Williamson, T. and Woodbridge, K. (2002) 'Values-added Practice (a Values-Awareness Workshop)', *Mental Health Today*, October, pp. 25–27.

Garcia, C. V. and Penketh, K. (2007) *Listen Up! Person-centred Approaches to Help Young People Experiencing Mental Health and Emotional Problems*, London: Mental Health Foundation.

Glasby, J. and Lester, H. (2004) 'Cases for Change in Mental Health: Partnership Working in Mental Health Services', *Journal of Interprofessional Care*, 18(1), pp. 7–16.

Glasby, J., Lester, H., Briscoe, J., Clark, M., Rose, S. and England, L. (2003) *Cases for Change: Community Services*, London: National Institute for Mental Health.

Glasby, J. and Littlechild, L. (2004) *The Health and Social Care Divide: The Experiences of Older People*, Bristol: Policy.

Glendinning, C. (2003) 'Breaking Down Barriers: Integrating Health and Care Services for Older People in England', *Health Policy*, 65(2), pp. 139–51.

Golightly, M. (2006) *Social Work and Mental Health*, 2nd edn, Exeter: Learning Matters.

Gordon, S. (2005) 'The Role of the Consumer in the Leadership and Management of Mental Health Services', *Australasian Psychiatry*, 13(4), pp. 362–365.

Gosling, J. (2010) 'The Ethos of Involvement as a Route to Recovery', in Weinstein, J. (ed.), *Mental Health Service User Involvement and Recovery*, London: Jessica Kingsley Publishers, pp. 30–44.

Gray, R., Parr, A-M., Plummer, S., Sandford, T., Ritter, S., Mundt-Leach, R., Goldberg, D. and Gournay, K. (1999) 'A National Survey of Practice Nurse Involvement in Mental Health Interventions', *Journal of Advanced Nursing*, 30(4), pp. 901–906.

Great Britain. *National Health Service and Community Care Act 1990: Elizabeth II, Chapter 19* (1990), London: HMSO.

Great Britain. *Carers (Recognition and Services) Act 1995: Elizabeth II. Chapter 12* (1995), London: HMSO.

Great Britain. *Mental Health (Patients in the Community) Act: Elizabeth II. Chapter 52* (1995), London: HMSO.

Great Britain. *Health Act 1999: Elizabeth II. Chapter 8* (1999), London: Stationary Office.

Great Britain. *Mental Health Act 2007: Elizabeth II. Chapter 12 Explanatory Notes* (2007), London: The Stationary Office.

Gregson, B., Cartlidge, A. and Bond, J. (1992) 'Development of a Measure of Professional Collaboration in Primary Health Care', *Journal of Epidemiology and Community Health*, 46, pp. 48–53.

Grella, C. E. (1997) 'Services for Perinatal Women with Substance Abuse and Mental Health Disorders: The Unmet Need', *Journal of Psychoactive Drugs*, 29(1), pp. 67–78.

Groves, P. and Farrell, M. (1996) 'Coping with Drug and Alcohol Misuse in', Watkins, M., Hervey, N., Carson, J. and Ritter, S. (eds), *Collaborative Community Mental Health Care,* London: Arnold, pp. 180–196.

Grumbach, K. and Coffman, J. (1998) 'Physicians and Nonphysician Clinicians: Complements or Competitors?', *Journal of the American Medical Association*, 280, pp. 825–826.

Guck, T. P., Guck, A. J., Brack, A. B. and Frey, D. R. (2007) 'No-Show Rates in Partially Integrated Models of Behavioural Health Care in a Primary Setting', *Families Systems & Health*, 25(2), pp. 137–146.

Gupta, N. (1995) 'Keyworkers and the Care Programme Approach: The Role and Responsibilities of Community Workers', *Psychiatric Care*, 1(6), pp. 239–242.

Hagebak, J. E. and Hagebak, B. R. (1980) 'Serving the Mental Health Needs of the Elderly: The Case for Removing Barriers and Improving Service Integration', *Community Mental Health Journal*, 16(4), pp. 263–275.

Hamer, S. and McNichol, E. (eds) (2006) *Leadership and Management: A 3-dimensional Approach*, Cheltenham: Nelson Thornes (Expanding nursing and health care practice).

Hamilton, L. (1996) *Audit of Patients with Schizophrenia on Depot Neuroleptics*, York: North Yorkshire Medical Audit Advisory Group.

Hammersley, R. H., Forsyth, A. J. M. and Lavelle, T. L. (1990) 'The Criminality of New Drug Users in Glasgow', *British Journal of Addiction*, 85(12), pp. 1583–1594.

Hammond, K. R. (1978) 'Toward Increasing Competence of Thought in Public Policy Formation', in Hammond, K. R. (ed.), *Judgement and Decision Making in Public Policy Formation*, Boulder, CO: West View Press.

Hannigan, B. (1999) 'Joint Working in Community Mental Health: Prospects and Challenges', *Health and Social Care in the Community*, 7(1), pp. 25–31.

Harrison, D., Dickinson, C., Bailey, D., Hall, A., Lavelle, M., McAnelly, A. and Watkins, H. (In preparation) '"A Learning Curve From Both Sides": The Impact of Service User and Carer Involvement in a National Study of Mental Health Workforce Change'.

Harrison, P. A., Martin, J. A., Tuasan, V. B. and Hoffmann, N. (1985) 'Conjoint Treatment of Dual Disorders', in Alterman, A. I. (ed.), *Substance Abuse and Psychopathology*, New York: Plenum.

Haswell, S. and Bailey, D. (2007) 'What is the Role of a Hospital Service User's Representative Scheme for Promoting Service User Involvement in Mental Health Care Delivery?', *Journal of Mental Health Workforce Development*, 2(1), pp. 12–22

Hawker, S. and Hawkins, J. M. (eds)(1995) *The Oxford Popular English Dictionary and Thesaurus*, Bath: Parragon.

Hayes, J. (2002) *The Theory and Practice of Change Management*, Basingstoke: Palgrave.

Health Education Authority (1997) *Mental Health Promotion: A Quality Framework*, London: Health Education Authority.

Hewstone, M. and Brown, R. (1986) 'Contact is not Enough: An Intergroup Perspective on the Contact Hypothesis', in Hewstone, M. and Brown, R. (eds) *Contact and Conflict in Intergroup Encounters*, Oxford: Blackwell, pp. 3–44.

Hickey, G. and Kipping, C. (1998) 'Exploring the Concept of User Involvement in Mental Health Through a Participation Continuum', *Journal of Clinical Nursing*, 7(1), pp. 83–88.

Hinshelwood, R. D. (1998) 'Creatures of Each Other: Some Historical Considerations of Responsibility and Care, and Some Present Undercurrents', in Foster, A. and Roberts, V. Z. (eds), *Managing Mental Health in the Community: Chaos and Containment in Community Care*, London: Routledge, pp. 15–26.

Horder, J. (2003) 'Forward', in Lethard, A. (ed.), *Interprofessional Collaboration: From Policy to Practice in Health and Social Care*, Hove: Brunner Routledge, p. xiii–xiv.

Hosking, D-M. and Morley, I. (1991) *A Social Psychology of Organizing: People Processes and Contexts*, Hemel Hempstead: Harvester Wheatsheaf.

Hudson, B. (1987) 'Collaboration in Social Welfare: A Framework for Analysis', *Policy and Politics*, 15(3), pp. 175–182.

Ignatavicius, D. and Hausman, K. A. (1995) *Clinical Pathways for Collaborative Practice*, Philadelphia; London: Saunders.

Ingram, R. (2004) *Towards No Secrets: The Use of Multi-agency Policies and Procedures to Protect Mental Health Service Users from Abuse*, London: Jessica Kingsley Publishers.

James, G. (1994) *Study of Working Together Part 8 Reports*, London: Department of Health.

Jarvis, T. J. and Copeland, J. (1997) 'Child Sexual Abuse as a Predictor of Psychiatric Co-morbidity and its Implications for Drug and Alcohol Treatment', *Drug and Alcohol Dependence*, 49(1), pp. 61–69.

Jones, A. (2001) 'Hospital Care Pathways for Patients with Schizophrenia', *Journal of Clinical Nursing*, 10(1), pp. 58–69.

Jones, A. and Bowles, N. (2005) 'Best Practice from Admission to Discharge in Acute Inpatient Care: Considerations and Standards from a Whole System Perspective', *Journal of Psychiatric and Mental Health Nursing*, 12(6), pp. 642–647.

Jones, R. V. H. (1992) 'Teamwork in Primary Care: How Much Do We Know About It?', *Journal of Interprofessional Care*, 6(1), pp. 25–29.

Judge, J., Harty, M-A. and Fahy, T. (2004) 'Survey of Community Forensic Psychiatry Services in England and Wales', *The Journal of Forensic Psychiatry and Psychology*, 15(2), pp. 244–253.

Kahneman, D., Slovic, P. and Tversky, A. (eds) (1982) *Judgement Under Uncertainty: Heuristics and Biases*, Cambridge: Cambridge University Press.

Katz, A. (1999) *Leading Lads*, East Molesey: Young Voice.

Kauffman, C., Grunebaum, H., Cohler, B and Gamer, E. (1979) 'Superkids: Competent Children of Psychotic Mothers', *American Journal of Psychiatry*, 136(11), pp. 1398–1402.

Keene, J. (1997) *Drug Misuse: Prevention, Harm Minimisation and Treatment*, London: Chapman and Hall.

Keene, J. (2001) *Clients with Complex Needs: Interprofessional Practice*, Oxford: Blackwell Science.

Kemp, P. (2010) 'Introduction to Mental Health Service User Involvement', in Weinstein, J. (ed.), *Mental Health Service User Involvement and Recovery*, London: Jessica Kingsley Publishers, pp. 15–29.

Kent, H. and Read, J. (1998) 'Measuring Consumer Participation in Mental Health Services: Are Attitudes Related to Professional Orientation?', *International Journal of Social Psychiatry,* 44(4), pp. 295–310.

Knapp, M., Cambridge, P., Thomason, C., Allen, C., Beecham, J. and Darton, R. (1992) *Care in the Community: Challenge and Demonstration,* Aldershot: Ashgate.

Kodner, D. and Spreeuwenberg, C. (2002) 'Integrated Care: Meaning, Logic, Applications and Implications – A Discussion Paper', *International Journal of Integrated Care,* 2(1), 14 November 2002.

Koffman, J., Fulop, N., Pashley, D. and Coleman, K. (1996) 'No Way Out: The Delayed Discharge of Elderly Mentally Ill Acute and Assessment Patients in North and South Thames Regions', *Age & Aging,* 25(4), pp. 268–272.

Kolb, D. A. (1984) *Experiential Learning: Experience as the Source of Learning and Development,* Englewood Cliffs, New Jersey: Prentice-Hall.

Krausz, M. (1996) 'Old Problems – New Perspectives', *European Addiction Research,* 2, pp. 1–2.

Kur, E. (1996) 'The Faces Model of High Performing Team Development', *Management Development Review,* 9(6), pp. 25–35.

Lee, M. (2006) *Promoting Mental Health and Well Being in Later Life: A First Report from the UK Inquiry into Mental Health and Well-being in Later Life,* London: Age Concern and the Mental Health Foundation.

Lee, M. (2007) *Improving Services and Support for People with Mental Health Problems: The Second Report from the UK Inquiry into Mental Health and Well-being in Later Life,* London: Age Concern.

Leichsenring, K. (2006) 'Providing Integrated Health and Social Care for Older Persons, a European Overview', in Leichsenning, K. and Alaszewski, A. M., *Providing Integrated Health and Social Care for Older Persons, A European Overview of Issues at Stake,* Aldershot: Ashgate (Public policy and social welfare, v. 28).

Lesser, J. F. (2000) 'Clinical Social Work and Family Medicine: A Partnership in Community Service', *Health and Social Work,* 25, pp. 119–126.

Lester, H. (2005) 'Shared Care for People with Mental Illness: A GP's Perspective', *Advances in Psychiatric Treatment,* 11, pp. 133–139.

Lethard, A. (2003) 'Introduction', in Lethard, A. (ed.), *Interprofessional Collaboration: From Policy to Practice,* Hove: Brunner- Routledge, pp. 3–11.

Leutz, W. N. (1999) 'Five Laws for Integrating Medical and Social Services: Lessons from the United States and the United Kingdom', *The Milbank Quarterly,* 77(1), pp. 77–110.

Lloyd, M. (2007) 'Empowerment in the Interpersonal Field: Discourses of Acute Mental Health Nurses', *Journal of Psychiatric and Mental Health Nursing,* 14(5), pp. 485–494.

Lloyd, M. (2010) *A Practical Guide to Care Planning in Health and Social Care,* Maidenhead: Open University Press.

Loxley, A. (1997) *Collaboration in Health and Welfare: Working with Difference,* London: Jessica Kingsley Publishers.

MacDonald, A., Carpenter, I., Box, O., Roberts, A. and Sahu, S. (2002) 'Dementia and the Use of Psychotropic Medication in Non-Elderly Mentally Infirm Nursing Homes in South-East England', *Age and Ageing,* 311), pp. 58–64.

Mann, A. H., Schneider, J., Mozley, C. G., Levin, E., Blizard, R., Netten, A., Kharicha, K., Egelstaff, R., Abbey, A. and Todd, C. (2000) 'Depression and the Response of Residential Homes to Physical Health Needs', *International journal of Geriatric Psychiatry,* 15 (12), pp. 1105–1112.

Margallo-Lana, M., Swann, A., O'Brian, J., Fairbairn, A., Reichelt, K., Potkins, D., Mynt, P. and Ballard, C. (2001) 'Prevalence and Pharmacological Management of Behavioural and Psychiatric Symptoms Amongst Dementia Sufferers Living in Care Environments', *International Journal of Geriatric Psychiatry,* 16(1), pp. 39–44.

Marshall, M., Preston, M., Scott, E. and Wincott, P. (eds) (1979) *Teamwork For and Against: An Appraisal of Multidisciplinary Practice,* London: British Association of Social Workers.

Mauksch, L. B. and Leahy, D. (1993) 'Collaboration Between Primary Care Medicine and Mental Health in an MHO', *Family Systems Medicine,* 11(2), pp. 121–135.

Mayes, K., Diggins, M. and Falkov, A. (1998) *Crossing Bridges: Training Resources for Working with Mentally Ill Parents and Their Children,* London: Department of Health.

McAndrew, S. and Samociuk, G. A. (2003) 'Reflecting Together: Developing a New Strategy for Continuous Involvement in Mental Health Nurse Education', *Journal of Psychiatric and Mental Health Nursing,* 10(5), pp. 616–621.

McCann, G. (1999) 'Care of Mentally Disordered Offenders', *Mental Health Care,* 3(2), pp. 65–67.

McClean, T. (2005) 'Interdisciplinary Practice', in Lishman, J. (ed.), *Handbook for Practice Learning in Social Work and Social Care: Knowledge and Theory,* 2nd edn, London: Jessica Kingsley Publishers.

McCurry, P. (2002) 'Mind the Gap', *Community Care,* 5–11 September, pp. 28–29.

McGrath, M. (1991) *Multi-disciplinary Teamwork: Community Mental Handicap Teams,* Aldershot: Avebury.

McNichol, E. (2007) 'Understanding Yourself as a Leader', in Hamer, S. and McNichol, E. (eds), *Leadership and Management: A 3-dimenional Approach,* Cheltenham: Nelson Thornes (Expanding nursing and health care practice), pp. 23–51.

McQueen, J. and Milloy, S. (2001) 'Why Clinical Guidelines or Care Pathways in Mental Health?', *Journal of Integrated Care Pathways,* 5(2), pp. 44–53.

McWhinney, I. (1997) *A Textbook Of Family Medicine,* 2nd edn, New York/Oxford: Oxford University Press.

Meltzer, H., Gatward, R., Goodman, R. and Ford, T. (2000) *Mental Health of Children and Adolescents in Great Britain: The Report of a Survey Carried Out in 1999 by Social Survey Division of the Office for National Statistics on Behalf of the Department of Health, the Scottish Health Executive and the National Assembly for Wales,* London: The Stationary Office.

Mental Health Foundation (1997) *Knowing Our Own Minds: A Survey of How People in Emotional Distress Take Control of Their Own Lives,* London: Mental Health Foundation.

Milewa, T., Dowswell, G. and Harrison, S. (2002) 'Partnerships, Power and the "New" Politics of Community Participation in British Health Care', *Social Policy and Administration*, 36(7), pp. 796–809.

Miller, C. and Freeman, M. (2003) 'Clinical Teamwork: The Impact of Policy on Collaborative Practice', in Lethard, A. (ed.), *Interprofessional Collaboration: From Policy to Practice*, Hove: Brunner-Routledge, pp. 121–132.

Miller, W. R. and Rollnick, S. (1991) *Motivational Interviewing: Preparing People to Change Addictive Behaviour*, New York: Guilford Press.

Milne, D. L., Keegan, D., Westerman, C. and Dudley, M. (2000) 'Systematic Process and Outcome Evaluation of Brief Staff Training in Psychosocial Interventions for Severe Mental Illness', *Journal of Behaviour Therapy and Experimental Psychiatry*, 31, pp. 87–101.

Mistral, W. and Velleman, R. (1997) 'CMHTs: The Professional's Choice?', *Journal of Mental Health*, 6(2), pp. 125–140.

Mohan, R., Slade, M. and Fahy, T. A. (2004) 'Clinical Characteristics of Community Forensic Mental Health Services', *Psychiatric Services*, 55(11), pp. 1294–1298.

Moore, B. (1996) *Risk Assessment: A Practitioner's Guide to Predicting Harmful Behaviour*, London: Whiting and Birch.

Morgan, S. (1996) *Helping Relationships in Mental Health*, London: Chapman and Hall.

Morgan, S. (1998) *Assessing and Managing Risk: A Training Pack for Practitioners and Managers of Comprehensive Mental Health Services*, Brighton: Pavilion Publishing.

Morgan, S. (2000) *Clinical Risk Management: A Clinical Tool and Practitioner Manual*, London: Sainsbury Centre for Mental Health.

Moxley, R. S. (2001) 'Leadership as Partnership', in Spears, L. C. and Lawrence, M. (eds), *Focus on Leadership: Servant-leadership for the 21st Century*, 3rd edn, New York: J. Wiley and Sons, pp. 47–52.

Mullen, P. E. (1984) 'Mental Disorder and Dangerousness', *Australian and New Zealand Journal of Psychiatry*, 18(1), pp. 8–17.

Myers, S. (2008) *Solution-Focused Approaches*, Lyme Regis: Russell House Publishing.

Najavits, L. M., Weiss, R. D. and Shaw, S. R. (1999) 'A Clinical Profile of Women with Posttraumatic Stress Disorder and Substance Dependence', *Psychology of Addictive Behaviours*, 13(2), pp. 98–104.

National Institute for Mental Health in England (NIMHE) (2003) *Redesigning Mental Health Access Booking and Choice Service Improvement Guide*, Leeds: NIMHE.

National Institute for Mental Health in England: North West Development Centre (2004) *Primary Care Graduate Mental Health Workers: A Practical Guide*, Hyde: National Institute for Mental Health in England.

National Treatment Agency (2006) *Models of Care for Treatment of Adult Drug Misusers: Update 2006*, London: National Treatment Agency.

Nettle, M. (1993) 'How Much Do You Value Our Experiences?', *Openmind*, (62), pp. 18–19.

Newnes, C., Holmes, G. and Dunn, C. (2001) *This is Madness Too. Critical Perspectives on Mental Health Services*, Ross-on-Wye: PCCS Books.

NHS Executive and HM Prison Service (1999) *The Future Organisation of Prison Health Care: Report by the Joint Prison Service and National Health Service Executive Working Group*, London: Department of Health.

NHS Health Advisory Service (1995) *Child and Adolescent Mental Health Services: Together We Stand; The Commissioning Role and Management of Child and Adolescent Mental Health Services*, London: HMSO.

NHSME (1993) *Nursing in Primary Care – New World New Opportunities*, Leeds: National Health Service Management Executive.

NICE (2006) *Guideline to Improve the Care of People with Dementia*, [CG42], London: National Institute for Health and Clinical Excellence.

Nies, H. (2006) 'Managing Effective Partnerships in Older People's Services', *Health and Social Care in the Community*, 14(5), pp. 391–399.

Nixon, B., Hooton, S. and Jones, A. (2008) 'Child and Adolescent Mental Health Services (CAMHS): Providing Services for Children and Young People with Learning Disabilities', *Journal of Mental Health, Education and Training Practice*, 3(3), pp. 39–52.

Nixon, C, and Northrup, D. (1997) *Evaluating Mental Health Services: How Do Programmes for Children 'Work' in the Real World?* Thousand Oaks, CA: Sage.

Northumberland Health Authority (1996) *Report to the Northumberland Health Authority of the Independent Inquiry Team into the Care and Treatment of Richard Stoker*, Morpeth: Northumberland, Northumberland Health Authority.

Norton, K. and Dolan, B. (1996) 'Personality Disorder and Parenting', in Gopfert, M., Webster, J. and Seeman, M. V. (eds) *Parental Psychiatric Disorder: Distressed Parents and Their Families*, Cambridge: Cambridge University Press.

Office for National Statistics (1999) *Social Focus on Older People*, London: Stationary Office.

Oliver, J., Huxley, P., Bridges, K. and Mohamad, H. (1996) *Quality of Life and Mental Health Services*, London: Routledge.

Onyett, S. (2003) *Teamworking in Mental Health*, Basingstoke/New York: Palgrave Macmillan.

Onyett, S. R. and Ford, R. (1996) 'Community Mental Health Teams – Where's the Wreckage?', *Journal of Mental Health*, 5(1), pp. 47–55.

Onyett, S. R., Heppleston, T. and Muijen, M. (1995) *Making Community Mental Health Teams Work*, London: Sainsbury Centre for Mental Health.

O'Rourke, M. and Bird, L. (2001) *Risk Management in Mental Health: A Practical Guide to Individual Care and Community Safety*, London: Mental Health Foundation.

Øvretveit, J. (1993) *Coordinating Community Care: Multidisciplinary Teams and Care Management*. London; Philadelphia: Open University Press.

Owers, M. et al. (1999) *Learning How to Make Children Safer: An Analysis for the Welsh Office of Serious Child Abuse Cases in Wales*, University of East Anglia/ Welsh Office.

Paterson, S., Moore, S. and Woodall, J. (2007) 'Exercise Referral and Offender Management in Relation to Mental Health: An Example from HMP Everthorpe', *The Journal of Mental Health Training, Education and Practice*, 2(3), pp. 23–24.

Patton, M. Q. (1990) *Qualitative Evaluation and Research Methods,* 2nd edn, Newbury Park, CA: Sage.

Paykel, E. S. and Priest, R. G. (1992) 'Recognition and Management of Depression in General Practice: Consensus Statement', *British Medical Journal,* 305(6863), pp. 1198–1202.

Pearsall, A. and Yates, L. (2004) 'Carer Perspectives', in Ryan, T. and Pritchard, J. (eds), *Good Practice in Adult Mental Health,* London: Jessica Kingsley Publishers, pp. 229–244.

Peck, E. (2002) 'Integrating Health and Social Care: Commentaries on the Case Studies in MCC 10.2', *MCC Building Knowledge for Integrated Care,* 10(3), 16–19, [online]. Available at: https://pierprofessional.metapress.com/content/rpm8n04454288862/resource-secured/?target=fulltext.pdfn (accessed 9 June 2011).

Peck, E., Gulliver, P. and Towel, D. (2002) 'Information, Consultation or Control: User Involvement in Mental Health Services in England at the Turn of the Century', *Journal of Mental Health,* 11(4), pp. 441–451.

Peck, E., Gulliver, P. and Towel, D. (2002) *Modernising Partnerships: An Evaluation of Somerset's Innovations in the Commissioning and Organisation of Mental Health Services,* London: Institute for Applied Health Social Policy, King's College.

Perkins, R. and Repper, J. (1998) *Dilemmas in Community Mental Health Practice: Choice or Control,* Abingdon: Radcliffe Medical Press.

Perkins, R. and Repper, J. (1998) 'Principles of Working with People Who Experience Mental Health Problems', in Brooker, C. and Repper, J. (eds), *Serious Mental Health Problems in the Community,* Policy, Practice & Research. London: Balliere Tindall.

Petersen, A. C. and Leffert, N. (1995) 'Developmental Issues Influencing Guidelines for Adolescent Health Research: A Review', *Journal of Adolescent Health,* 17(5), pp. 298–305.

Petersen, I. (2000) 'Comprehensive Integrated Primary Mental Health Care for South Africa. Pipedream or Possibility?', *Social Science & Medicine,* 51(3), pp. 321–334.

Pilgrim, D. and Rogers, A. (1996) *A Sociology of Mental Health and Illness,* Buckingham: The Open University.

Polak, P. (1993) 'Recovery from Mental Illness: The Guiding Vision of the Mental Health Service System in the 1990s', *Psychosocial Rehabilitation Journal,* 16(4), pp. 11–24.

Prochaska, J. O. and DiClemente, C. C. (1992) 'Stages of Change in the Modification of Problem Behaviors', in Hersen, M., Eisler, R. M. and Miller, P. M. (eds), *Progress in Behavior Modification,* Sycamore Press, Sycamore, IL: Sycamore Press, pp. 184–214.

Public Health Insititute for Scotland (2003) *Needs Assessment on Child and Adolescent Mental Health: Final Report May-2003,* Glasgow, Public Health Institute for Scotland.

Quinton, D., Gulliver, L. and Rutter, M. (1995) 'A 15–20 Year Follow-up of Adult Psychiatric Patients: Psychiatric Disorder and Social Functioning', *British Journal of Psychiatry,* 167(8), pp. 315–323.

Ramon, S. and Williams, J. E. (2005) 'Towards a Conceptual Framework: The Meanings Attached to the Psychosocial, the Promise and the Problems', in Ramon, S. and Williams, J. E. (eds), *Mental Health At the Crossroads: The promise of the Psychosocial Approach*, Aldershot: Ashgate, pp. 13–24.

Rawson, D. (1994) 'Models of Interprofessional Work: Likely Theories and Possibilities', in Lethard, A. (ed.), *Going Interprofessional: Working Together for Health and Welfare*, London: Routledge.

Reed, J. (1997) 'Risk Assessment and Clinical Risk Management: The Lessons from Recent Inquires', *British Journal of Psychiatry*, 170 (Supplement 32), pp. 4–7.

Rees, G., Huby, G., McDade, L. and McKechnie, L. (2004) 'Joint Working in Community Mental Health Teams: Implementation of an Integrated Care Pathway', *Health and Social Care in the Community*, 12(6), pp. 527–536.

Reith, M. (1998) *Community Care Tragedies: A Practice Guide to Mental Health Inquiries*, Birmingham: Ventura.

Repper, J., Felton, A., Hanson, B., Stickley, T. and Shaw, T. (2001) 'One Small Step Towards Equality', *Mental Health Today*, December 24–27.

Rethink (2009) 'Supporting Young People with Mental Health Problems', *Rethink Policy Statement 8*, London: Rethink.

Robert, G., Hardacre, J., Locock, L., Bate, P. and Glasby, J. (2003) 'Redesigning Mental Health Services: Lessons on User Involvement from the Mental Health Collaborative', *Health Expectations,* 6(1), pp. 60–71.

Roberts, V. Z. (1999) 'Is Authority a Dirty Word?', in Foster, A. and Roberts, V. Z. (eds), *Managing Mental Health in the Community: Chaos and Containment*, London/New York: Routledge, pp. 49–60.

Richards, G. and Horder, W. (1999) 'Mental Health Training: the Process of Collaboration', *Social Work Education,* 18(4), pp. 449–458.

Robinson, G., Beaton, S. and White, P. (1993) 'Attitudes Towards Practice Nurses – Survey of a Sample of General Practitioners in England and Wales', *British Journal of General Practice*, 43(366), pp. 25–29.

Rorstad, P. and Checinski, K. (1996) *Dual Diagnosis: Facing the Challenge – The Care of People with a Dual Diagnosis of Mental Illness and Substance Misuse*, Kenley, Great Britain: Wynne Howard.

Rose, D., Ford, R., Lindley, P., Gawith, L. and Kensington Chelsea and Westminster Mental Health Monitoring Users' Group (1998) *In Our Experience: User-focused Monitoring of Mental Health,* London: The Sainsbury Centre for Mental Health.

Rosenberg, S. D., Drake, R. E., Wolford, G. L., Mueser, K. T., Oxman, T. E., Vidaver, R. M., Carrieri, K. L. and Luckoor, R. (1998) 'Dartmouth Assessment of Life Instrument (DALI): A Substance Use Disorder Screen for People with Severe Mental Illness', *American Journal of Psychiatry,* 155(2), pp. 232–238.

Ross, F. (1992) 'Barriers to Learning', *Nursing Times,* 88(38), pp. 44–45.

Rothmann, A. A. and Wagner, E. H. (2003) 'Chronic Illness Management: What is the Role of Primary Care?', *Annals of Internal Medicine*, 138(3), pp. 256–262.

Rowe, R. and Shepherd, M. (2002) 'Public Participation in the New NHS: No Closer to Citizen Control', *Social Policy and Administration*, 36(3), pp. 275–290.

Royal College of Psychiatrists (2006) *Raising the Standard: Specialist Services for Older People with Mental Illness*, London: Royal College of Psychiatrists.

Ryan, P., Ford, R. and Clifford, P. (1991) *Case Management and Community Care*, London: Research and Development for Psychiatry.

Ryan, T. (1997) 'Risk Management and People with Mental Health Problems', in Kemshall, H. and Pritchard, J. (eds.), *Good Practice in Risk Management 1*, London: Jessica Kingsley Publishers, pp. 93–108.

Ryglewicz, H. and Pepper, B. (1992) 'The Dual Disorder Client: Mental Disorder and Substance User', in Cooper, S. and Lentner, T. H. (eds), *Innovations in Community Mental Health*, Sarasota, FL: Professional Resource Press.

Sainsbury Centre for Mental Health (2001) *The Capable Practitioner: A Framework and List of the Practitioner Capabilities Required to Implement the National Service Framework for Mental Health*, London: Sainsbury Centre for Mental Health.

Sainsbury Centre for Mental Health (2006) *Our Choices in Mental Health: Improving Choice for People Who Use Mental Health Services and their Carers (Briefing 31)*, London: Sainsbury Centre for Mental Health.

Sayce, L. (1989) 'Community Mental Health Centres – Rhetoric and Reality', in Brackx, A. and Grimshaw, C. (eds), *Mental Health Care in Crisis*, London: Pluto, pp. 158–174.

Scheid, T. L. (1996) 'Burned Out Emotional Labourers: An Analysis of Emotional Labour, Work Identity and Burnout', *The American Sociological Association Meeting*, 1996, New York.

Scottish Executive 2005, *Getting the Workforce Right: A Review of the Child and Adolescent Mental Health Workforce*, Scottish Executive, Edinburgh.

Secker, J., Pidd, F., Parham, A. and Peck, E. (2000) 'Mental Health in the Community: Roles, Responsibilities and Organization of Primary Care and Specialist Services', *Journal of Interprofessional Care*, 14(1), pp. 49–58.

Shaw, J., Appleby, L. and Baker, D. (2003) *Safer Prisons: A National Study of Prison Suicides, 1999–2000 by the National Confidential Inquiry into Suicides and Homicides by People with Mental Illness*, London: Department of Health.

Shepherd, G., King, C., Tilbury, J. and Fowler, D. (1995) 'Implementing the Care Programme Approach', *Journal of Mental Health*, 4(3), pp. 261–274.

Shia, N. and Marriott, S. (2002) 'Introducing a Mental Health Training Programme For Practice Nurses', *Mental Health Practice*, 5(5), pp. 36–38.

Shiers, D. (2001) 'Preface, A Family-centred Approach to Integrated and Community-based Mental Healthcare', in Chambers, R., Boath, E. and Wakley, G. (eds), *Mental Healthcare Matters in Primary Care*, Abingdon: Radcliffe Medical Press, p. vi–viii.

Silverman, M. (1989) 'Children of Psychiatrically Ill Parents: A Prevention Perspective', *Hospital and Community Psychiatry*, 40, pp. 1257–1265.

Simpson, A. (1999) 'Creating Alliances: The Views of Users and Carers on the Education and Training Needs of Community Mental Health Nurses', *Journal of Psychiatric and Mental Health Nursing*, 6(5), pp. 347–356.

Smith, J. A. and Osborn, M. (2003) 'Interpretative Phenomenological Analysis', in Smith, J. (ed.), *Qualitative Psychology: A Practical Guide to Research Methods*, London: Sage, pp. 51–80.

Smith, L. and Bailey, D. (2010) 'What Are the Barriers and Support Systems For Service User-Led Research? Implications for Practice', *Journal of Mental Health Education, Training and Practice*, 5(1), pp. 35–44.

Smith, M. and Beazley, M. (2000) 'Progressive Regimes, Partnerships and the Involvement of Local Communities: A Framework for Evaluation', *Public Administration*, 78(4), pp. 855–878.

Social Exclusion Unit (2002) *Reducing Re-offending by Ex-prisoners*, London: Social Exclusion Unit.

Social Services Inspectorate (2003) *Improving Older People's Services: An Overview of Performance*, London: Department of Health.

Stein, M. A. and Test, L. I. (1978) 'Community Treatment of the Chronic Patient', *Schizophrenia Bulletin*, 4(3), pp. 350–364.

Stickley, T. (2006) 'Should Service User Involvement Be Consigned to History? A Critical Realist Perspective', *Journal of Psychiatric and Mental Health Nursing*, 13(5), pp. 570–577.

Stone, H. and Taylor, A. (2000) 'Forensic Psychiatry Services', in Gregoire, A. (ed.), *Adult Severe Mental Illness*, London: Greenwich Medical Media Ltd., pp. 257–282.

Strathdee, G. and Jenkins, R. (1996) 'Purchasing Mental Health Care for Primary Care', in Thornicroft, G. and Strathdee, G. (eds), *Commissioning Mental Health Services*, London: HMSO, pp. 71–84.

Swanson, J. W., Holzer, C. E., Ganju, V. K. and Jono, R. T. (1990) 'Violence and Psychiatric Disorder in the Community: Evidence from the Epidemiologic Catchment Area Surveys', *Hospital and Community Psychiatry*, 41(7), pp. 761–770.

Telford, R., Boote, J. D., and Cooper, C. L. (2004) 'What Does It Mean to Involve Consumers Successfully in NHS Research? A Consensus Study', *Health Expectations*, 7(3), pp. 209–220.

Thomas, P. (1994) *The Liverpool Primary Health Care Facilitation Project 1989–1994*, Liverpool: Liverpool Family Health Services Authority.

Thornicroft, G., Rose D., Huxley, P., Dale, G. and Wykes, T. (2002) 'What are the Research Priorities of Mental Health Service Users?', *Journal of Mental Health*, 11(1), pp. 1–5.

Titterton, M. (2005) *Risk and Risk Taking in Health and Social Welfare*, London/Philadelphia: Jessica Kingsley Publishers.

Tew, J., Gell, C. and Foster, S. (2004) *Learning from Experience: Involving Service Users and Carers in Mental Health Education and Training*, Nottingham: Higher Education Academy, NIMHE and Trent Workforce Development Confederation.

Thorley, A. (1997) 'Dual Diagnosis: The Challenge of Comorbid Psychiatric Disorder and Substance Misuse', (unpublished paper) cited in Barker, I, (1998) 'Mental Illness and Substance Misuse', *The Mental Health Review*, 3(4), pp. 6–13.

Tucker, S., Hughes, J., Scott, J., Challis, D. and Burns, A. (2007) 'Commissioning Services for Older People with Mental Health Problems: Is There a Shared Vision?', *Journal of Integrated Care*, 15(2), pp. 3–12.

Tucker, S., Baldwin, R., Hughes, J., Benbow, S. M., Barker, A., Burns, A. and Challis, D. (2009) 'Integrating Mental Health Services for Older People in England – Fom Rhetoric to Reality', *Journal of Interprofessional Care*, 23(4), pp. 341–354.

Tuckman, B. W. (1965) 'Developmental Sequences in Small Groups', *Psychological Bulletin*, 63, pp. 384–399.

Tversky, A. and Kahneman, D. (1973) 'Availability: A Heuristic for Judging Frequency and Probability', *Cognitive Psychology*, 5(2), pp. 207–232.

Underdown, A. (2002) '"I'm Growing Up Too Fast": Messages from Young Carers', *Children & Society*, 16(1), pp. 57–60.

Unsworth, C. (1987) *The Politics of Mental Health Legislation*, Oxford: Clarendon Press.

Ussher, J. (2000) 'Women's Madness: A Material-Discursive-Intrapsychic Approach', in Fee, D. (ed.), *Pathology and the Postmodern: Mental Illness as Discourse and Experience*, London: Sage, pp. 207–230.

Valimaki, M. (1998) 'Psychiatric Patients' Views on the Concept of Self-determination: Findings from a Descriptive Study', *Journal of Clinical Nursing*, 7(1), 59–66.

Valios, N. (2000) 'Making a Splash', *Community Care*, 20–26 April, pp. 20–21.

Vasiliou-Theodore, C. and Penketh, K. (2008) 'Listen up! Young Peoples' Participation in Service Design and Delivery', in Jackson, C., Hill, K. and Lavis, P. (eds), *Child and Adolescent Mental Health Today: A Handbook*, Brighton: Pavilion Publishing, pp. 129–139.

Walker, S. (2001) 'Developing Child and Adolescent Mental Health Services', *Journal of Child Health Care*, 5(2), pp. 71–76.

Ward, M. and Applin, C. (1998) *The Unlearned Lesson: The Role of Alcohol and Drug Misuse in Homicides Perpetrated by People with Mental Health Problems*, London, Wynne Howard Publishing.

Warne, T. and Starke, S. (2004) 'Service Users, Metaphors and Teamworking in Mental Health', *Journal of Psychiatric and Mental Health Nursing*, 11(6), pp. 654–661.

Watkins, T. R. (1997) 'Mental Health Services to Substance Abusers', in Watkins, T. R. and Callicutt, J. W. (eds), *Mental Health Policy and Practice Today*, London: Sage.

Watts, F. and Bennett, D. (1983) 'Management of the Staff Team', in Watts, F. N. and Bennett, D. H. (eds), *Theory and Practice of Psychiatric Rehabilitation*, Chichester: Wiley.

Webb, A. and Hobdell, M. (1978) 'Co-ordination between Health and Personal Social Servces; A Question of Quality', in Carver, V. and Liddiard, P. (eds), *An Aging Population: A Reader and Sourcebook*, Sevenoaks: Hodder and Stoughton/OU Press, pp. 336–348.

Wellard, S. (2002) 'The Drugs Don't Work', *Community Care*, 31 October–6 November, pp. 32–33.

West, M. A. and Farr, J. L. (1989) 'Innovation at Work: Psychological Perspectives', *Social Behaviour*, 4, pp. 15–30.

West, M. A., and Poulton, B. C. (1997) 'A Failure of Function: Teamwork in Primary Health Care', *Journal of Interprofessional Care*, 11(2), pp. 205–216.

West Midlands Regional Health Authority (1991) *Report of the Panel of Inquiry Appointed by the West Midlands Regional Health Authority, South Birmingham Health Authority and the Special Hospitals Service Authority to Investigate the Case of Kim Kirkman*, Birmingham: West Midlands Regional Health Authority.

WHO (2001) *Mental Health, A Call to Action by World Health Ministers*, Geneva: World Health Organization.

Wildridge, V., Childs, S., Cawthra, L. and Madge, B. (2004) 'How to Create Successful Partnerships – A Review of the Literature', *Health and Information Libraries Journal*, 21 (Suppl. 1), pp. 3–19.

Williams, J. and Keating, F. (2000) 'Abuse in Mental Health Services: Some Theoretical Considerations', *The Journal of Adult Protection*, 2(3), pp. 32–39.

Wilson, A. (1994) *Changing Practices in Primary Care: A Facilitator's Handbook*, London: Health Education Authority.

Wilson, A. and Charlton, K. (1997) *Making Partnerships Work: A Practical Guide for the Public, Private, Voluntary and Community Sectors*, York: Joseph Rowntree Foundation.

Wood, N., Farrow, S. and Elliott, B. (1994) 'A Review of Primary Health Care Organization', *Journal of Clinical Nursing*, 3(4), pp. 243–250.

Woodcock, M. (1989) *Team Development Manual*, 2nd edn, Aldershot: Gower Publishing.

World Health Organization and World Psychiatric Association (1997) Organization of Care in Psychiatry of the Elderly: A Technical Consensus Statement, Geneva: World Health Organization and World Psychiatric Association.

Zubin, J. and Spring, B. (1977) 'Vulnerability: A New View on Schizophrenia', *Journal of Abnormal Psychology*, 86, pp. 103–126.

Index

227